KRISTA'S PROMISE

KRISTA'S PROMISE

KRISTA FORD

BOOKLOGIX®
Alpharetta, Georgia

The author has tried to recreate events, locations, and conversations from his/her memories of them. The author has made every effort to give credit to the source of any images, quotes, or other material contained within and obtain permissions when feasible.

Copyright © 2024 by Krista Ford

All rights reserved. No part of this book may be reproduced or transmitted in any form or by any means, electronic or mechanical, including photocopying, recording, or any information storage and retrieval system, without permission in writing from the author.

ISBN: 978-1-6653-0827-4 - Paperback
ISBN: 978-1-6653-0828-1 - Hardcover
eISBN: 978-1-6653-0829-8 - eBook

These ISBNs are the property of BookLogix for the express purpose of sales and distribution of this title. The content of this book is the property of the copyright holder only. BookLogix does not hold any ownership of the content of this book and is not liable in any way for the materials contained within. The views and opinions expressed in this book are the property of the Author/Copyright holder, and do not necessarily reflect those of BookLogix.

Library of Congress Control Number: 2024917794

∞This paper meets the requirements of ANSI/NISO Z39.48-1992 (Permanence of Paper)

092024

*I would like to dedicate my memoir to God,
and to those who believed in my vision.*

CONTENTS

1	Tracy, California, 1984	1
2	Homeless Trust-N-Gym	11
3	Goin' Back to Indiana	15
4	Cot to Bed	21
5	My Body Is My Hobby	29
6	Rainbow and Timing	35
7	BIO	43
8	The Strength of One	57
9	The Intro	67
10	One of the Four Agreements	75
11	Ruby Slippers	85
12	Wanna Come Out-N-Play?	93
13	Pure and Uncut	103
14	A Lot of "Ologies"	109
15	Qualified Solo	121
16	Over the Water	129
17	Red Light, Green Light	137

18	I Can and I Am	145
19	Спаси́б = Spasiba	153
20	Pumpmama4u	163
21	Run, Skip, Hop, Jump	171
22	Krugerrand	181
23	Hopscotch	191
24	My Pit Crew	203
25	Good Nature	209
26	Blueprint	217
27	Monopoly Game	223
28	Black Cool Runnings	229
29	Discipline Is My Destiny	243
30	Not Alone	247
31	628.2 LBS	255
32	Repetitive Stupidness	261
33	Bionic Woman	271

Epilogue 287
Author's Note 291
Acknowledgments 293

1

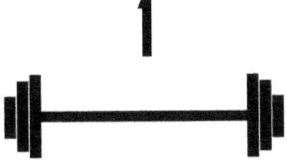

TRACY, CALIFORNIA, 1984

My alarm clock was some sort of delivery truck with the loudest brakes I have ever heard. It was very effective though, as I was up right away. I already had an apple in my jacket pocket, and after a quick shower, I was good to go. In less than ten minutes, I was out the door, and the warm California sun kissed my cheeks. I couldn't help but smile.

Two days after my high school graduation from Ben Davis High School in Indianapolis, my mother called Mamie Anderson, my cousin, and arranged for me to spend the summer with her. Or so she told Mamie that *lie* — in truth, she was kicking me out of the house, but I didn't care. I was ready to get the Hell out of that house and away from that wicked woman — my adopted mother, Catherine Ford. So onward and forward, to California, somewhere I knew I loved even though I had only been there one other time in my life at thirteen years old. I was so excited I could barely sleep until I got there. California sure didn't disappoint. It was warm but not too hot, with an almost-always gentle breeze — perfect really.

I jogged six blocks to the park. The sun was already out, so I kept a slow pace. I'm not sure if this was a dog park, but lots of dogs and their owners came to this park in the mornings to exercise and play. Yesterday, I met a young, energetic golden retriever, Oliver. His owner, Jeanette, had recently undergone some sort of surgery that made taking Oliver to the park impossible. Yesterday had been their first day back, and Oliver was completely out of his mind with joy. Jeanette had been resting on a bench when I walked by, and Oliver must have sensed I love dogs, because he came bounding toward me. At the end of his tether, he wiggled and, I swear, he smiled at me. I couldn't resist him, so I said hello to both.

Oliver was so happy he jumped up at me and continued wiggling. After the introduction, Jeanette asked if I would like to play with him off the leash. That sounded good to me, so we ran and played while Jeanette laughed and cheered us on. He was fast but so was I. We ran and chased each other until we were both winded. I think I had him on agility, but I knew it was only because he was a pup. When we were played out, Oliver let out a big, satisfied sigh, and flopped down beside Jeanette. He didn't have a care in the world. His life was paradise.

I remembered a time when I felt that way. I was very young, and a man with kind, loving eyes looked at me and, for the first time in my life, I felt a true connection with another person. I'm not sure what I was feeling, but I could tell he loved me—I just knew it. And in that instant, I loved him right back too. His name was John Ford and he and his wife, Catherine, adopted me and I went home to live with them. And my world, for a beautiful moment, was paradise.

Oliver brought me back to reality with a playful yip. It was game on as I took off around the grassy perimeter of the park, with Oliver on my heels. I gained some ground when he had a squirrel moment (which turned out to be a chihuahua) but, by the time we got back around to Jeanette, Oliver was well on his way to catching up to me. It seemed like he got quicker by the minute. He was amazing. I said my goodbyes and told Jeanette to hurry up and get better so the next time we could tag team to keep up with Oliver.

I still had enough time to run up to the bicycle shop. Kelly smiled as I walked in. He knew why I was there. Almost every day for the past two weeks, I had been coming in to look at the best-looking bike in the shop. A royal blue Schwinn girls' ten-speed. It was beautiful. The blue reminded me of blue ribbons,

TRACY, CALIFORNIA, 1984

fitting for the best bike on the floor. And, I still couldn't believe it, but I will be buying it tomorrow. Then I could go anywhere! Not that Tracy, California, was a gigantic city, like Indianapolis, but I could get anywhere once I had that bike—and way faster too.

Kelly noticed my excitement. "Tomorrow, Krista?"

"Yep," I replied, my smile telling him what he already knew.

Little did I know that after I left the shop, that bike was cleaned, inspected, tires aired up, and the whole bike polished to a sheen. Kelly's heart went out to the spunky, curly-haired teenager who was on fire for this bike. He knew what it was like. He had mowed lawns and raked leaves in his neighborhood to earn enough money for his first bicycle. He was almost as excited for me as he had been for his first bike. For a finishing touch, he put a "Manager's Special" sign around the handlebars and marked the price down as far as he was allowed.

When I left the bike shop, I ran the ten blocks to the gym. My haven. A place where I felt welcome and felt like I belonged—like I was with my extended family. We were working back and biceps, Linda and I. She was the owner of the gym and had agreed to work out with me and teach me the basics of lifting weights. She had a good knowledge of weight training and was sharing her knowledge, and I was soaking it up like a sponge. I liked lifting weights. I really liked it, and my body liked it. My muscles and joints felt stronger and healthier every day with every workout. Man, I found something I was very good at, almost without trying. My body just did it, like it knew what to do.

We had a great workout; and I wrote everything down, like I always did. Every set and weight, and how many repetitions. I wanted to make sure I had it all down, I didn't want to forget a thing. Not that I could ever imagine forgetting any of this. I knew I could never quit lifting, no matter what. That's how much I loved it. It was already my favorite part of the day. What I didn't know then was where this incredible sport would take me.

After a quick shower and a change of clothes, I was off to

work. I was super excited tonight. Not only was it payday, but I got to be Chuck E. Cheese tonight. The manager saw how easily I interacted with the kids and how they crowded around me when I was horsing around with them. He had asked if I wanted to do the job of being Chuck E. Cheese. Tonight was to be my first night. My friend Nena gave me a thumbs-up when I was putting on the costume. We both giggled knowing it was going to be a good night. Being Chuck E. Cheese was the best job in the place if you ask me, and I was so happy to be chosen.

It was a full house, with Billy and his twelve eight-year-old friends comprising the largest group. They were a rowdy bunch of boys, as we always expected, and me, being so excited about my bike and getting to be Chuck E. Cheese, was dancing and cavorting all over the place. Within minutes, almost all the kids in the place were laughing and squealing at my dance moves. That was one of the loudest nights in the history of Tracy's Chuck E. Cheese. It was the best work night ever. Nena and I had become quick friends, and she was laughing at me too. We were best buds after that night.

Tonight was my last night I'd be running home. Tomorrow, my bike! I tucked my few personal items into my pockets, said my goodbyes, waved to Nena across the room, and was out. I started off slowly but built speed as the familiar California breeze blew across my face. I was running, and my body felt so strong.

Morning came gently and I was thankful to be awake before the screechy truck made its arrival. I had just woken up a few minutes before and enjoyed my talk with God, thanking him for one more day of life, one more opportunity.

Oh yes, my bike! No wonder I woke up early! I put on some comfortable shorts and tennis shoes and grabbed the few items I would need for that day. It was a beautiful sunny morning, with just a few scattered clouds in the sky and a bird chirping in the distance. I almost started to sprint to Kelly's bike shop, but before I got too far down the street, I realized I needed to go to the

TRACY, CALIFORNIA, 1984

bank to cash my paycheck, but my bank didn't open for another twenty minutes. So, I decided to take the long route and look in the store windows as I walked, trying to take my time. (That is hard to do when you have a bike waiting!)

In a few short blocks, I was in an area with lots of windows to look in as I walked. The first store I came to was a glittery jewelry store, then a clothes store, and—ooh—an ice cream shop (I took note of this for sure), then an art supply place, and a drugstore. All that in one long block. As I got closer to the drugstore, I couldn't believe my eyes. *No way!* In the window was the latest Barbie doll, but not just any Barbie. I needed to take a closer look. As I crept up to the window, I saw she was a Peaches 'n Cream Barbie. Wow, I couldn't wait to tell my sister, Stacey! I hadn't thought about Barbies for a long time, since we were children.

This made me think of Stacey. Growing up, we each had our own Barbie dolls. Our Barbies were white and that was fine, they were our Barbies and we loved them. They went shopping and traveling with us, and my Barbie wanted to travel the world and see exotic places. Oh, and we had the Barbie camper, plane, and house that enabled our Barbies to go traveling whenever and wherever they wanted and go. We would hear of a place or see something on television, and we would pack up our Barbies and our camper and go. They would see the sights of the destination, eat the local food, and go shopping so they would have lots of pretty clothes to wear while they were there. We spent hours playing with our Barbies.

We also had this kitten, Fancy, who got into the Barbie camper one time, and when we came into play, there she was, sound asleep in the camper. Well, we took that to mean she wanted to play Barbies with us, so she got to be the Barbie cat. We had a few doll dresses that fit her, and she patiently let us put them on her. Then she was officially part of the Ford Barbie family—Stacey, Krista, Fancy, and the Barbies. That was our little family. And that, in a word, described my sister, she was my family.

I smiled at the memories. It still amazes me that two sisters could be so opposite. Taking a trip in our time machine to the future looked like this: Stacey spent her high school years studying and getting good grades. I spent most of my high school time on the track and field team, softball team, playing powder puff football, golf team, and anything ROTC. Her good grades paid off. She would start her freshman year of college in fall, where she was studying to become a registered nurse. I was so proud of her. She's my only sister and I love her. I got my share of teasing because I was biracial, and she stood up for me in my first fight ever when I was a freshman in high school, and she was a senior. We both got in trouble for that and sent home, and I remember my wicked mother telling Stacey in front of me, "Don't ever take up for Krista again and jeopardize your graduating from high school." I was shocked because my mother said it like she only had one daughter standing there.

On and on I walked, as the minutes slowly passed. Fortunately, I came to a sporting goods store with plenty of windows to keep an anxious girl occupied for a few minutes. The latest clothes were the main attraction in the window, but I liked to look at the equipment. Bats, balls, tennis rackets, gloves, and all kinds of accessories for lots of different sports. But nothing for lifting weights. I could not understand how this fabulous activity was not mainstream. Not yet anyway. Maybe I could change that.

Finally, enough time had passed that the bank would be open. I was less than a block away, so I started to sprint. When I ran up to the door, I think I scared the dear lady who was preparing to unlock the doors, but when she saw my ear-to-ear grin, she realized I meant no harm. She let me in and, unable to remain quiet, I told her all about the bike, and that I was there to cash my paycheck to go get it. She laughed at my eagerness, cashed my paycheck straight away, and told me to hurry up and go get my bike. With money in my pocket, I ran all the way to the bike shop, at least twelve blocks. When I got there, Kelly was

TRACY, CALIFORNIA, 1984

putting a few new-edition bikes out on the sidewalk. He saw me running up and joined in my excitement.

"Today's the day, right?" he called as I got close enough to hear.

"Yep, Kelly, I'm ready!" I dashed into the shop to see her polished shiny blue and chrome. What was this? A sign on her handlebars told me her price had been reduced! I couldn't believe my good luck. Kelly came in and we did our transaction for the bike. And just like that, she was mine. I hugged Kelly so hard for his kindness and generosity, I think I might have cracked his ribs, but I couldn't help it. He and this bike just changed my life. As I was walking my bike to the sidewalk, Kelly slipped a chain with a lock over my shoulder.

"You're going to need this, Krista. "Now go, take your bike on a spin," and I was alone on the sidewalk with the most incredible bike ever.

I climbed on and started to pedal, and, in a few short pumps, I was gliding along the sidewalk. Soon I was at a side road that would take me to a long stretch. I remembered from the taxi ride to my cousins. It was a wide road that seemed to go on forever. That would be the road for me that day. I quickly came to the highway and when I turned onto the shoulder, I started to pedal hard. Before long, I had to stop pedaling or I might've lost control of my new precious bike. Once I slowed down a little, I couldn't help but get her going again.

I chose this road to see what this bike could do, but I realized I was finding out what all those hours in the gym had done for me as well—I was strong, very strong. I had always been athletic and probably stronger than all the girls in my high school, but this was different. I could feel the *power* in my legs I had never felt before. This surprised me in a good way. I felt like I was finding out what my legs could do for the first time. I could tell the difference, like night and day, from last summer when I rode a bike in Indiana. My legs felt strong in a way I had never felt before. I think this bike ride was my first hint that lifting weights was really doing something to transform my body, not just a fun pastime.

Linda, the owner of the gym and my training partner, had been talking to me about bodybuilding since the first day we met. She wanted me to train for that sport. She thought I was a natural because my symmetry was already apparent, and my muscles were naturally strong and responded quickly. And, she said, the main thing I possessed that would make me a good bodybuilder was my passion. For me, there is no other way to live. I do things with all the passion I have, or I don't do it at all.

Well, I didn't have to make any decisions about it right then, so I just kept on pedaling. The road became a long, slight incline and I had to start working a little harder. Perfect, this was what I was looking for, a challenge for this bike. At first, my legs were pumping as hard as I could, but I had to ease off a tiny bit to let my breathing get caught up. I had run enough track to know I couldn't keep a full sprint going indefinitely, so I set a fast, steady pace I thought I could maintain for the entire incline. On and on I went until my thighs were burning bad! But I was determined to grind through the pain to get to the top of this incline—a few more feet and I was on top. Wow! I pulled my bike over and stepped down off the pedals and onto the road. My legs felt like I had just done a heavy leg workout, but different too, they were rubbery, and I had to laugh at myself for being all gimpy up here on top of this hill. On the way back down the incline, I noticed how blue and vast the sky seemed. It was beautiful and I was so happy on my bike, in the sun. A day just didn't get better than this.

When I got back to the gym, I put my bike in its prearranged spot in the closet and got into my workout clothes. Yay, it was bench day! Linda and I had a good workout. I was up to benching about 165 pounds now. After a long hot shower, I was ready to go to work. I smiled knowing my bike would take me there and back.

When I asked if they would let me ride my bike around the

block with the Chuck E. Cheese suit on, they all laughed. I pleaded my case—you know, an advertising type of thing. Unfortunately, the answer was no, but it was a fun idea. I almost couldn't resist doing it anyway, but I didn't want to get fired; so, I just had to laugh visualizing it.

> **"FOR WE LIVE BY FAITH, NOT BY SIGHT"**
> **(2 CORINTHIANS 5:7 NIV).**

HOMELESS TRUST-N-GYM

I was at the door before I knew it, and I slipped inside, locking it behind me. A sigh escaped my lips as I strode forward, passing the Smith machines, the squat racks, and all the individual weight machines, making my way to the stairs. At the door to the women's locker room, my reality began to set in again.

Here I was, seventeen years old. I thought I was going to spend the whole summer with my cousin—that's what my mother told me. Apparently, she told my cousin I was going to be visiting for two weeks. So, after many months of bliss, I was told I could no longer stay at my cousin's; her husband, Horace, was getting progressively more ill and eventually had to be admitted to the hospital. She was under so much pressure and had to care for him—a long-term guest in the house was more than she could handle. So, that was the end of that.

Thankfully, Linda, the owner of the gym, said I could sleep upstairs where the aerobic room was while I earn enough money for an apartment. I was so thankful for Linda's generosity, but I would have to wait till the gym was totally closed at eleven p.m. and everyone was gone for me to use my key to get in. Linda didn't want anyone to know that I was staying upstairs. So, some nights I would sleep on a park bench not far from the gym before I could go in. I wondered what I did to get into this kind of situation. Was I a bad person? Did I do something wrong? Why did this happen to me? I was doing my best to do the right things and make the right decisions. The tears of frustration began to well up in my eyes and I couldn't hold them back. I was safe, here in the gym, but I was scared out of my wits for my life.

A voice inside me said, *Let it out, Krista, just let it out, baby.* It sounded like something my favorite Aunt Bobbie would say. Oh Lord, I missed her, and another wave of tears fell. It felt like there wasn't a single person who truly cared about me out here. If something happened to me, nobody would even know.

I asked God again that night why this was happening to me. I pleaded for an answer or understanding at least. I didn't really get an answer, but I knew He was there. I could feel it in my spirit. He was the one constant in my life. "Be strong and of good courage; do not be afraid or dismayed, for the LORD your God *is* with you wherever you go (Joshua 1:9)," my grandmother's voice in my head. I know grandma, and my mind flashed back to memories of going to church when I was young. Sunday school was the best. Magnificent stories were told about God and Jesus. My favorite was Moses, how God had found favor in Moses and chose him to lead the people to the promised land. I loved God and I knew He loved me too.

So, my conclusion for the night was I was where He wanted me to be. I decided my only real option was to wait and try my best to have patience and faith. I didn't think God's plan was for me to die out here, so, whatever I had to go through, I was determined to go through it and give it my best shot. I wanted God to know that if this was His plan for me, then I would do my best. Whatever happened, I would be of good courage. So, I lay down on my little rug, put my head on my rolled-up sweatshirt, and looked up at the ceiling. I would know every tile before I left this place. Finally, my tears began to subside, and sleep miraculously found me. Funny thing about life sometimes, I think it doesn't take you having a degree from college to obtain a PhD in life.

The summer/fall of 1984 had been so exciting and wonderful, joining the gym, meeting new friends, getting a job, and learning about lifting weights. Not even realizing it, I had stumbled upon something that had captured my heart and energy. Little did I know at the time it would turn into the greatest passion of my life. And now I had met Linda, the first of many people who would influence my fledgling weightlifting career. This time was full of bike rides, alone and with Nena, romps with Oliver, and happy fun nights being the best Chuck E. Cheese ever. But, by summer's end, I had a sinking feeling that I was not going to be able to get the apartment I so desperately wanted. I just could not save enough money each month to make it happen. I fought the feeling as long as I could but, eventually, I had to face reality and I knew I had to return to Indianapolis. It didn't help that Grandma was asking for me to come back, bless her heart. And my Aunt Bobbie had been pleading with me for some time now. So, finally, I gave in and made the tough decision. I promised myself I would return to California someday—hopefully to live again.

And my beautiful bike? She made her way right back into Kelly's bike shop, for sale, as the most pristine used bike ever, not a scratch on her. I'm sure Kelly overpaid me because there was more money in his envelope than there should have been, but he wouldn't let me give any of it back.

After dropping off my bike, I walked slowly back to the gym. Linda had finished packing my things and had my suitcase down by the front door of the gym. Linda would be dropping me off at the airport and we were leaving at about the same time Linda, and I usually worked out, so all our workout buddies were there. As Linda and I began to make our way toward the front door, I started to hear, "Bye, Krista!" and "Bye, we'll miss you!" When I turned around, everyone was waving and smiling and wishing me well. I didn't realize how much my gym buddies had become my family.

I smiled and yelled back, "Bye, you guys. I'll see you soon!" but I had a feeling I probably wouldn't. I put my hand over my heart before I turned to leave. With considerable effort, Linda and I got my bag loaded into her car—I couldn't believe my meager lot of clothes and lifting gear could weigh so much. Then we were off. My time here had come to an end, but I was so grateful I had met such good people and had learned so much about lifting weights here. Linda helped me get checked in and get my bag up to the counter. Once that was done, we walked outside and said our goodbyes.

As she was walking away, she turned around and said, "I want to see you in a magazine someday, Krista."

I smiled at her, shook my head, and said, "Ya, ya, ya."

"I mean it, Krista, you have what it takes." I just looked at her. "Really, Krista, you are a natural if I have ever seen one. You *must* do this!" Up until then, I was just enjoying reading magazines about lifting and bodybuilding, but I had no concept of what it took to compete.

I could tell she wasn't going to let me go without this, so I said, "Okay, Linda, I'll compete in a bodybuilding show, but not till I'm ready, okay?" She accepted that and we smiled. I turned toward the terminal and took in my last deep breath of California air. Ninety minutes later, I was on a plane back to Indianapolis.

> "NO MIND HAS IMAGINED WHAT GOD HAS PREPARED FOR THOSE WHO LOVE HIM" (1 CORINTHIANS 2:9 NLT).

3

GOIN' BACK TO INDIANA

I boarded my flight back to Indy with a bunch of emotions running through my head. I was thankful for all the experiences in Cali, and I felt blessed to have made so many friends there, especially Linda Tracy. And, how funny, she had the same last name as the city, Tracy. She patiently taught me about sets and repetitions and to rest my muscles. She also introduced me to bodybuilding. That, right there, was the greatest thing ever—a sport where you are the builder and the sculptor, where you can build and chisel yourself to your best physique. Also, a sport where unbounded energy and stamina are blessings. A perfect sport for a girl like me.

However, I was heading back home, and the feelings of betrayal were starting to poke their ugly heads out again. How could my mother pack up all my clothes and tell my cousin I was going to spend the summer with her? Growing up, I stayed away from gangs, didn't drink or smoke, and didn't get pregnant as a child/teenager. I just went to school, played sports, and made lots of friends. Now that I was going to be back home, at some point I would see her, and my stomach tightened at the thought. Thankfully I was going to stay with my grandmother.

As the plane began to taxi out to the runway, my heart raced. Flying was so thrilling to me. I had flown several times as a child and was always enthralled by it. This flight was nothing out of the ordinary, except for the girl walking toward the plane standing a little straighter and maybe even a little taller. A teenage girl who left for a fun summer vacation, but came back a determined young woman, and a survivor.

As always, it seemed to take forever to get off the plane, but eventually, my turn came. I was striding up the ramp at full speed, and then there she was—my beloved granny. I had never seen a sweeter face in all my life. She gathered me up in her warm, ample arms and I fell into her, as I had done a million times before. I was home.

The ride back to Granny's was nothing but me talking nonstop about bodybuilding, the gym, my first job at Chuck E. Cheese, my bike, and the wonderful time I'd had in Cali. Well, except for the homeless part—I brushed over that as best I could so as not to upset her. We pulled up to my granny's apartment/townhome, and I couldn't believe my eyes—there was my aunt Bobbie. I jumped out of the car and ran to give her the biggest hug ever. I was so happy to see her. We had a lot to talk about and catch up with. She helped me get my bulging suitcase out of Granny's car and stash it up in the bedroom that would be mine until I got myself set up here. Stacey would come over later.

Granny, Bobbie, Stacey, and I all stayed up late, talking and just enjoying each other's company. Granny was the first to turn in while Bobbie, Stacey, and I stayed up well past midnight. She was in her third year of nursing school, and it was getting very interesting. With all the prerequisites out of the way, she was really getting into the essence of nursing. She loved it too; I could tell by the tone of her voice.

I told my aunt and sister all about bodybuilding and showed how my muscles were growing. It seemed my sister and I found a path that suited us. Finally, late into the night, we all fell asleep.

Chirping birds made me realize it was morning. Since I was still in yesterday's clothes, I went up to the bedroom to find a change of clothes. I unzipped my suitcase and laughed out loud at why my suitcase had been so heavy. As I opened it, out spewed at least two dozen *Muscle and Fitness* magazines that had been in the gym. Linda must have stuck them in when she finished up my suitcase. It made me laugh, but those magazines were my bodybuilding lifeline for months to come. Thank you for everything, Linda!

Since it was Sunday morning, we would be going to church, and I was very excited to see everyone again. I hoped I could rejoin the choir too—that was one of the best things about church, singing in the choir with my cousin Lenita. I hoped she would be in church that day. Before long, I could smell bacon cooking. Granny was up doing her Sunday morning breakfast.

I ran down the stairs into the kitchen where my sweet granny was and helped set the table for breakfast. My aunt Bobbie had to leave and a few minutes later, Stacey staggered in and then, laughing, shook her head when she saw me racing around the kitchen, doing everything as fast as I could. Some things never changed, I guess.

After our wonderful breakfast (quite the change from granola bars and instant oatmeal), I felt like a sausage. I was so full, but I felt so good. We piled into Granny's car and off we went to Our Savior Lutheran church. As we pulled up into our parking space, I saw Lenita's car pulling in.

"Go!" said Granny when she saw the look on my face; and waved me off with her hand. I jumped out of the car and sprinted across the lot, catching Lenita just as she was climbing out of her car. She screamed and jumped up and down when she saw me, and we hugged and hugged. I held her hand as we went into the church, I did not want to let go of her—I loved my cousin with all my heart.

I spent most of the church service looking around to see who all was in church that morning. There was Tim Lewis, our choir director, and Cleveland Lewis, some church friends, and Mrs. Sweat, my Sunday school teacher. I caught her eye, and she gave me a quick wink. Up in the choir, next to Lenita, was my aunt Joyce, Lenita's mother, and just loved all of us kids and always wanted to know what we were doing.

Oh, outstanding! The choir began to sing my favorite song, *God Is*. I looked up at Lenita and she was singing with heartfelt joy that was undeniable. My heart swelled to see her up there belting it out. Aunt Joyce squeezed my hand, she knew that song was my favorite.

After church, Lenita and I went around to say hi to everyone. All my church family wanted to know all about my time in Cali and of course that's all I could talk about anyway, and soon, a small crowd gathered around me as I talked about all my Cali adventures. Bodybuilding and weightlifting were front and center of course. Everyone could feel my excitement as I showed the various poses I learned from Linda. I could have shown pictures, but the *Muscle and Fitness* I had in my hands that morning did not make it to church. Granny made sure of that. However, by the time I was done, I think everyone in church knew what bodybuilding was all about.

As I settled into my life back home in Indy, I was thinking hard about what kind of a job I needed. I knew the amount of money I made at Chuck E. Cheese was not quite enough to get an apartment of my own. A higher-paying job is what I needed. I was already known locally as an athlete, but when people saw me that summer and knew I was looking for a job, they kept saying I should apply to UPS. So, that's what I did.

I wasn't nervous about the interview. Talking to people always came easy to me, but this interview was different. I had to do physical tests, like picking up a big, fifty-pound box and moving it around, on and off some shelves. There was a cardio portion which was a piece of cake after riding my bike all summer, and then a hop, skip, and jump type of thing. Apparently, it was a good interview. I know I was having fun doing all those tasks with ease. The next day when the call came, I got the job! Wow! This was *huge* for me. Now I knew I could take care of myself. I could rent an apartment and I vowed to do the very best I could for UPS. Thank you, God, for this job.

> "BY MIRACLES, WONDERS, AND SIGNS"
> [ACTS 2:22 NIV].

4

COT TO BED

I started my job at UPS in late February 1985. I was hired on as a "Loader and Unloader." What this job entailed was either loading or unloading the eighty-three-foot trailers. (Usually, you did one or the other all day.) As with most new hires, I started unloading. These huge semitrucks would come into the hub and back up to the big dock doors. They were packed from top to bottom with boxes of all shapes and sizes. There were two giant decks in these trucks and when I saw how tightly they were packed, I couldn't believe it. I don't think another box could have been crammed in there. The unloaders would climb into the trailers and start unloading the boxes onto these rollers. The boxes would roll down onto conveyor belts and then roll down the corridor and out of sight. This unloading job was hard work, but it was fun. Several of us would try to go box for box with each other. Soon I could keep up with the fastest of the unloaders. Our supervisors sometimes would come to check on us and we'd be there working hard but laughing. They couldn't understand how we thought it was so fun. The loading portion of the job took a little more thinking and planning and, of course, time. I eventually became good at this too and when my first job review came around, I got quite high marks for my hard work and maybe for bringing some fun and laughter to the group. Mostly it was just my competitive spirit rising to each day's challenge. This job was a blessing for me and a perfect fit.

I would come home tired but excited to tell Granny all about my day and what went on. She was extremely pleased I had landed this good job. She told me every day about how proud she was of me. She always had a hearty meal for dinner ready for me, and I ate like I was starving. I think my body was making up for the lean time I had just gone through. Regardless, Granny cooked, and I ate—simple as that. And I slept, oh my goodness, like I hadn't slept in months. As I sank into my bed at night, happy but exhausted, I realized my bodybuilding would have to take a back seat for a minute while I got myself acclimated to my job and the level of physical exertion it required. I wanted to find a gym so bad; it was all I could do to *not* go out and look at them. But I knew what would happen if I did. I would find one, love it, and join *instantly*. I knew my priority was to get my apartment. All my money was being saved for that. So, once I had my apartment, I could look for a gym. *One step at a time.* And thanks to this job, my muscles were certainly not shrinking.

There were several of us who really enjoyed our jobs, like Arnold Sampson. He was tall, handsome, and the sweetest guy. We worked side by side on many shifts and, after a few months, we spent time together outside of work. Arnold became my first real boyfriend. We had good times, going out to movies, eating meals, and just spending time together. It's funny I can remember always having a boyfriend as young as five years old.

As my life became busier, I worried I might be a little too much for Granny. I didn't want to wear her out—she was my sweet Granny, but undeniably getting on in years. I only had about a third of the amount I'd need to get into an apartment. Fortunately, my Aunt Bobbie had been thinking the same thing about Granny and offered me to stay with her at her house. Gratefully, I accepted her offer. I would be okay for a while longer. And that would mean another UPS check. I was closer to getting my apartment!

And speaking of my Aunt Bobbie, she was the one who gave me my first set of weights when I was about ten years old. She knew I was naturally strong and impulsively bought them while shopping for my birthday presents that year. I played with them but, at the time, I wasn't exactly sure what to do with them. I think I did curls because I had seen someone do that on television, maybe Jack LaLanne. I loved them because they were shiny and heavy and no one else had them. But best of all, they were from my favorite Aunt Bobbie. How could she have known at the time what weights would mean in my life? Maybe, all those years ago, it was a gentle nudge from God.

When Sunday came, I was back in the choir, standing and singing next to Lenita. I told her how my situation had changed, and how I couldn't stay at my Aunt Bobbie's too much longer. She was very sympathetic but she didn't have a place of her own yet either so she couldn't really help. What I didn't know was Mrs. Higgins overheard our conversation that day and she slipped away to make some inquiries of her own.

The following Sunday, Mrs. Higgins approached Lenita and me after church and asked how we were doing. Lenita told Mrs. Higgins her latest news, she had just been promoted in her job and told us of her new responsibilities.

"That is wonderful news, Lenita. They are lucky to have such a hard worker like you." Then Mrs. Higgins turned to me. She already knew I got the job at UPS (I'm pretty sure the whole church did) so I confessed the only pertinent news I had. I wouldn't have a place to stay after a few more days and I'm only about halfway to an apartment money-wise.

"Well, Krista," Mrs. Higgins began, "I've seen how hard you're trying, and I know you need a place to live. I just found out there will be a vacancy at the end of the month in the apartment building across the street from where my husband and I live. I have spoken to the apartment manager, she's a friend of mine, and if you can come up with the rest of the money at that time, she will save it for you." I did the math quickly in my head and knew I'd still be short, but not by much. I couldn't say a word, I just hugged her. She knew what that meant.

I would come up with the money somehow. I had to. I was running out of options.

"Oh, and Krista, will you come stay with us until that apartment becomes available?" she smiled hopefully. Now I really couldn't say anything, I just hugged and hugged her, and she ushered me off to some privacy as I fell apart in her arms. The fear of being homeless again, combined with her loving gesture, was just too much. Mrs. Higgins held me and reassured me that everything would be okay.

And that's the way it went. I went from being kicked out of my mother's house at seventeen years old two days after graduating high school to being kicked out from my cousin Mamie's in Cali, to homeless and living in a gym, to my granny's, my Aunt Bobbie's (and after an unfortunate disagreement about money, asked to leave as well), to the Higgins's house. The Higginses welcomed me and made me feel comfortable. Their two children, Harvest—we called him Junior—and Rowena, were friends of mine from church and they were both happy to have me become a part of their family for a while. Mrs. Higgins was the sweet, generous hostess, going out of her way to get me anything I needed or wanted. And bless her heart, she cooked some gigantic meals for the now five of us. I was still eating like I was starving; I couldn't help it.

Mr. Higgins knew I would soon tire of taking the bus and getting rides from friends. So, being very knowledgeable about cars, engines, and all that, he told me when I was ready to get a car, he would take me and make sure I got a good car and didn't get taken advantage of. *What a good man*, I thought, as I accepted his offer. Eventually, I *would* need a car. Apartment first though!

Waiting for the apartment seemed to take forever. That was okay with me, I was really enjoying life with the Higgins's. I was with them for almost a month, and when the apartment did become available, I was ready. I was *so* ready. I was swinging-from-the-rafters ready! However, I was still $200 short. When I told Arnold, he told me he'd been saving also, and he had the $200 I needed! And with this news, it was official, I was going to be on my own again. A little more prepared this time though. And I am so grateful for the people who assisted in getting me to this point. No kindness shown to me went unnoticed.

My first apartment was a HUD-subsidized apartment named Colonial Square. It was a one-bedroom basic apartment, but it was my first home and I loved it. At first, all I had was a military cot from Mr. Higgins, and my blanket, pillow, and a small array of stuffed animals. I remember a koala bear from Lenita (I gave her a gray elephant), my teddy bear from Aunt Bobbie, a little lion from Granny, and some other ones I acquired along the way. But that apartment was my home and I decorated it with everything I had. Pictures of my friends, magazine pictures of my favorite bodybuilders, anything that meant something to me got hung on the walls. As I lay on my cot that first night, looking up at the ceiling, I spoke to God with my eyes and heart full of tears of joy and thanksgiving. I made a vow to God and myself I would never be homeless again. I would always have a roof over my head I could call my own and no one could take that from me and tell me to get out.

Eventually, I acquired a chair, a sofa, and finally a table. And as luck would have it, I even got a television when a family close to the Higginses got a larger one. I felt like I had it all—my church family, my family members like Lenita, my Aunt Bobbie, my granny, a good job, a nice boyfriend, and now a home of my own.

After another few months, I had saved enough money to start thinking about a car. Mr. Higgins took me to look at some. I think we went looking two or three times but when I saw the shiny 1975 maroon Chevy Monte Carlo sprawled out in her space at the lot, like she was tanning on a beach, it was over.

That was the car for me. Fortunately for all involved, that princess of a car passed Mr. Higgins's rigorous inspection. And $500 later, she was mine! Mr. Higgins taught me probably everything I know about cars to this day. He left nothing to chance. He made sure I knew how to take care of her and take care of her I did.

Once I had my car, I could drive to work, and go anywhere I wanted. Of course, where I wanted to go—I'm sure you can guess—was to all the gyms I could find. I asked Arnold to go around with me to look at all the gyms. As luck would have it, I found Gold's Gym West, just a five-minute drive from my apartment. The second I had the money to join, I did. And I was back! I couldn't wait to begin lifting again, and I did so with vengeance! I worked out as hard, or harder, than I had in Cali. Before, Linda had been guiding me, now I had the reins, and I was going full speed ahead. I had a bodybuilding competition somewhere in my future I had to get ready for. Now that the essentials had been divinely taken care of—my job, my apartment, and now my car, TYG—I could focus on my training. I had been out of the gym for nearly three months.

When I couldn't sleep at night from a lot whirling around in my mind, I would get up at midnight, put on my jogging clothes and my earphones to listen to my music, and sprint down my stairs, out the door, and down the street up to the gym and back. It's funny, I always felt close to God when I did this. Whatever was on my mind that night slowly creeped back out when I got back home. It's like that was my quiet time with God and my own spirit of thoughts. It was so peaceful and tranquil; you could hear a pin drop. The funny thing was that I never was scared to be out there on the streets in the middle of the morning. I've always felt like God had his protective arms around me, keeping me safe from any harm or danger. I would exhaust myself physically and mentally and just go home and crash. I did this a lot to clear my mind and spirit.

> **"DO NOT BE ANXIOUS ABOUT ANYTHING"**
> **[PHILIPPIANS 4:6–7 NIV].**

5

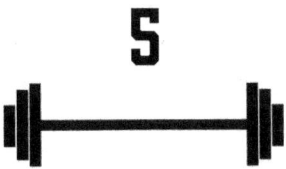

MY BODY IS MY HOBBY

Gold's Gym West was my new home away from home. I couldn't help myself; I was there every spare moment. I soon made friends with other lifters and bodybuilders. As each day passed, I was getting stronger, and my muscles were responding to the new training program I had set up for myself. Since I was training for a competition, I needed to focus on my symmetry and build up any muscles that were lacking the development of others. I determined my weaker points to be chest, triceps, and biceps, and I worked in extra sets and exercises for those weak points. For the next few months, I did everything I knew to do to get ready for bodybuilding.

As winter set in, I realized there was a lot about this sport I didn't know. How to pose, for instance, was completely foreign. How to pick music, how to walk out on stage, and what position I would be in while waiting for my music to start. All these things were coming closer to the forefront of my mind, and I knew I would need some help. I started asking around the gym who might be a good trainer for me. And, as luck would have it, only one name was mentioned over and over—Melissa Reardon.

We met and hit it off immediately. She had competed several times before, so she knew the ropes of this sport. We did a few workouts together as she assessed me. She must have liked what she saw because we began to train in earnest after that. We trained hard through the winter. She focused especially on the lower body, which I liked because that had become my favorite as well. She thought I could be ready for the Indiana Bodybuilding Championship Competition to be held at the end of the summer of 1985, about six months away. I would be nineteen years old in my first bodybuilding contest. Once I had that date in my head, I lived, ate, and breathed bodybuilding. I couldn't wait. All that energy went into the weights and my physique showed it. My whole body felt tight and strong.

Melissa and I worked on stage presence and posing—not just posing at yourself in the mirror but using the stage light and slight angles to accentuate your strongest points. The judges are seated lower than the stage, so you need to be aware of how to show your body to them. I'm glad I had Melissa because there was a lot more to this than I knew. She helped me pick my music and helped put my posing routine together.

Things with Arnold had quieted down this past year, probably due to my intense training schedule, but we remained friends and he cheered me on in my bodybuilding career.

During these months of heavy training, I acquired a few more things for my apartment. I got a real bed and some chairs for the dining room table. However, most of my extra money was spent on trying to eat healthily. Prior to this, I could eat anything I wanted, but bodybuilding requires a certain level of food discipline. It was tough, but I did it. I ate chicken, tuna, turkey, fish, raw vegetables, and amino acids and vitamins. I probably had more than that, but those are the things I remember eating (of course, all the while dreaming of a Big Mac).

I am thankful I learned so much about nutrition at this age. It wasn't fun at all to eat so healthily like that, but my body sure reaped the benefits. I was muscled up nicely, lean but not skinny, and my symmetry was good. Melissa helped me pick out my posing suit. It was canary yellow, and it looked bright and beautiful on my light skin. And almost before we knew it, the day had come. I was ready and I was so excited. I couldn't wait to get on that stage. Most people get nervous before getting on stage, but not me—that stage was exactly where I wanted to be.

The morning portion of the show was where all the judging happens, compulsory poses with the other competitors in your class. I'm five feet six, so I was in the tall class of women. There were fourteen women in this class, and looking at everyone in my class, I figured I would place somewhere in the middle of the pack. Some of the women had been training for years and the density of their muscles was phenomenal, while others looked a little smooth. I was young but I had been athletic all my life and it showed. We did all the compulsory poses for the judges and our routines without music, then a little more judging was done.

By the night show, I was chomping at the bit, practically screaming, "Call my name! I want to be on that stage right now!" When my turn finally came, I had to keep myself from sprinting out on the stage. I strode confidently out and assumed my position. When my music began, I started my routine just as I had practiced it dozens of times. When I did my first double biceps pose, the crowd started to clap—*Oh good, they like me.* (A bunch of my gym friends were there probably making most of the noise.) Then when I shook my thigh and snapped a quadriceps flex, whistles and cheers—*that* was way louder than just my friends. I almost went off script and posed for the audience, but I held myself in check and finished my routine as I was supposed to do. When the music ended and my time on stage was over, I did a quick double biceps pose and then held my hands up and out to the crowd, who applauded louder than I had heard up until now. I felt good.

When everyone had posed and it was time for the awards, Melissa and I were very excited. Neither of us expected me to win, but we both thought I would be somewhere in the top half of the pack. The way the awards were presented was last place working up to first place. Well, the first name that was called was mine. The crowd went crazy with boos. I didn't understand—I thought they liked me. And then I got it . . . they weren't booing me, they were booing the judges' placement of me. But it was already official, I had gotten fourteenth place—a.k.a., last place. You can't get no more last than that. Sometimes you just have to laugh at yourself.

Well, I learned a lot that day. It was a little disheartening to get last place when clearly the crowd liked me a lot. Didn't the judges like my posing? Was I too muscular? What was it? No one would tell me. I left confused but feeling like I had done my part to the best of my ability. Once Melissa and I got back into the gym, we would figure out what went wrong and what we could do better next time.

Oh yes, there would be a next time. I don't quit that easy.

Melissa and I trained harder than ever. We pored over *Muscle and Fitness* magazines, trying to get an exact read on what the judges were looking for in a female bodybuilder. We trained every muscle in my body with precision. We even made up some exercises to fine-tune certain areas. Fall turned into winter, and winter into spring as we trained. All my energy went into my training, and the rest of my life went by in a blur. I still made it to church every Sunday (my only day off from the gym), where I kept up with Lenita, the Higginses, and the rest of my friends and family. My job was not so exhausting anymore, I just thought of it as my cardio for the day and treated it as part of my workout.

During this spring, I met another bodybuilder at UPS named Joe Jones, he was a union rep who heard about my competition from the gym. Joe was tall, maybe six feet three, and pushing 260 pounds, all of it muscle. He also trained at Gold's Gym West but at a different time than I did. We became friends and had endless talks about bodybuilding and weights. He was currently in training for a competition also, so that made our lifestyles compatible, and we began to spend some time together—mostly in the gym, encouraging and inspiring each other. Some people thought we were brother and sister because we looked so similar. We laughed because we certainly weren't brother and sister, we were a couple.

One day I was training and in walked Lenda Murray! I knew her in an instant, I had seen so many pictures of her in my *Muscle and Fitness* magazines. She was tall and dark, beautiful really, all muscled up and balanced perfectly, like no physique I had ever seen. She was one of the top female athletes in this sport and she had a dazzling smile that told you she *loved* to train. Once she began, I watched her every move, hoping to learn something, and was just fascinated to watch her training routine. She was amazing and I left that day knowing I had seen a great woman. A beautifully muscled, Black, athletic woman, destined for greatness. After Carla Dunlap, she was one of the next pioneers in our sport and it was my privilege to watch her train that day.

Training continued until Melissa, Joe, and I all thought I was ready. I was bigger, stronger, and more symmetrical this time. We chose the 1987 South Bend Amateur Bodybuilding Championships to be held at Saint Mary's College by Notre Dame in South Bend in the fall. Melissa and I choreographed my posing routine to showcase my best body parts (back and legs) and I picked a bright, fuchsia-colored posing suit. On the day of the competition, before I left my apartment, I took out a picture from my first contest. I took a hard look at myself in the mirror and compared what I saw to the picture I held in my hand. There was a bigger difference than I realized. I was twenty-one now; and had spent the last three years training my body *hard* for this day, and it showed. I was ready. When I walked on stage, I knew I looked good, and once again, the crowd loved me, cheering at each pose. The judges must have thought I looked pretty good too because I placed third this time and was given a big trophy to take home. Melissa and Joe were proud of me, and we all celebrated afterward.

Joe was getting close to his competition date and, since I was already in condition, we decided to enter the mixed pairs division of the contest. We put a posing routine together and practiced it until we had it down. We had matching suits, and all was going well until two days before the contest. I had an attack of "I have to have a Twinkie really bad, and I have to have it right now." If it had been only one Twinkie, I think I would have been okay, but a twelve-pack, not so much! So, with all that sugar and sodium, my body swelled up and I looked more like a chubby baby than a bodybuilder, nothing like I'm supposed to look. And with only two days to go, there was really no way my body could recover from this. So, unfortunately, I let Joe down. I felt so bad I had lost my self-control like that. Joe did quite well in his individual class, and I hoped that made up for me messing up our mixed pairs competition. We remained friends but that damaged things between us for a while, and I swore to myself if I ever gave my word to someone, I vowed I would not break it again. I could hear my granny's words, "Do unto others, Krista . . ." I know, Granny, because it sure feels awful when you let someone down, especially someone you really care about.

By the way, I *did* do a lot better in that second bodybuilding contest than the first, but truth be told—can you believe it—there were only three girls in my class that day. So, you get the math, haha—once again, dead last. But I did my best and that's what mattered to me. However, two last places and a Twinkie-self-disqualification are not exactly the stats I was hoping for. Bodybuilding is a very difficult sport, to say the least. I guess I just had to try even harder!

> **"I PRAY THAT ALL MAY GO WELL WITH YOU AND THAT YOU MAY BE IN GOOD HEALTH"**
> **[3 JOHN 1:2 ESV].**

6

RAINBOW AND TIMING

The next week found me right back in the gym, determined to become the best bodybuilder I could be. While I was working my back, doing some pull-downs, a guy came up to me and introduced himself as Bob Sidebottom. He said he'd been watching me work out and had heard about my bodybuilding competitions.

"Maybe you should think about powerlifting, you would be a good powerlifter," he said. I had heard of powerlifting but didn't know much about it.

So, I said, "How so?"

"Well," he began, "with bodybuilding, who sets the standards? And who decides what the perfect body must look like? That is very subjective. And you must take into account the judges' personal preferences. Maybe they prefer a certain body type. You've seen pictures of Franco Columbo, right?"

"Yes."

"How about Frank Zane?"

"Yes," I had seen him too.

"Well, what if nine out of ten judges prefer the look of Frank Zane?"

I stifled a giggle as I thought, *I must be Franco Columbo in this analogy, right?* But I understood his point.

So, I said, "I can understand that."

"But with powerlifting, if you lift the most weight, you win regardless. It doesn't matter what you look like. Just like a race, whoever gets to the finish line first, wins."

I said something remarkable like, "Huh," but that made sense and I knew I should consider this sport. Bob was anxious to share with me what he knew, and we made plans to start training together. Funny thing Bob said to me in the beginning, "If you don't like powerlifting you can go back to that sissy sport if you want to," and we both laughed. To this day it's a bittersweet rivalry between powerlifters & bodybuilders.

Bob's track reference got me thinking back to my days of running track in high school. My favorite events were the relays, especially the 4x400, where I ran the anchor leg. Running the final leg of the 4x400 relay was a challenge I loved. I might have several girls ahead of me when I got the baton. It's everything you can do not to put on the one-hundred-meter speed and run them right down. Having a good strategy and a good day on the track, I could've probably caught them. The final hundred meters is where you find out what you're made of. Are you going to quit, or will you keep forcing those legs to drive onward, despite how heavy they've become, and keep driving your arms harder when you almost can't breathe anymore? I loved that race because it never beat me, I never quit or eased up. I gave 100 percent all the way to the finish line. But the best part of that race was being a part of the relay team. Us girls developed a special bond, like a little family, and coming down that home stretch, seeing the three of them all screaming, jumping up and down, and cheering for me, knowing they were depending on me, I couldn't quit—I wouldn't—not ever. And they knew that. We were a great team—a team no one was anxious to race. I loved competing in track. I was a strong sprinter too and, through my high school years, I ran the one hundred, two hundred, and four hundred at one time or another, and usually ran the lead leg of the 4x100 relay. You give it all you've got for a few long seconds (well, for a sprinter) and, if you're the fastest, you win. It wasn't quite that easy, but if I could get out of the starting blocks fast enough, and I usually did, I was able to win most of my races. So, there it was: If I did my best on the track, I usually won, but when I did my best on the bodybuilding stage, I did not win. (I couldn't even beat one person, to be precise). So, powerlifting would be more like track. If you lifted the most weight, you would win.

And when I said it that way to myself, my mind flashed back to my high school track coach, Mr. Ritter, who said, "Krista, you would be a great weightlifter." This was said while I was doing some wind sprints. I thought it odd at the time for him to say such a thing, I was one of the top sprinters in the state, and my sights were set on the Olympics. Why would he even mention a different sport? At the time, I must have given him a deer-in-the-headlights look and we never talked about it again, but I never forgot him saying that. So, now I've heard it again and, while it did strike a chord in me, I wasn't ready to quit bodybuilding. I had just spent the last three years of my life training for it and despite what those judges thought of me, I knew my physique showed my hard training. I just had to figure out what the judges wanted to see. (Which ended up being the story of my bodybuilding life.) However, I can say the concept of "whoever lifts the most weight wins" did appeal to me, I knew I could out-lift probably every one of those bodybuilder girls, and probably sprint faster than them too!

For the next year, my training was all over the place. I didn't have a competition to train for, which meant, for the first time, I didn't have a date circled on my calendar that determined my training routine. So, on days I could meet up with Bob, I trained with him, doing his powerlifting routines. Bob was about twenty years my senior, and he had already been powerlifting for many years. He had his routines down to a science. He worked on the major body parts twice a week, once heavy and once lighter, and weights were increased in small amounts. This was a different way to work out for me and it took several months of paying close attention to learn his theory—and Bob really understood how to train for this sport. I was getting stronger, and I could feel it. I learned how to squat like a powerlifter, changing the placement of the bar on my back. *Oh, I liked that.* I finally felt "perfectly balanced" under the bar. It's hard to describe when the light bulb goes on and you "get" something. But I got it, and I got it good. This was the first of the three lifts to capture me—the squat.

On days when I was with Melissa, we trained for bodybuilding. That was old school and comfortable now—I knew exactly how to make my muscles respond. When I was by myself, I did the exercises I especially loved, mostly back and legs. The gym was my second home and sometimes I would come back later, well after my workout, and get on the treadmill or stationary bike and do some cardio while I let my mind wander.

During these wanderings, my mind often went back to the summer three years earlier, and the feelings of betrayal from my mother. Now that I was back in town, I saw my mother from time to time, at holidays or family functions. My granny and Aunt Bobbie always included me in family events, and I felt comfortable with them, but I just couldn't think of a thing to say to my mother. We were polite but that was about the extent of it. Even though I was now twenty-one years old, I still wanted a mother. (Maybe I should clarify, I wanted a mother who *wanted* to be my mother.) But how can you ache for something you've never had? That's how I felt about our relationship.

My adopted father was the one who loved me. He was the one who chose me, pointing at me the second he saw me. He didn't look any further—I was the one he wanted, and we had an instant and deep love. He would be my hero forever from the day he picked me up at the adoption agency in Boston Massachusetts and held me in his arms, to our home in Framingham Massachusetts then onto living in a ranch-style house with a stone facade on the east side of Indy, on Gladstone Street, where my sister and I each had our own room. We had toys and dolls strewn across our beds and floors, and my life went from uncertainty to paradise overnight, literally. My father was a great big blessing from heaven. Because of my father, I finally had a family.

Sadly, when I was about five years old, my parents got divorced. I remember my sister and I were sitting on the living room floor watching television, some cartoons or something. Our mother came in and told us that she and Daddy were getting a divorce. We said something like "oh, okay" and got right back to our show. That's how much we comprehended at the time. Over the years, I wondered what happened, but I never asked—our father was just not around anymore. Shortly after that, we moved to the Meadows apartments, a subsidized housing, and the three of us lived in a small two-bedroom apartment. It was kind of scary, but I didn't mind sharing a bedroom with Stacey. We did have twin beds to sleep in separately.

I didn't see my dad as much after that. He unfortunately began drinking at some point and it seemed to be getting out of control. He would pass away due to this several years later.

So, I wondered if my birth mother and family would want a relationship with me. Or, at least, we could meet and get to know each other a little and maybe she could tell me about my birthfather and any family history that would be of interest to me. At first, it was just a thought and curiosity, but then it became a desire that grew with intensity. I so wanted to feel love from a mother—I never felt that growing up and I wanted to feel a mother's love while I still had a little youth left. When and if I found that love with her, I wanted to languish in it forever. I couldn't help but fantasize that she wished she hadn't given me up, and she loved me, and she was looking for me. The thought was comforting, and somehow that was enough for now.

During this time, I also began to think about my employment situation. I was making good money at UPS, but it was only part-time. I wanted to work full-time at UPS, but an opportunity didn't happen for that. So, I began to look around and I quickly found a full-time job at a local Target warehouse. It was slightly less pay per hour but lots more hours that made up for it, and it was somewhat like my UPS job. I was still in a warehouse, but with this job, I was packing trucks instead of unpacking them. Each store in the region would order products for their store for that week and we filled those orders, got the boxes on the trucks, and got them on their way to the various stores. A woman on the next line over, Anna, was white, soft-spoken but funny and very sweet. We talked and laughed during our shifts and soon were like best friends. Within months, we were spending a lot of time together and with her thirteen-year-old daughter—well, as much time as any thirteen-year-old wants to hang out with her mother. We both had apartments and spent many evenings together watching movies or just talking. I told Anna about my desire to find my birth mother and how I was still struggling with my adopted mother's rejection. Anna was there to listen, to comfort, and to help me with the decision to look for my birth mother. During these conversations, Anna and I became very close as I was baring my soul to her. Anna was a mother and from her perspective, she thought my birth mother could, should, and hopefully would be receptive to meeting me.

Over the course of about a month, I finally made the decision to look for her. I had no idea how to do this, so I hired an agency to find her. Once that was in the works, I let them look for my mother and tried not to think about it. That's hard to do when your heart leaps every time your phone rings. *Is it them? Did they find her?* Patience, when you're sitting on the sidelines, is pretty much impossible but I hung in there. What else could I do but wait? But doing nothing is torment and I was crazy with anticipation and apprehension.

Anna knew how hard waiting was for me, so she planned fun outings for us to keep my mind otherwise occupied. One day, she drove us out to this nature preserve or park. It was serene and quiet with all sorts of birds and wildlife, and there were benches to sit on and look out over the land and trails into the woodsy part of the park. That was what appealed to both of us, and we explored the trails for hours. It was an exciting but calming trip for me, and when we got back to Anna's, exhausted from our adventure, we lay back on Anna's bed and both of us fell asleep. I draped my arm over her as we slept and, later in the evening when we both woke up, I started to pull my arm away, but Anna's hand was on my arm, and she held on.

I looked into her face, and she leaned over and kissed me. It was a sweet, simple kiss, just like that—so I kissed her back. And that was the beginning of a beautiful journey we took together in the weeks and months to follow, a life-altering first for both of us. This would be my first gay relationship and Anna and I were a couple like a girl and a guy. She was my girlfriend at this point for sure and I had no regrets about this wonderful human being that came into my life.

> "THAT WHOSOEVER BELIEVETH IN HIM SHOULD NOT PERISH BUT HAVE EVERLASTING LIFE" (JOHN 3:16 KJV).

The key word here is *whosoever*!

7

BIO

The best thing to do when you're waiting for something to happen is to stay busy. I was training almost daily with Bob now, I was getting the hang of choosing my weight amounts based on the sets and reps we were going to do, and I was getting stronger. At first, I didn't realize it, but then all at once, something must have clicked in my form, and I started putting up some good numbers. When I started squatting close to 280 pounds, the gym would go quiet as I got ready to lift. I thought it was funny, but I was lifting an amount of weight not many people had seen a woman do. I wondered how strong I could get. The thought was intoxicating, and I couldn't help it, I trained harder and harder, heavier and heavier. After about four months, Bob and I both thought I was ready for a powerlifting meet. We chose the Tower Club Powerlifting Competition to be held in Indianapolis ten weeks later in July. I hoped the powerlifting judges would like me better than the bodybuilding judges did.

When I said this to Bob, he just said, "All you must do is lift the weight, just like you do, slow and strict, no worries at all. Your numbers will speak for themselves. Everyone's going to love you in this sport, Krista, I promise you. I'm willing to bet, on competition day, you're going to know in your heart that this is *your* sport! It is, Krista—it *is*." I was putting up some good numbers so maybe he was right. But Bob loved this sport so much, I think he thought everyone should love it. He was making it sound like it was already a done deal. I wasn't so sure, having had a few not-so-great moments on the stage. But I loved lifting heavy, and I felt strong so maybe it would be different this time. Bob planned out my ten-week-till-competition regimen like a scientific project. I trusted Bob implicitly and did exactly what he told me in those ten weeks leading up to my first competition. If it didn't go well, I didn't want it to be because of him—this was on me, and I was going to do it right. There just wasn't any other way to do things for this girl.

About halfway through the ten weeks, while I was lying on my bed watching television after my workout, the phone rang. I figured it was Anna because we were supposed to meet up later that evening. But the voice on the other end was not Anna's—it was Susan Drake; the CEO of the Boston Connection Adoption Agency I had hired to find my biological family. I literally could not speak.

She eventually realized I was still on the line, and she said simply, "Krista, I have news for you. Can you come to Boston?" *Oh, my Lord, what does this mean? Did she find her?* My heart was in my throat, but as soon as I found my voice, I bombarded her with questions. Yes, she had been found, and yes, she had agreed to meet me. That was about all Susan could tell me. Not even sure what was happening, arrangements were made for me to fly to Boston and stay for a few days. Fortunately, this was going to be over the weekend, so I would only have to miss one day of work. I told Anna, who was thrilled for me. She promised to cover for me at work and not tell anyone my news. This was a very private and emotional journey for me, and I didn't want everyone looking at me funny when I came back to work or asking me a bunch of questions. The only other people I told were my cousin Carolyn in California and, of course, Lenita. I knew they would keep my secret, and they did.

The next eleven days were the longest of my life. I couldn't wait to meet the woman who had brought me into the world.

Somewhere along the line, I got some paperwork and I found out that my mother's name was Christine. I said her name over and over, and over and over. I was in a daze, to say the least. I barely remember working or training during that time but apparently, I did. I still had a job to come back to and my training was right where I left it. Once I got that phone call, there was nothing in the world that mattered except this trip. I was going to meet my mother! And that's all I thought of until the day arrived.

It was the spring of 1989 when I flew from Indy to Boston. Anna drove me to the airport for the flight. She was so excited for me. We walked the length of the terminal and finally got to my gate. She held me close as I was trembling, and I just couldn't stop. I was so excited and nervous, I couldn't even sit down. If I were a drinker, this would have been the time, but I'm not, so I just had to suffer through the waiting on pins and needles. Anna stayed with me while we waited for boarding, and I didn't realize I was clinging to her; she had to pry me off when it was time for me to board. She smiled and I could tell she was truly happy for me and as I walked away, she waved at me every time I turned back around to look at her.

And then I was by myself on the ramp and the reality of everything set in. *I am going to meet my mother! Christine.* I kept saying it to myself . . . well, not *just* to myself for long. Once I was seated on the plane, I immediately told everyone within earshot that my birth mother had been found and I was on my way to meet her. I couldn't keep my mouth shut; this was monumental for me. Complete strangers shared in my excitement and asked questions I had no answers for. Ninety minutes passed in a flash, and I was in Boston, and she was in the terminal waiting for me! I've never fainted but I thought I might when I tried to get out of my seat, I was so nervous. Suddenly an older lady grabbed my arm and practically yanked me out into the aisle.

"Come on, we all want to see this!" I heard some laughter at the stranger's excitement. She bustled me smartly down the aisle and up the ramp, and then I was there. My moment of truth. *I am going to find the piece of myself I have been missing my whole life, who I am.* It was always "who am I?" before that day, but that was the day I would *know*.

Out of the corner of my eye, I saw a big white sign with KRISTA printed on it. Behind the sign were three women and two children. I couldn't move; I just stood there. But before I could even think, *One of these women is my mother*, I found myself already looking at her—and I *knew* her. I don't know how, but I did, without a doubt. My mother and I locked eyes, and it was like the whole rest of the world had fallen away and all I could see was her face. Just laying my eyes on her for the first time, my heart was pounding so hard, the world went silent. She was still probably twenty feet away, but it was like we were the only two people in the world. I was captivated. She knew me too. I wasn't wearing a Krista sign, yet she still knew me when she saw me. I think I started to love her right then.

I felt a little pat on my shoulder, "Go on honey, go to her," and the older lady gently pushed me into motion, and the twenty feet between us began to shrink. The small group of passengers that followed me off the plane to meet her held a collective breath as I walked toward her. *Well, maybe now I'll faint*, I thought, but I didn't, and suddenly, a wave of emotion welled up inside of me, and I walked straight to her, my arms reaching out. She took a few tentative steps toward me, and we embraced. I think I cried a little, I was so thankful, first that she was alive, and she had been found, and she answered the letter from the adoption agency, and she agreed to meet me, and she was here, and we were together again for the first time since I was born. I couldn't let her go for a long moment. I couldn't even look away and acknowledge the claps and cheers from my flying companions, but I think they understood.

When I could finally take my eyes off her, she introduced her sister Gloria and two of Gloria's three children who were almost my age. Then their mother, my grandmother, who was named Gloria also. Well, this totally exceeded my expectations, a mother, an aunt, cousins, and a grandmother! I looked back and forth between the three women and just couldn't believe my eyes. There was something familiar on each face. I didn't understand what it was, but even though I knew I was seeing these women for the first time, I felt like I had seen all their faces before.

The ladies had thought ahead, knowing I was going to have a million questions, and they had made reservations at a pizza place (famous for real Italian pie) where we could eat and talk.

First, they told me about their family. They were a second- or third-generation Naples Italian family, and very Catholic. So, when Christine turned up pregnant, from a Black man no less—a fact that would mar the family reputation irreparably—they couldn't let that happen. So, Christine went to "art school" during her pregnancy and returned after I was born, and that was that. A nice tidy little package. And the three women at the table were three of only four women who knew of my existence. Christine's other sister, Jeannie, knew but didn't live close enough to meet the others in Boston. So, the story of "me" was buried good and deep, with these four women in the archives of their family secrets.

Later, we all went to my new Aunt Gloria's house where I would stay for the duration of my visit. Christine was married and her husband had no idea about me so obviously I wouldn't be staying with her. But I didn't care, I was here in Boston and getting to know my mother. After talking well into the night, my mother and my newfound grandmother left for home. My Aunt Gloria had a nice guest room and as wound up as I felt, I fell asleep almost immediately exhausted. My last thought was that I would spend the next day with Christine—just her and I, a whole day with my mother. It was a blissful night and I slept hard, contented.

In the morning, Gloria and I had breakfast together as we waited for Christine. I asked Gloria about the family and learned what I could about the family history. Other than having bad eyes, there were no major health concerns, nothing that ran in the family. I found out they had four brothers too. Uncles! This was getting better and better. I was excited to meet them too, but Aunt

Gloria said that could not happen. They didn't even know about me. No men in the family knew Christine was pregnant, and had given birth to me—still, to this day. Wow. Gloria's description of their father was somewhat of a *Godfather*-type of man, very Italian, gruff, but with a secret kind heart. She said if her dad had known about me, he would have wanted to keep me in the family, but Christine's mother made the decision about me without his knowing, and that was that.

Christine pulled up to Gloria's right at nine and picked me up. Once we were in her car, she said she had somewhere important to take me. We drove about forty-five minutes out of the city to a somewhat rural area where she pulled up to a large house. By the time we got there, I knew this was where Christine had come during her pregnancy. An elderly white lady came out of the house to greet us, and Christine introduced her as Sally. Sally had opened her home to unwed mothers for some thirty-plus years. Sally and Christine embraced, and I saw the connection these two had, then Sally beamed at me—a child she helped bring into the world. We stayed about an hour; the whole time Sally was smiling at me. We walked around the house and I saw the room Christine had called hers while pregnant with me. This home was a place full of kindness, acceptance, and love. Christine's family had made a good choice to send her here. As we were getting ready to leave, Sally looked deep into my eyes, held my cheeks in her hands, and kissed my forehead. Even if she couldn't tell me what she knew about me, that act told me I was loved.

After our visit with Sally, we were both getting hungry, so we made our way back to the city to get something to eat. Christine drove us to this nice restaurant right by Plymouth Rock at the harbor. As I sat across from her, I studied every inch of her face. Her jawbone was the same as mine, and her eyebrows were shaped like mine, but her hair was long, straight, and light brown, held up in a ponytail—very unlike my curly dark brown hair. She was a few inches shorter than I was, about five feet four, and slender. Her skin was very light and her eyes were hazel. She was elegant really, in her fitted jeans, a light blouse, and Converse sneakers. We got our menus and shared a giggle as we both reached for our glasses at the same time, and I saw that her hands were the same shape as mine. I had never seen another person with any of my features, let alone this many, and how bizarre . . . I was looking at a white woman.

After we had eaten, we had some tea and continued talking. My first question to her was, "Did you name me?"

She said, "Yes, I did. Krista is like Christine, and I wanted you to have a part of me." That touched my heart. Even though she was giving me up, she wanted me to take a piece of her with me.

"My middle name is Noelle; did you give me that name too?"

"No, I named you Krista and the N was for my family name." Napolitano. That told me she loved me at the time. I wondered if she wanted to keep me. But something inside of me held onto that question. I just couldn't ask her. Maybe I didn't want to know the potential answer.

During our conversation, I found out that she was an animal lover like me, artistic like me, and she drove fast just like me. When I asked about my father though, Christine started to clam up and then there was an awkward silence for a while. She did say something to me I felt like she was lying about. She and my father were at a party, and she was date raped. I just didn't feel from her energy that she was telling the truth. I think she and my father were girlfriend and boyfriend and, from his description, he was very handsome, but they had to keep their interracial relationship on the hush-hush because—in the 1960s—that was a no-no for sure. The other story she told me was that she tried to abort me with a wire clothes hanger. I just thought when she said that, *Who says these hurtful things, that you tried to kill me, to the child you put up for adoption some twenty-three years ago.* The next day I would find out from Aunt Gloria that Christine had some real mental issues.

After we finished our conversation at the restaurant and walked around Plymouth Rock, she said she had somewhere else she wanted to take me. It was a place where our mutual love for animals made us both at ease, an elaborate stable where she boarded several of her Arabian show horses. She let me help feed and brush them. Then she showed me a little of what they do in a show. She rode one around the arena and its mane and tail flowed like silk as the horse lifted its manicured feet in a prancing sort of way. The horse's movements were mesmerizing, and I couldn't stop staring in awe at its prance. The movement looked so effortless, almost like it was floating. I could see why Christine loved these Arabian horses. She said they were quite an expensive pastime though. As the day was winding to a close, in one moment I felt like I had known Christine my whole life, and then in the next moment, she was someone I just met yesterday. She seemed totally open and honest about some things and then evasive and possibly even untruthful about other things—at least, that is how her answers to my questions came across. It was a very strange feeling. After all, I wasn't here to cause family problems, I just wanted to know the truth about my birth family and maybe even become a part of it.

Before Christine dropped me off at Gloria's, she said she had a few things to give me. She gave me a painting of some flowers she had done. It was a beautiful painting; she was quite talented. Next was a little crop (a short horse whip), and then she pulled out a piece of a bracelet and handed it to me. She said nothing about it, but I could feel the weight of her gesture. The bracelet meant something to her with regard to me. Maybe my father had given it to her, but she didn't say, and I didn't ask. There was something fragile about Christine, I couldn't put my finger on it but sometimes she seemed like she might fall apart. I didn't know if this was because of me being here, or if she was always this fragile. I just couldn't tell.

The next morning, I asked Gloria a few more pointed questions about Christine. She said Christine struggles emotionally and is in therapy and the family does their best to protect her. That's why all of them had accompanied her to meet me, they didn't want her to be alone. When I asked about my father, Gloria said Christine had gone to a party with this man and things turned bad and he forced himself on her. But when I asked Christine earlier about him, she seemed protective of him. Had she loved him? What I did get out of Christine was that she saw him once, years later, on a street in Boston but they hadn't spoken. She wasn't even sure he saw her. She was already married and expecting my half-brother Jason at the time. What could she have said?

After my two-day emotional marathon, I boarded my plane to Indy, emotions conflicting, spinning, and spiraling in my thoughts. I just didn't believe some of the answers I was given. I'm street savvy enough to know when people are not being straight with me, and some things just did not ring true. I couldn't figure out what they had to gain or lose by not telling me the truth. I guess the big thing I thought was being covered up was whether I was wanted or not. Was I the product of two young lovers? Did I see something flash in her eyes when "he" was mentioned? Or was Christine date raped like I was told? And why does all this secrecy matter anymore? Which made me wonder—did my father even know about me? Did he know Christine was pregnant? My questions went on and on. However, I knew I had to be patient. Christine said she wanted to have a relationship with me, and we could write letters to each other for now and see how that goes. I had to be happy with that. I mean, it could have gone better, but I was truly rejoicing we were going to give our relationship a try. I was already writing a letter to her on my flight back home. This was my only chance to have a relationship with my mother, so I had to proceed at her speed. I could do that. Whatever it took.

I arrived at the Indy airport happy, confused, exhausted, and exhilarated, all at the same time. Anna was there, a nervous smile on her face, not knowing what to expect. I was a nonstop chatterbox all the way home to my apartment. Anna listened and took it all in, saving her questions for later. Once we got to my apartment and went through my nightly rituals, like brushing my teeth and putting on my pajamas, I continued to tell her everything. Before I knew it, I was in bed, still talking to her, as my eyes closed, and I drifted off to sleep.

> "GOD THE FATHER IS THIS: TO VISIT ORPHANS AND WIDOWS IN THEIR AFFLICTION" [JAMES 1:27 ESV].

My adopted family (Father, John Ford).

Christmas 1967 with my new family. Mother Catherine Ann Ford, sister, Stacey Lynn Ford, and me, Krista Ford.

My first summer (1980) in Tracy, California, and Stockton with cousins.

Cousin Lenita Poindexter and I at Our Savior Lutheran Church in Indianapolis, Indiana, singing in the church choir.

My job working at Chuck E. Cheese's in Tracy, California, seventeen years old.

Stacey Lynn Ford (my sister) and I.

My first car, 1975 Chevy Monte Carlo in front of my first apartment in Indianapolis, Indiana.

My first apartment with Eric Beer (Boyfriend).

Stacey and Bob "Doc" Sidebottom once they became a couple.

KRISTA'S PROMISE

*Logan Airport Boston, Massachusetts,
meeting my Biological Family for the first time in 1989.*

NPC Indiana Bodybuilding Contest, nineteen years old (my first, 1985).

8

THE STRENGTH OF ONE

I made my way through the next few days in a bit of fog, my whole life had completely changed. I met my mother, Christine. My first letter to her was written, and rewritten, at least three times. At last, it sounded okay. I've never been at a loss for words before, until now, but I did my best. I had slipped it into the mailbox the previous evening and now waited anxiously for a return letter.

Work was good. No one looked at me funny or asked any questions when I came back, which was fine with me. Anna had kept my secret. But as I looked around at my world, it seemed different somehow. I felt bigger, empowered.

Bob was already at the gym when I got there in the afternoon. We had four weeks left before the competition. We had a small team to take to this meet, Bob, me, Ron, and Marty—some other powerlifters from Gold's Gym West who trained with us from time to time when our schedules allowed. Bob and Marty had competed before, but it was mine and Ron's first powerlifting meet. I had no idea what to expect but I knew I was in good hands. Bob and Marty would show us the ropes and take care of us along the way.

The next few weeks were intense. I had missed one workout, going to Boston, so I tried to make up for that every day. I didn't want to lose any strength or focus. I wanted to do well and have a good experience on stage. The only way to do that was to lift heavy, so that's what I did. I thought of Christine during my workouts, wondering if she had ever lifted weights. I didn't think so. In my letter, I told her I was getting ready for my first powerlifting meet, I told her about Bob and my other lifting buddies, and I shared my excitement with her I felt over this new sport. Maybe Bob was right. Maybe this would be the sport for me. I wondered if she would ever see me compete. I hoped so. Competing was what my life was about.

Almost two weeks passed, work and workouts were all going fine. I drove home one Tuesday evening and stopped at the mailbox, and there it was, a letter from Christine! Wow! I was so excited; I tore it open right there at the mailbox. It was a two-page letter answering all the things I asked her about. She updated me on the status of the horses, told me about her work as a secretary, and a few family outings they had gone on. Then she asked me how my training was going, getting ready for my first competition.

I stood in front of my apartment building for a few minutes, rereading every word, my heart feeling full. My mother's words, how precious. I think I read her letter three times before I could even walk into my apartment. I knew right where I would put the letter. I acquired a purple velvet box, and this is where I would put them. The bracelet she had given me was already in there, along with all the papers I had gotten from the adoption agency. I placed the box on my dresser, right next to my bed, closed. The painting of the flowers she had given me hung right above the box, the first thing I saw every time I walked into my bedroom.

Finally, the day arrived. Competition day! I had a good night's sleep and woke up feeling rested, ready, and excited. Marty, Ron, Bob, and I met up at the gym early in the morning and Bob drove us all to the meet, the Total Power Club Powerlifting Championships in Avon, Indiana. I was the ripe ole age of twenty-two years, and the first thing we all did was weigh in. I weighed in at 154.5 pounds so I would be competing in the middleweight class. That was fine with me, I didn't know any difference. After we all weighed in, Bob suggested we go get some breakfast. As soon as that was said, I realized I really was hungry. We hadn't eaten breakfast so we would weigh in as light as possible. Bob said if there was ever a tie of weight lifted, whoever weighed less would be the winner. That made sense. So, we all piled back into Bob's car and went to get some breakfast.

Once back at the gym, which was small for a gym let alone a competition site, we started getting our gear out and ready.

Bob was constantly talking to me. "Listen for your commands, don't move unless they tell you to. They are going to give you the okay to start your squats. So go get under the bar, back out of the rack, and set up. Get your body into your perfect lifting position. Really feel it, okay? Because once you appear to the judge that you are set, you can't move your hands or feet." He made sure we understood that point. "Then nod at your judge," he continued, "that signals to him you are ready, and he will say 'squat,' usually with a hand signal accompanying the command. Then you squat and come back up and just stand still, don't rack your bar yet. You must wait for the judge to give you the command 'rack.' The judge won't give the command until he verifies that your knees are locked, and you are fully upright. Then, once he gives you the rack command, you walk your bar forward to the rack and put it down."

I paid close attention and nodded my understanding. Bob continued, "I will be on the side of you. Listen to me. I will tell you if you're low enough and I will talk you through your lift. There will be a rule briefing soon and the judges will tell us all the specifics, but, bottom line, listen to the judges and listen to me and you'll be fine."

Out of the corner of my eye, I saw my sister, Stacey! I couldn't believe she had been able to make it, as she hadn't been sure the night before. She couldn't make the bodybuilding contest, but she was here for this. I introduced her to my teammates, and I had to brag about her, my sister the RN nurse who had just landed a great job at the VA medical center in Indianapolis. Bob seemed quite impressed with her. And then I saw Anna, my girlfriend, walking in. I left Stacey with Bob and ran over to get her. I gave her a hug and a kiss and took her over to meet my sister and friends. After the introductions were made, Anna and Stacey sat together with our big pile of gear surrounding them.

At about that time, I felt a tap on my shoulder. I turned and there was Joe Jones, my bodybuilder ex-boyfriend from UPS and the gym. He gave me a quick hug and said, "I had to see this, Krista. You go do your thing." And he went to take a seat in front of the platform.

The rules briefing was just like Bob said it would be and then we were ready to go. Women and lightweight men lifted in the first flight and then the bigger guys in the second. I would be the first of our little group to lift, so the three of them were all gathered around me. I was wrestled into my suit, Bob wrapped my knees, and when I stood up, he tightened my belt, and I was ready to go. I felt strong and confident I could do this. I didn't know what weight was on the bar because Bob decided my numbers and just told me to lift it. I unracked the bar, took a few steps back to get out of the rack, then got into my stance and looked at the judge. He was looking right at me, so I started my squat. I heard Bob's voice at my side as I squatted, "Down, down, down, okay, up, slow," and I came up and stood still at the top. After the rack command, I walked forward and put the bar back down on the rack, then I looked up and saw two red lights and a white one in a little box in front of the platform. Two red lights meant two judges declared the lift was no good. And two out of three is the official result—the lift was no good. I knew my form had been good. I heard Bob beside me the whole way, and I know I went deep enough in my squat, so what went wrong? As soon as I got off the platform, I asked Bob what happened.

He calmly said, "Your squat was perfect, Krista, just like we practiced. No worries there."

"Okay, what then? Come on, Bob."

"Well, you didn't give your head judge a chance to tell you to squat. He must give you the command. You just went." After a moment of stunned silence, I realized he was right. I was so eager and nervous, I just got set up, made sure the judge was watching, and squatted. Well, I won't do that again. And I never did. (Beating the command like that normally gets you three red lights.)

So, twice more I squatted, down deep and back up, after the command of course, and both times I saw three white lights. Bob was nearly leaping around when we got away from the platform, he was so excited.

"Krista, you just squatted three hundred pounds!"

"What?" I exclaimed.

"You did it, you squatted three hundred!"

I couldn't believe it; I had gotten maybe 280 in the gym before this.

Stacey was there, almost as excited as Bob, "Wow, Krista, you are *so* strong!" We were so opposite growing up—her loving books, and me loving sports—but I think she understood me down to my bones that day. She could tell what this meant to me.

Anna smiled at me and gave me a quick hug. She was enjoying finally getting to see what I'd been talking about for the last six months. She laughed and said, "This is way more exciting than I thought it would be." And then, "Wow, I knew you were good at this, Krista, but I didn't know you were *this* good! This is amazing!" She was so excited for me, so proud of me, and so happy for me. She was having a blast, and so was I. This was turning out to be a great day.

Then it was on to the bench press. I tried to remember everything Bob told me. "Keep tight, get your feet solid and far under you, and once you get set up, don't move your hands or feet. Wait for the 'press' and 'rack' commands, and never, never, never, and I do mean never, let your booty come off that bench. That's an automatic bad lift." I thought my form was good and solid, but I certainly was not over-confident.

The guys got me into my bench shirt, wrapped my wrists, and finally cinched on my belt. When my time to lift came, I got into position on the bench, followed the commands, and listened for Bob. My lift was good, with three white lights, and Bob was right there.

"Yeah, Krista, you got this, you're doing great." Another lift, which was also good. And then it was time for my final bench attempt. I got in position and got myself as tight as I could. When I lifted the bar off the rack, I could tell it felt a little heavier than I was expecting but I tried not to think about it. I trusted Bob and I knew he wouldn't put anything on my bar I couldn't lift, or almost lift, so I'm going for it. I got the bar down to position and waited for the "press" command. One split second of doubt went through my mind—this was *heavy*. But when I heard 'press', I pressed *hard*. And from what I could hear, the crowd was cheering and clapping, and the bar went up and kept going up and then I locked it out. Fortunately, I remembered to wait for my 'rack' command.

Bob, once again, was leaping around, very excited. "You just benched two twenty-five, Krista! Oh my gosh!" As I watched his antics, I hoped he'd have enough energy left to do his lifts.

There was one woman in my class who looked nothing like a powerlifter, she looked like Brigette Nielsen—the actress and ex-wife of Sylvester Stallone. She was tall, slender, short blond, haircut and beautiful. She lifted good amounts, not as much as I did, but very impressive for a slender tall woman. She loved this sport too, and I talked to her between lifts and cheered for her when she lifted. As I looked around, I saw all types of bodies, tall and slim, short and stocky, and everything in between. What Bob said all those months ago came back into my mind. "Just lift the weight, it doesn't matter what you look like." Nice.

After our flight was done benching, it was time for the deadlift. The main thing with the deadlift is having the bar slide smoothly up your legs. When it starts slowing down, the natural tendency is to try to "hitch" it up by getting under the bar with your knees and bumping it upward. That's a no-no, a very bad lift! I tried to remember everything I had learned. And then it was my turn to lift. Once again, I wrestled into my suit and tightened my belt. If you have not seen a dead lifter walking up to the platform, it is serious and comical all at the same time. It looks like a cross between a cartoon character and a zombie. Nobody laughs though because we all look like that. (I heard later that Stacey and Anna had gotten a pretty good laugh at me, which is fine. I used to be Chuck E. Cheese, remember? This suit had nothing on a mouse suit, believe me.) So, once on the platform, hands chalked up, baby powder down my shins so the bar could slide easily, and facing the judges, I got my feet set, grabbed the bar, and pulled. And up it went, no problem, light almost. When the judge signaled for me to put the bar down, I put it down slowly like Bob showed me. And when I looked up, I saw the three white lights. I think I am going to like this sport; I like seeing white lights. My second lift went well, and then it was time for my final lift. When I stepped onto the platform, I started to count the weight loaded on the bar, but Bob must have seen me doing that.

He started yelling, "Go, Krista, go now, you've got this!" which was enough to distract me from adding up all the weights. I got set up and pulled that bar again, a wee bit slower this time, but I kept it moving. I remembered that, if it's still moving up, it can go as slow as it takes. And then I was up, locked out and I waited for my signal. I could already hear Bob screaming on the side and I knew it was a good lift. I saw the white lights and it was done. I went eight for nine in my first competition. That was what Bob was hoping for and he had chosen my weights appropriately. And that last deadlift was 325 pounds, more than I had ever done. Bob totaled up my lifts in his head and was shouting 850, 850, over and over.

And then Ron was there, adding to the commotion, "That's what I'm talking about, Krista! Oh yeah!" and a minute later he whispered in my ear, "This is you, Krista," and he looked right into my eyes, and I knew exactly what he meant.

I knew I lifted more than the other women, so did that mean I won? I hoped so. The day was long, Bob, Ron, and Marty all lifted, and I did what I could to help the guys with their equipment. The three of them were in different classes and in the end, all three of them won their classes. Bob in the 220 class, Ron in the 242 class, and Marty in the 181 class. When the awards were presented, each lifter was called out by name and given their award. When the women were announced and the announcer got to my class, I held my breath, could it be true . . .

The announcer said simply, "And with a total of eight hundred fifty pounds, the winner of the women's middleweight class is Krista Ford." Bob patted my back as I walked up to the stage. When I got there, I received my first award for powerlifting. I thanked the presenter and turned to leave the stage. It was true, I lifted the most weight and I won. I smiled at Bob, who was sporting the biggest grin I had ever seen—he was beaming at me. And he was standing close to my sister, who was beaming just as big. Did something happen between the two of them that I missed? (I would check into what was going on with them later.) I came back to our group and sat down by Anna and Stacey, feeling content and happy. And for now, I would just languish in my victory, surrounded by my sister, my girlfriend, and my gym family.

After all the awards were presented, there was a bit of a lull, and it seemed like everyone was waiting for something. Nobody said anything about it, so I just waited with our group. I was happy for all of us, we had all won our classes. I read the inscription on my trophy, "Tower Club Powerlifting Championship Women's Middleweight Class First Place." With all four of us winning our classes, I didn't think that day could get any better, but it was about to.

The announcer made his way back to the platform and began, "And without any further ado," he boomed, "We're ready to call back two of our lifters for the final presentation." I was thinking someone must have made a big record or something when I thought I heard my name being called. I looked so confused, and the guys started laughing at me, motioning me to go to the platform. I didn't know why; as far as I knew, I was done. I hadn't broken any records.

As I stepped up onto the platform, the announcer continued, "By means of the Schwartz Malone formula, Krista Ford, you are 'Best Lifter' for the women." I stood dumbfounded while another trophy was handed to me. Best lifter, what did that even mean? I smiled at the applause as I made my way off the platform.

Bob gave me a big hug and said, "That means you were the best female lifter today, Krista, pound for pound." I let that sink in for a minute. I didn't just win my class, I won over all the other women lifters, big, small, and in-between.

I blinked and it finally hit me; I was at home here. And in that moment, I knew. *This* was my sport.

Later that night, I had a long talk with God—me doing most of the talking as usual. I thanked Him for my physique and my body's ability to respond and develop. And my strength! Wow, thank you especially for that. This was the sport I could go to the top with. I know I still had a ton to learn, but I could be the best in the world. "I will do my part; I will train with everything I have, and I will go through anything You put before me. Most opportunities, people, places, and things have been suggested or introduced to me, and I've always had a free spirit and mind to at least explore the possibilities.

> "THE LORD IS MY ROCK, AND MY FORTRESS, AND MY DELIVERER; MY GOD, MY STRENGTH, IN WHOM I WILL TRUST" [PSALM 18:2 KJV].

9

THE INTRO

When I got back to the gym the following week, word of our performance at the powerlifting meet had made the rounds. I was greeted by lots of shouts and pats on my back. People I didn't even know were saying hi to me and congratulating me. It was as if I gained heightened status overnight, people were watching me now.

Bob, of course, was not going to let us soak it up and lounge around for long. Literally, within minutes, we were back at the weights. Bob and I had decided our next competition would be in two months, in Canton, Ohio, a big meet in the mecca of powerlifting. This had been decided on our return trip from the Total Power Club meet and we were all excited to get back into our training and excited for a big meet. The Total Club meet had about thirty lifters, and the Ohio meets usually had about one hundred lifters. I couldn't even imagine that many powerlifters in one place at the same time. I don't know if Bob was as excited as I was. All I knew was I couldn't wait.

Meanwhile, I had written a nice long letter to Christine, my mother. I told her all about the competition, how I won my class and then was surprised to learn what the Best Lifter was and that I won that too. I think I told her everything I knew about powerlifting, and about the upcoming meet. I had given my cousin Carolyn's information to Christine in Boston, but I reminded her of it. I wanted Christine to be able to get in touch with me via Carolyn if she needed to and I was off competing somewhere. This might have been a little premature on my part, but when I get excited about something, I'm a hundred paces down the road already.

Training was going well. Even though we weren't currently doing any maximum lifts right now, I could tell my strength was increasing. I was anxious to see what I would lift in the next competition. It was happening in small incremental increases. Bob made sure we increased our weights slowly, so as not to get unnecessary injuries. I was blessed beyond measure to be mentored in this sport by Bob. He knew how to train for it, and he was patient with the body's response to the training. And he was old enough to know you can't master this sport in a month or two, a fact he tried desperately to convey to us newbies chomping at the bit to go heavier and heavier. In the end, Bob won, and we lifted what he told us to. I will give credit where it is due, thanks to Bob, none of us got hurt. He took good care of all of us.

When we trained alone, I asked Bob a question about my sister. "Have you ever dated a Black woman?"

He said, "No!"

I said, "Would you?"

He said yes, so, I mentioned my sister to him. Stacey told me growing up she only wanted to be with a white man. I told her not to ever tell Daddy that and we both laughed. I remember that like it was yesterday. So, Bob finally took the hint and called Stacey. Bob was a good man; I could attest to that. If anyone was good enough for my sister, it was Bob, and when he did call her, she was flattered but not surprised because I had already hinted at it. They really *had* made a connection at the meet; I wasn't mistaken about that. Someone had finally turned the head of my shy introverted sister.

So, Bob began to see my sister, and they were a couple for fifteen years prior to his sudden passing at the early age of fifty-six. This was Stacey's first-ever boyfriend in life, and he was so special to me as well—after all, Robert "Bob" Sidebottom introduced me to the wonderful sport of powerlifting, which has turned into my passion and love.

Anna and I were happy and enjoying our newfound interests together. We started a women's softball team at Target and played several teams from Walmart and some city teams. On the softball field was where Anna was a rock star. She could catch anything by running backward, forward, sideway, jumping, diving, leaping, whatever it took, and she would catch it nearly every time! I just laughed and shook my head every time she did it. She just knew she had it, and she did. Anna was shy with most people usually, but out on the field with our buddies, she really let her true self out. There were high-fives and little dance moves we did when our team made a good play. Anna had fans too; she got quite a few whistles and cheers after her plays.

One day, we were playing a game and her estranged soon-to-be ex-husband was in the stands. We didn't know why he was there, we never found out, but he didn't like all the attention she was getting. He didn't like it one bit. We were just hoping he wouldn't do anything crazy, he could yell and call us names all he wanted, but I draw the line if someone tries to hurt one of my friends. I'm thinking, *Not gonna happen, buddy. Just sayin' don't even go there.* Well, a team of girls was no threat to this big boy, and he charged into our midst as soon as the game ended. I was gathering up bats and equipment when he came onto the field and our whole team gathered protectively around Anna. The girls started telling him to leave Anna alone and to please just go. Not feeling threatened by us, he stood his ground and demanded Anna leave with him. Anna shook her head no and held onto the teammate she was next to. Seeing her so scared like that, I couldn't take it anymore. I grabbed a bat out of the bag and threw the loaded bag down. Anybody who's ever been on a baseball field knows what a bat bag sounds like.

"You're leaving now!" I said in a voice that didn't need my Louisville slugger to convince him I meant it. I was eyeballing a home run right around his head. He eyed me levelly and decided he was not going to take me on and turned to leave. A few of us "escorted" him for a way, just to make sure he left. Then we ran back to see if Anna was okay. She was doing much better when we got back, so everything ended well, but something like that never should have happened in the first place. What a creep.

That night, when we were alone, Anna teased me that she thought I really was going to knock him in the head with the bat. We laughed but I couldn't completely deny it. I will protect those I care about; how could I *not*? However, I probably would have hit him in the leg. The truth was, I hoped my muscles and the way I was wielding that bat would be enough, and thankfully it was. But I certainly don't like it when someone puts me in a position like that; watching my girlfriend get abused or take on the bully myself, neither being an acceptable choice. But once that day was over, our lives thankfully fell back into our normal routine. Our softball season continued without another incident, and Anna was back to her fun-loving ways out on the field. I learned a lesson in resilience from Anna that year.

I got another letter from Christine. In this one, she congratulated me for my powerlifting meet. She told me she wasn't surprised I won the whole thing, with my athletic ability and intense drive. She caught me up with her family—well the ones I met anyway—and everyone was doing well. She told of the local happenings around Boston, the weather, and anything newsworthy. She told me she still had Carolyn's information handy, so that was good. Her letter was nice, and I read and reread every word. As soon as I finished reading her letter, I began one to her in response. I was so thankful she was in my life now. My own mother. Christine was the one who had given me life, and I thought it was okay if I told her I loved her. I hadn't said it to her until now, and I know she gave me up, but she did make the choice to have me, and I loved her for that, so I told her.

Bob was waiting for me when I got to the gym, grinning from ear to ear. I had no idea what was up, so I looked around the gym to see if someone special was there or if something was happening, but nothing looked out of the ordinary. Then it hit me, that ear-to-ear grin I'd seen only once before, at the meet when he met Stacey! I started laughing and he did too when he knew I understood why he was so happy. He'd obviously gone on a date with her.

I was glad for the two of them, but I didn't want to hear all the details, so I gave Bob a taste of his own medicine, "Come on, Bob, the weights aren't going to lift themselves, let's get to it." He obliged but had a hard time wiping the smile off his face. It was squat day, and I hadn't met anyone yet who could keep a smile on their face on a heavy squat day, so eventually, his smile did fade but I could still see it in his eyes. He really liked my sister, and I was as pleased as anyone could be.

We were lifting heavier weights now, with the meet just two weeks away, and as I suspected, my numbers were higher than before. Bob kept us from getting too far ahead of ourselves, but I thought I might be able to hit close to an 880 total. That, or better, was my goal. Everything was on schedule. This meet was large enough to have the standard weight classes and Bob and I decided I would compete in the 165-pound class, so I needed to start weighing myself every day to make sure I was where I needed to be. Bob didn't want any last-minute surprises, and neither did I, so weigh-ins were now a part of our daily training. Bob also discussed nutrition with me, making the case that good nutrition produces a good, strong body. He'd been telling me that from the start, and the bigger the meet, the higher the stakes. I guess this meant not as much candy would be consumed for the next few weeks. Then I had the mortifying thought that Bob had seen my gym bag pocket containing granola bars and candy in varying quantities and I decided right then to minimize the goodies in there. Bob's not a snoop, so I know he didn't see it, but he was right, and my gym bag lost a few pounds later that day. And never again, since then, did my gym bag hold more than just essential food, one granola bar, and one candy bar, that was it. Junk food was not a legitimate dinner any longer.

As the day drew nearer, the tension and anticipation in our little group grew in intensity. Training was hard and heavy. One day to break the tension, Ron and I started horsing around. Not with the weights, just laughing and goofing around. Finally, Bob had to speak up. "This is where the rubber meets the road, you guys. You're pushing your body to its limits. One false move, loss of concentration, balance check, whatever booboo you might do, could be a disaster and cause you serious injury." Bob made sure we understood this. He didn't want us to get complacent because we knew all of this from before. "You must be this careful every time, especially the last few weeks. This is the time when people get hurt. You're lifting as much as your body possibly can, and you know how heavy it feels, right?" He looked around at us and we all shook our heads in agreement. "However, when you lose control of the weight, that's when you find out how heavy it *really* is. If you've ever seen someone fall under a squat, you'll never take that bar for granted again, I guarantee it." He looked at us all seriously. "I just don't want that to be any of you. So, no horsing around anymore till after the meet, okay? I can't take it, really you guys." We all agreed and stifled the urge to call him Dad.

One week before the meet, I came home to a message to call my cousin Carolyn. So, I showered, ate dinner, and then settled into my recliner to call my cousin back. When I heard her voice, I instantly knew something was wrong. I sat up straighter. She could barely speak; she was so upset. When she finally calmed down enough to talk, all she could say was, "Oh, Kris, I need to tell you something."

"Okay," I said to a silent phone. "Just tell me, Carolyn, whatever it is, just tell me." "Okay," she started. "I need to know first, are you sitting down, Sweet Pea?"

Now, I didn't know this at the time, but I remembered hearing it somewhere before: Heartbreaks are tough, but you got to remember that God will never take something away from you without the intention of replacing it with something much better.

> "TO EVERY THING THERE IS A SEASON, AND A TIME TO EVERY PURPOSE UNDER THE HEAVEN" [ECCLESIASTES 3:1-22 KJV].

10

ONE OF THE FOUR AGREEMENTS

I was already sitting down, but when she said my childhood name, I knew it was bad. My throat constricted and my heart started to pound. Finally, she began to speak, "I've just been on the phone with your mother, Christine, for about the last hour."

Oh, thank you, God, she's alive. That was my first thought when Carolyn called. "And then she said Christine doesn't want to be in contact with you anymore," she choked out. "I'm sorry, Kris, I'm so sorry."

"What?" I think I said it because it made no sense at all. I had just gotten a beautiful letter from her two weeks prior. What happened? I could hear Carolyn talking in the background, but I didn't hear the words, my mind was reeling, I felt like I might be sick, my stomach was upside down. After a moment, it was quiet, and Carolyn was saying my name.

Finally, I answered her, and she asked if I heard what she said. "No, I'm sorry."

"Christine said she got a letter from you telling her you loved her, right?" Carolyn inquired.

"I do love her, Carolyn, she's my *mother*, my *real* mother!" I was getting agitated.

"Well, the way she took it was that you are a lesbian and you loved her like that, and she thought that was unnatural." The rest of the conversation was a bit of a blur, but I got that Christine was sending me a letter explaining all of this. "I think she's crazy, Krista. Seriously, I think she has lost her mind. She is not right in the head." I didn't have a thing to say. I couldn't even believe this, *what* did she think? And *how* could she think this? Where does this even come from? What is going on?

Some two hours later, Carolyn was finally ready to let me off the phone. She got me through that first initial shock, the denial of "There's no way she would think that," and then realizing and trying to acknowledge that my mother wanted to end our new reunion. I was devastated and shocked beyond words. But there, in the back of my mind, I didn't like the nagging feeling that I thought this might happen. There were several evasive answers I had gotten from her in Boston; I never thought she was being totally straight with me. But to go to my cousin to tell her to tell me that she didn't want to talk to me anymore? How weird was that? I was somewhat calmed down when Carolyn and I hung up, but the night would prove to be a long one.

By morning, I was in a nasty funk. I felt like Christine had only agreed to meet me out of curiosity. And once she met me, she found her first opportunity to bail on me once again in my life. *Wow*, I thought. How she could have gotten the wrong idea from my letter was just plain impossible—well, if I were dealing with a rational person. Carolyn thought she had lost her mind, literally. Maybe she couldn't handle getting to know me, the child she created with her young black male lover, and then going home to her perfect little life with her white husband and son (my half-brother, Jason, by the way), who didn't even know he had a sister. Maybe she *was* crazy, driven that way by her young life's choices. I don't know. I was trying to do everything at her speed. What did I do wrong? Once again, here in this place of confusion. If I didn't do anything wrong, then why did this happen?

A few of the guys at the gym tried to find out what was wrong with me, but I did not have a word to say. After a few attempts, the matter was dropped, and the weights were once again the focus. I could feel Bob's eyes on me throughout the workouts, but I just couldn't say anything to him, or anyone for that matter. I'm totally ashamed of this discovery. He didn't even know I was looking for my mother. I felt the dirtiness of shame. My own mother—I was her flesh and blood—and still, she didn't want me anymore. That burned. Why bother meeting me if she was just going to dump me once her curiosity was satisfied? That's heartless, I think. And if I wasn't so appalled and aghast at her, I would have . . . I don't know what I wanted to do. I wanted to cry but I was too mad. I wanted to scream but I was too repulsed. It was over. She was done with me. What *could* I do?

Anna did her best to console me, but how could anyone ease the pain of almost getting something you've wanted your whole life, just to have it slip through your fingers the second it's within your reach? Sometimes there are sorrows that have no time or space, they just consume you, your heart, your spirit, and your joy. This was one of those times. There was no easing this pain, not today, not next week, maybe not ever.

It was three days until the competition. I knew my numbers were good, but my heart was certainly not. I went through the motions. Everything was right on schedule, my form was solid, I was strong. However, for all intents and purposes, I was not even there. I was on a pier in Boston, remembering a privileged lady riding a horse, a lady who would never look my way again. My own mother.

When I got home from work the day before the competition, I got the letter. I looked at the envelope, at my mother's handwriting. This would be the last letter I would ever get from her. I took it inside and sat it on the table. From what Carolyn had told me, I already knew what was going to be in it. Christine thought I had an "unnatural love" for her, whatever that meant. Well, I knew what she thought that meant, but I still couldn't understand how she arrived at that conclusion. I thought again, *Maybe she is crazy. Whatever*. I left the letter on the table and went to the gym.

Bob was there when I arrived, and he looked at me closely. He knew something was wrong, but he was enough of a gentleman not to pry. Mostly we just went over our plan and did a little stretching and cardio.

We made our arrangements to get to Canton and then he put his hand on my shoulder and gently said, "Krista, I know something's wrong and I'm sorry." He then faced me and continued, "I'm here, Krista, okay? I'm here, whatever you need." I was looking down so he couldn't see my eyes, which threatened to overflow. I shook my head, and he gave me a quick pat and then he was gone. I got on the stationary bike, and I rode till I couldn't ride anymore. Probably not the best pre-competition strategy, but I just couldn't be still, I had to keep moving. It was dark outside and very late in the evening when I finally quit riding and went home. My legs felt tight, I had ridden for over two hours. I never considered myself an endurance athlete, but I was that day.

Morning came and I was awake before my alarm. I didn't sleep too much, kind of on and off all night. It was competition day, I should have been buzzing with excitement, but no. The envelope still sat on the table unopened. My legs felt tight, and I was just plain old cranky, there's no other word for it. My gym bag, with all my competition gear, sat by the front door, ready for another exciting day. I sat down at the dining table and looked at the letter. I was curious but not ready for any more surprises, so I let it sit. If she doesn't want to be in my life, then so be it. I made it this long without her, I can keep going without her. Obviously not the outcome I dreamed of when meeting my mother, but if she's done with me, I don't know how to have a relationship with her. And with that thought, I picked myself up and headed for the door.

I picked up Anna and met up with Bob (and Stacey) at the gym. We had already decided to take both cars as Bob had some friends in Canton and he wanted to stay a while. He also told me that his friend Larry Parsley was going to be joining us and would help handle us. Anna and I also planned to stay one more day. So, we followed Bob all the way to Canton. Thankfully, Anna took a nice long turn doing the driving, so I would be rested. However, rested was not how I felt; I was tight in my quads and hips and just didn't feel like myself. Normally, I'm quiet before a competition but just about to bubble over inside, I'm so excited. I felt like I might be going to the grocery store, with all the excitement I had. I hoped my attitude would change when I got to the meet site and saw all the lifters and equipment. This was going to be my second meet ever. Canton Open was the name of the competition, and I was the ripe ole age of twenty-three years old.

When we got to Canton, we made our way to the hotel hosting the competition. We were all getting hungry so, once inside, we headed straight for the weigh-in area. I was a little surprised, I was over 165 pounds a few days ago, but I hadn't had much of an appetite the last few days, and weighed in at 162.5—well under my 165-pound class. Bob weighed in and made his 220-pound class, and that part was done. Then we had to get our gear checked. I finally looked around and I was amazed. This meet was big and organized. There were people all over doing various jobs like setting up the platforms, weighing competitors, and checking gear. Weights were being wheeled over to the racks, and I could see a warmup area on the other side of the room. The room itself was a big conference room, and vendors were setting up their booths around the perimeter. Our gear was thoroughly checked; wraps, belts, shirts, singlets, squat suits—everything! Then we were free until the rules briefing, so we went to get some long overdue breakfast. We'd been on the road for over four hours.

When we got back to the hotel after breakfast, we checked into our rooms, brought in our luggage and I laid down for a power nap. When I woke up it was almost time to go. Bob and Stacey knocked on our door a few minutes later and all four of us made our way back to the competition. There were a lot more people in the room now and I started to feel the excitement. We secured a spot for Stacey, Anna, and our gear, and headed over to the rules briefing. I was glad for the reminder of all the little rules of powerlifting, all the dos and don'ts. And again, I would be lifting in the first heat. Bob would lift in the first heat also, but on a different platform. I thought it was exciting to have two platforms going at the same time.

While the crowd was still gathered around for the rules briefing, the meet director, Pat Leonti, announced that Janice Roge-Henderson was in the house, and she had just returned from Worlds and had won the 148-pound class. That was one weight class down from mine! I couldn't wait to see her. What does a world champion in this sport look like up close? I finally saw her a few minutes later when the crowd began to disburse. What I saw first was that Janice had a big back, gigantic for a female, and strong hips and legs underneath. She wasn't very tall, which made her back even more impressive. I won't lie, I was a little starstruck—I watched her until I had to warm up.

My quads and butt were still sore, and they were sluggish feeling. I got my warmup lifts done and I felt strong enough, I guess. The weights felt heavy that day, but I knew it was my heart that was weighing me down. If my first squat was any indication of how the day was going to go, I was in big trouble. I just didn't feel right under the weight. Maybe my muscles were so sore and fatigued they weren't responding like they normally would. I don't know, but it felt like a ton of weight going down and even more coming back up. Not at all what you want to feel on your opening lift. I did get the lift, three white lights confirming it, but it woke me up and kind of scared me. I couldn't explain what happened, why the lift looked and felt so difficult. Bob appraised the situation and gave my next weight amount to the meet official. I would certainly be paying more attention during this lift, that's for sure. I got my second lift easily enough, another three white lights confirming it, although I could still feel the soreness. Bob gave my next amount to the official and then he had to leave me and go warm up for his lifts. Larry stayed with me for my last lift. And my third lift, well, let's just say it went down easy enough, but not so much on the coming up part. The spotters on each side had to assist me, which automatically earned me three red lights—not a pretty sight. It made me cringe, literally.

My benching went fine, in fact, the same exact numbers as my first meet. I knew I was stronger than that, but I just couldn't pull it out of myself. Same thing in the deadlifts, the same numbers as my first meet. My heart just wasn't into it that day and it showed. I was disappointed in myself that my lifts weren't what they should have been, and that I let the distraction of Christine's rejection get the better of me. That couldn't happen again, I needed to get stronger mentally, so I could shut out any distractions when it came to competition day. Easier said than done, I know, but my performance was not what it should have been. In the end, I went eight for nine, and five pounds less than the first meet. Disappointing but nothing compared to the day Bob had.

Somewhere about the time of my deadlifting, Bob was having the worst bench day of his life. He didn't get his first lift, which always puts a substantial damper on your confidence; and he didn't get his second, which was the same weight as the first attempt. (In powerlifting, you can repeat the same weight or go up in weight, but you can't go down to a lower weight.) On his third attempt, still the same weight, his wrists popped forward and the weight fell onto his chest. I don't know how much weight was on the bar, in the 350-pound range, but when the bar falls that suddenly, the lifter's chest takes the brunt of it, despite how close the spotters are. It goes down fast and hard, probably like being kicked in the chest by a giant mule. And to add insult to injury, since he didn't get any of his three bench attempts, he was disqualified, what we call "bombing out." It's devastating when it happens, and Bob was quiet for the rest of the meet, not to mention he was hurting, probably more than he let on.

Several things happened that day that were blessings though. The first was after my first deadlift, the head judge called me to him from the platform after my lift. He said, "You're flexing your biceps when you pull, your elbows are bending." He smiled at me and added, "I don't want to see you tear a bicep today. I want you to be out here competing for a long time. So, you must always keep your arms completely straight when you're pulling, okay?" I thanked him and knew I would look at my deadlifting form right away, I wasn't aware I was doing that. The other blessing was seeing, and then meeting Janice Roge-Henderson. After my benching, as I was walking back to the warm-up area, we passed each other.

She smiled at me and laughingly said, "Hey, do you think you have enough holes in your ears?"

I laughed right back and said, "Yep, six on the right and four on the left," and we both laughed. I congratulated her on her win at Worlds and then we parted ways, walking in opposite directions. Our powerlifting paths would cross again very soon.

After the meet, we all went to dinner: Bob, Larry, Stacey, Anna, and me. We had a delicious pizza and called it an early night as Bob was not feeling very well, and Stacey wanted to take him home to relax.

After that, Anna and I talked about going to the NFL Hall of Fame, I wanted to see whatever they had about Walter Payton and Tom Landry—I always liked Tom's hat. But, in the end, we decided to drive straight back home. I vowed to see the NFL Hall of Fame someday, but not this time. We gathered our belongings and headed for home. The drive was quiet, as I went through the events of the day. I was disappointed with my numbers, I knew I could have done better, but that was my best for that day. Going into this meet, I had a few things on my mind like the conversation with my cousin about Christine's phone call about me. It was enough to have me a tad off my focus for the day, then I was concerned for Bob and wondered how sore he would be after his incident.

On the bright side, I met a world champion and I was happy to look at another first-place trophy. I placed it on my dresser next to the ones from the first meet. Even though I didn't have a great performance that day, I was still loving it. And I loved the people

I met in this sport. Everyone was so supportive of each other; it was like you already knew everybody. That thought made me smile.

That day, Bob got hurt, even after his many years of competing, knowing all the common mistakes, and having good focus. That could have easily been me, hurt on the platform. After seeing that happen to him, I vowed not to let anything get in the way of my focus again.

> "ALSO DO NOT TAKE TO HEART EVERYTHING PEOPLE SAY" [ECCLESIASTES 7:21-22 NKJV].

11

RUBY SLIPPERS

Back home after the meet, life returned to normal. The nine-page typed letter from my mother was opened, read, reread, and put right back into the envelope. No surprises there, other than wondering how some people's minds work. I took all the things she had given me and in anger and rage, ripped everything to shreds and threw everything away. I tried to look for the positives in her rejection. She gave me my life, and she gave me creativity, sensitivity, and passion. So, thank you, Christine N. (and you're welcome I did not spell your married name out). I do hope to stumble upon my half-brother (Jason) someday, just to meet my only blood sibling (that I know of), but I'm not holding my breath for that. He *is* my brother. I couldn't help feeling this in my spirit though, I have been rejected by two mothers in one lifetime, isn't that some sh--.

After recovering from the initial shock of Christine's decision, my focus went back to the weights, the one thing I could always count on. Once again, I tried to train harder than before. I buried myself in my training and that is all I did. I worked at my job, of course, but my real day began when I walked through the gym doors. Bob, Larry, and I studied every aspect of my technique to see where we could make improvements. The main thing we changed was widening my stance slightly in the squat. I trained with my new stance and got it solidified in my muscle memory. I felt strong and balanced in my squats, even better than before. I couldn't wait to compete again. Bob had recovered from his bench incident and was anxious to compete again too. We decided to enter the Tower Power (Columbus Open) meet in May 1990, a full eight months after the Canton meet. This meet was a national qualifier. What that meant for me was my total weight lifted would determine if I qualified for junior nationals or senior nationals. Junior and senior nationals have nothing to do with age, they are strictly lifting classes. Junior nationals are for the good lifters. Senior nationals are for the elite lifters. Could I lift enough to qualify for senior nationals? The qualifying amount for senior nationals that year was 894 for my 165-pound class. If I could lift that much or more, I could skip junior nationals altogether. I began to envision it in my mind, seeing myself lifting the weight I needed. I could do this.

During the next eight months, I could honestly say God and lifting were my only focuses in life. I wanted to compete in this sport and get stronger and stronger. One day, I wanted to be like Janice Roge-Henderson, a world champion. I was nowhere near lifting that much yet, but I was determined, and I believed I could do it. I believed God gifted me with a body that responded to sports. And what I would do with that gift was take it as far as I could. I just had to keep training and stay healthy.

Anna and I were good. She arranged bike rides and dinners for us, and we still had fun working together. She was a true friend during this time. I trained and slept, trained and slept, and she kept me fed and once again planned excursions for us on our down days. My favorite was when Anna and I went for one of our bike rides. I think my legs could tell the difference between a real bike and a stationary one, and all they wanted to do was go faster and faster. Anna did her best to teach me moderation, but when I'm focused, I have a hard time pulling in the reins. At this time in my life, I thought if training hard was good, then training harder must be even better. I have learned over the years that even if you are training harder, you *always* need to listen to your body; give it a chance to catch up with your spirit (and mine always signals full speed ahead). Your heart, mind, and spirit might be ready to compete at the national level, but your body requires weeks, months, or even years, to be ready for this level. I was pushing myself hard, but between Anna and Bob, everything was going according to plan. By spring, we were all in great shape, healthy, happy, and strong.

As the time grew closer for the meet, Bob and I felt ready. It would be just us two competing, and Larry would accompany us and be our handler. Arrangements were made and suddenly the day was upon us. Bob and Larry picked me up and we were on our way. The trip was a blur as I fell back to sleep, and only awoke as we were entering Columbus. It was a beautiful city, and I took in the skyline as we made our way to the meet. I was excited, but it felt a little different this time. I was more dug in, set in my mind what I was going to do. This was a national qualifying meet for APF Senior Nationals, where the big girls and boys played.

I had to lift more than 894 if I wanted to compete at senior nationals this year, which was only two months away, in July, a month before my twenty-fourth birthday, and almost exactly a year since my first powerlifting contest in Indy. To say I was nervous would be an understatement. In my mind, my entire life was on the line. This meant everything to me. I wanted to compete on the national level more than anything. I wanted to show the world I had finally found my sport and would not stop until I had climbed to its mountaintop, God willing. The rejection from Christine, and the nonacceptance from my adopted mother—not feeling wanted or included by either mother—I wanted to prove to them, myself, and the entire world, that I *was* worthy. Worthy of acceptance, inclusion, and love.

Larry pulled into the parking lot of the high school hosting the competition. We piled out and hauled our gear in for our check-in. This meet was Columbus Open, and we were met by the meet director, Jeff Chorpenning, and he was so welcoming and kind. His mother was even there at the meet, greeting the competitors, welcoming everyone, and wishing everyone good luck. She was a sweet lady, and out here supporting her son. Now there's an awesome mother.

We got weighed in, our gear checked, and then—you guessed it—breakfast! I got bacon and eggs, toast and hashbrowns, more than a normal breakfast but I needed serious energy. This was the day I found out if I was good or if I was *elite*, a junior national or senior national.

My new squatting stance felt great; and allowed me to put 330 pounds toward my 894 goal. The bench went well also, another 225 pounds. I was at 555 going into the deadlift. I needed 339 pounds more to qualify. I thought about these numbers on my way back to the warm-up area after the bench. Then I saw a girl warming up who caught my attention, she was in a higher weight class than me, I think 181 or 198, and I could tell, she was a superstar, like Janice. She had a giant back, thick strong legs, and big developed shoulders, just like Janice. She had some wild and crazy blond hair, and something about it made me think of Twisted Sister; so, I was already smiling at her when she approached me and introduced herself as Lynn Boshoven.

"That was some nice benching out there, very good technique," she said to me.

"Thank you!" Wow, I couldn't believe someone like *her* would be complimenting *me*. She asked if I was trying to qualify for senior nationals.

"Yes," I said, "I'm trying."

She said, "You and I will both be there, okay?"

I said, "Okay," and we shook hands, but I still had a long way to go.

Larry gave my first lift amount to the officials, and I lifted it, no problem, and added another 310 to my total. Now I was at 865. The second deadlift was 330, so I was at 885. One lift to go—or nine pounds, however you want to look at it.

My bar was loaded. This was it, my final lift. Once again, I wasn't sure of the amount, but I knew it was going to be more than 339, the minimum I needed to qualify. Could I do it? I could probably lift it in the gym, where I'm relaxed and focused. But here, after eight expenditures of my strength and energy already, did I have enough left in me to lift this final weight? I certainly hope so.

My name was called, and the sixty-second clock began. I had one minute to begin this lift. A quick prayer and I was up on the platform. I looked over at Larry and Bob, who was done benching, had joined him. Bob was looking at me, seriously, and nodded once. That said to me, "You've got this." I got my feet in place, met the eyes of my head judge, and then reached down to get my hands around the bar. For me, right hand grips over the bar, left hand grips under the bar. I was all set. I looked up, and then pulled. Some deadlifts pop right up and then there's some you pull on for what seems an eternity before you can lock it out, showing the judges you are standing fully upright and still holding the weight. This lift was somewhere in the middle but leaning more toward a slow pull. I felt a trickle of sweat run down my face, but I refused to let it distract me, and finally, I got that bar up. I could see Bob from the corner of my eye, while I was looking at my judge, waiting for my "down" command. Bob was staring at the box, waiting for the lights.

After I put my weight down and turned around, I saw the final of three white lights come on.

I could hear Bob and Larry screaming on the side. "You're going, Krista, you're going!" I knew what they meant; I'm going to *senior* nationals. My last deadlift was 350 pounds, making my total 905 pounds. I beat the qualifying amount by eleven pounds!

I couldn't help myself; I was jumping up and down, "I'm going to senior nationals! I'm going to senior nationals!" Bob and Larry corralled me back to the warm-up area where I continued to jump until I could finally stop, but I couldn't hold still, and I walked back and forth across the room about twenty times.

The next flight of dead lifters started a few minutes later, but long enough for me to repeat those words to myself at least a dozen times. Senior nationals! Senior nationals! Then it was time for Lynn to lift. Her opening squat was an astronomical amount, in the high four hundreds, close to five hundred pounds! And for an opener! As she took her pre-lift breath, all the way in and then a teeny bit out, I took my breath in unison with her and watched her every move, moving ever so slightly with her, trying to imagine I was lifting the weight myself. It was incredible to see, perfect. Wow, this was the best female lifter I had ever seen lift. Without a doubt, she would be at senior nationals, and lots more like her. It really would be the big league, with some big lifters. I had a reality check moment when Lynn squatted over five hundred pounds. I would need to bring my absolute A-game. I felt grateful to be in the group qualified to compete with these powerful women, capable of lifts I could only dream of. I couldn't wait to go. I couldn't wait to see this with my own eyes, the absolute best in my sport!

During the lifts, Larry told me that my total was very close to another lifter in my weight class, Shelly Warren. Of course, I wanted to win the competition, but the main thing was qualifying. As it turned out, Shelly out lifted me by seventy pounds. So, I placed second, but I was qualified for senior nationals, so I didn't really care that she beat me.

Well, that's not 100 percent true. I'm about as fierce of a competitor as ever existed, so yes, that hurt a little, truth be told. But I can live with it, I was going to senior nationals. And, no big surprise, Lynn got Best Lifter that day. Bob lifted well, but just missed his qualifying total, so, I would be the only one going from our gym, Gold's West Indy.

One highlight so inspiring to me from this meet was a blind gentleman who was competing. He did the full power meet, three squats, three bench presses, and three deadlifts. His handler walked him up to the equipment then the man oriented himself to the bar with his hands and got set up. He was so calm, the audience was dead silent, and he did his lifts. All without the sense of sight. I can't imagine squatting with my eyes closed. To see a person lift a loaded bar blind was very impressive and humbling. My hat's off to you, you brave and strong young man.

The drive back home seemed to fly by. All I kept saying in my head was, "I'm going to senior nationals." I couldn't quite believe it, but it was true, I had qualified. Somewhere during the drive home, Bob suggested I drop down to the 148-pound class for nationals. I had a moment of hesitation, remembering starving myself for bodybuilding, and how weak that made me feel. I needed to be as strong as I could be, not feeling hungry and wimpy. Thankfully, Bob had seen that time of my life and assured me it would be nothing like that, just cut out a little snack or candy here and there. Bob figured if I could lose weight and maintain my strength, I'd be a more efficient lifter, pound for pound. I could see the logic in that, it made perfect sense. So in the end, it was decided, I would be in the 148-pound class for nationals. That Bob, he sure was persuasive.

They dropped me off at my apartment, and I carried my gym bag in one hand and my trophy in the other. Anna had stopped by and was waiting to hear all about the meet. She helped me in with all my gear and when she couldn't wait any longer, she asked hesitantly and very quietly, "Did you qualify?"

I put my arms around her waist, picked her up, and spun her around, looked right into her eyes, and said, "Yes, I did! I'm going to senior nationals!"

She hugged me tight, and said, "I knew you could do it, Krista." And then, "Where's it going to be at? And when is it? I want to go."

I laughed at her eagerness and said, "It's in Pittsburg in two months." And with that, suddenly I was exhausted and all I wanted to do was sleep. And bless her heart, once again Anna put me to bed, me mumbling all the way about senior nationals. With just three competitions under my belt, I skipped junior national level and went straight to the second-highest level of powerlifting. This made me smile as I thought, *Wow, I'm going to play with the big girls and boys now.*

The title of this chapter goes hand-in-hand with Dorothy from the movie, *The Wiz*, clicking her heels three times for her wish to come true. That was me with my wish to qualify for APF Senior Nationals.

> "THE LEAST OF YOU WILL BECOME A THOUSAND, THE SMALLEST A MIGHTY NATION. I AM THE LORD; IN ITS TIME I WILL DO THIS SWIFTLY" (ISAIAH 60:22 NIV).

12

WANNA COME OUT-N-PLAY?

The next two months were a blur of activity. No sooner had we just done our pre-competition cycle of training for the Tower Power meet, now we were already a week behind in doing it again, back-to-back. In hindsight, maybe that wasn't the best idea in the world, but right then, that was the *only* idea in the world. The only idea that mattered, anyway. Bob and I trained just like always, but this time our workouts were built specifically around me and my needs. Bob said he was relieved not to be competing this year. He wanted to focus on me and help me have the best experience at nationals and put up some good numbers for Indiana. That's exactly what I wanted to do too, so we were both on the same page.

Training was rigorous. Bob and I both wanted the same result, for me to lift the same weight, or more, at the lighter weight class. I would have to lose fifteen pounds to make that happen. This was the only part of the training I was not looking forward to. My new eating style was acceptable, but I hoped it wouldn't last forever—I do love my sweets and treats. But what I really wanted was to make a good showing at my first nationals. That was way more important than any box of chocolates. So, each morning I prayed for the strength to do every repetition I needed, stay focused, keep my technique right, don't snack, and don't get hurt. It would be a whole year for another chance at nationals if I got hurt now. I wasn't worried, but I was certainly as careful as I could be.

Bob kept saying, "There's no room for error, no distractions, no deviations from the plan, Krista. Everything's got to be perfect." Bob was a real training guru. He had every repetition planned for me until nationals. That was fine by me, I knew if I lifted what he put on the bar, I was on schedule. So, there was nothing for me to worry about, in theory, but any time I thought about being at nationals in Pittsburg, or how many days were left, my heart went galloping off at full speed and my stomach balled up into a knot. I don't think I've ever been so nervous in my whole life. I was going to lift with the big girls, the girls I read about in the magazines. Newsflash, Krista, you're not just lifting *with* these girls, you're lifting *against* these girls. And my stomach did another somersault.

One thing I did the day after we got back from Columbus, when I knew I was qualified, I called Inzer Advanced Design (John Inzer company, former powerlifter) and ordered a new squat suit, a deadlift suit, knee wraps, and a single ply bench shirt. The reason I called was because the only choices for colors listed on the order forms were red, navy, and black. There had to be other colors, so I called and put my order in: a red bench shirt, and black and red wraps, both of which were standard. But I was able to custom order a purple deadlift suit, and a pink squat suit! It wasn't pastel either, leaning more toward the neon side, very bright, very nice. All that set me back almost a whole paycheck, but I was making an investment in myself, and I wanted to give myself the best chance I could.

And what can I say, I wanted to look good doing it too.

The fifteen pounds stubbornly melted off, and my six-pack was more solid and full than ever before, showing the core strength I'd gained since I started powerlifting. That was one good thing losing fifteen pounds did for me. I got to see how my body was slowly, very slowly, morphing from a bodybuilder body into a powerlifter body. My back was getting thicker and denser, and I could tell my thighs were too. I had been so focused on training, I didn't even pay much attention, but after losing that body fat, I could see the difference. I was nowhere near as thick and powerful looking as Janice or Lynn, but I looked a little less like a bodybuilder now, and that was fine with me. One kind of physique looks great posing on a stage. The other physique looks like she could carry the entire world. *That's* who *I* wanted to be. So, I was headed to APF Senior Nationals in Pittsburgh, Pennsylvania.

The flight to Pittsburg was exciting as was the drive to the hotel. We got into the hotel lobby and headed to the elevator, the doors opened to none other than the strongest woman in the world, Dawn Reshel-Sharon, standing inside wrapped in a robe and towels. I knew her instantly; I'd seen her pictures numerous times in *Powerlifting USA* magazine. She smiled at us, and I introduced myself and Bob. She said she had been in the steam room trying to shed a few pounds to make her weight class. She was very friendly, and I liked her right away. She wished me good luck and disappeared down the hall.

Bob and I got up to our rooms and dropped off our gear and went to see where the event would be taking place. It was a grand hotel with a huge ballroom—maybe two or three rooms combined into one gigantic ballroom. It was huge! I couldn't even imagine what it would look like tomorrow with up to three hundred lifters, and I wondered how many platforms would be going up. The vendors were setting up their booths around the perimeter and bringing in their equipment, supplements, T-shirts, and all sorts of things lifters could buy to remember this event. People were wandering around, talking, and looking at everything. Then, as I started looking at the people individually, it seemed like a *Powerlifting USA* magazine came to life right in front of my eyes. There was Louie

Simmons, his wife Doris, some of his group from Ohio, and a host of faces I knew from the magazines, Laura Dodd, Curtis Leslie, Steve Goggins, Scott and MaryEllen Warman, Dr. Mariah Liggett, Ed Coan, Terry and Nancy Dangerfield, and Dave and Mary Jeffrey.

Somehow, I was introduced to one of Louie Simmons's lifters, Amy Weisberger. She was another first-timer, so we bonded right away. We remembered seeing each other at the Canton open powerlifting meet, so we talked awhile—she was as nervous as I was, and we laughed about that. We parted ways when I had to go weigh in.

I weighed in at 147.8 and once that was done, I asked Bob if we could go eat—like right now. He overruled my "all-you-can-eat-buffet" idea, and we ended up getting some chicken, vegetables, and pasta. At least one of us had some sense. And how nice was that, weighing in the night before? At the smaller meets, everyone weighed in during check-in, just a few hours prior to competing, so this was greatly appreciated.

By evening, after seeing all the big lifters in the sport, I was so nervous, I wasn't sure I was going to be able to go through with this. My stomach was in knots, and I was sweating for no reason. By nightfall, I was exhausted. I know I must have slept some, but a good part of the night was spent walking, praying, stretching, looking out the window, anything, just to make the time pass. When morning finally arrived, my nerves had not calmed even a little. After breakfast, and by the time we got down to the ballroom, my nervousness had made its way to my intestines and I spent the next eternity... well, you get the picture. Like I said, I had never been so nervous in my life. Eventually, I emerged, and I felt hopeful the intestinal revolt was over, the nervousness, not so much. This is where Bob's experience came shining through. He got me to stop looking (ogling really) at all the other lifters and just focus on what I needed to do.

"Krista, calm down, okay? It's just me and you, just like always, okay? Just another day in the gym," and he kept talking to me quietly and slowly, calming me down enough to pay attention to what I needed to do. I started my squat warmups, doing the best I could not to look at anyone else.

Just stay focused and do what you came here to do, I told myself. Bob was by my side the entire time. And then it was time to get my suit on. Once your suit is on, there is no turning back. I worried about another bout of intestinal revolt—I didn't even want to imagine that happening on the platform. This is when I stopped and bowed my head and asked God to please get me through this. This one I could not do alone; I was a wreck.

After a few deep breaths, I felt a little calmer, and the sight of my pink squat suit brought a smile to my face. *Even if I'm not the best lifter out here today, I bet I'll be the only one with a pink squat suit,* I thought. And I was. Once I was suited up, I did my last two warm-ups, and I was ready to go.

I heard the announcer say someone's name, and then he said, "Ford, you're on deck," meaning I would be the next lifter. I already knew the judging would be very strict. The rules were reviewed and there would not be any slack at the national level. The lift must be perfect. Then I heard, "Ford, you're up," and I knew the one-minute clock had begun. I walked onto my platform, my eyes on the bar, and I got set up under it, raised it off the rack, and backed it up into place. I looked at my judge until he said "squat" and his hand motioned down. I did my squat, came back up, and everything felt good. I expected three white lights, just by the way the lift felt—but I only got two. So, I did something wrong, but it was a good lift. Thankfully, that first lift was a good lift, because whatever I did wrong, I must have done it two more times. That first squat was the only squat I got, the other two were red-lighted and no good. I was thankful I got that first lift, otherwise, I would have bombed out and that would have been the end of nationals for this year—and in the squat no less, my favorite.

Benching was next and things started to come together. I was still a nervous wreck, but once the squat was over, I settled down a little. My new bench shirt felt good, and I only got one red light during my three benches, so all three lifts were good. After the bench, I went into the women's restroom, and Mary Jeffrey, one of the best in the world in the 123 class, approached me.

She said, "You are doing really well out there, is this your first nationals?" I said it was and she continued, "You're a good lifter. You keep coming back year after year, and you *will* be a national champion someday, that's what I see in you." I don't know what she saw, but I took her words straight to heart. She was one of the best in the world and if she said so, I believed her. I would be a national champion someday.

After that boost of encouragement from Mary, I went after my deadlifts with a vengeance. My purple deadlift suit was striking, and I was turning heads as I walked to the platform. (Apparently, I turned heads with my pink squat suit, but I was so nervous I didn't notice.) Once on the platform, I got set and pulled. I got my first lift easy enough, one of those that goes right up. The second lift was a little slower, but I got that one too. The third one, however, was a different story.

My bar was loaded, and I got up on the platform, bent over, got my hands around the bar, lowered my rear, leaned my head up, straightened my back, and pulled. And pulled. And pulled. And, well, this one wasn't even leaving the platform. Kind of comical, seeing someone pulling with all their worth, veins bulging everywhere, eyes bugging out, and nothing's happening, no movement whatsoever. When that happens, you might as well let go and laugh at yourself. That bar was not going up. I did get my first two deadlifts, so I was happy. And I was done! Despite my extreme nervousness, I felt good about my performance. I finally let the breath out I think I'd been holding since qualifying. I did it. I made it to the senior national level in my new sport—and in just one year. I wondered what would happen next year, and the year after that. To say I was on fire for this sport was an understatement.

At least now that my lifting was over, I could watch everyone else. Mostly I watched Janice Roge-Henderson finish up her deadlifts. She was the leader in our weight class. There were six girls in the 148-pound class this year. Janice won, and the other four girls took second through fifth. And me? Please don't feel bad I got last place again, because I didn't see it that way, not this time. I lifted six of nine lifts, lifting a 319 squat, a 236 bench, and a 374 deadlift. My total was 929, twenty-four pounds more than two months ago, and with me being fifteen pounds lighter. I qualified to lift at this level, and I had done my best. I didn't bomb out like a lot of people do their first time at nationals; I went home with the sixth-place certificate. So yes, I got sixth out of six, but, unlike my bodybuilding days, I didn't view it as last place. I looked at this like I was the sixth best in the nation that day, and someday—I didn't know when—but someday, I *would* be the best.

When our flight was done lifting, and we all were back in the warmup area, I took a moment to congratulate Janice.

I made sure she remembered me by touching my earrings and saying, "Remember me? From the Canton meet." She remembered me and I congratulated her on her victory. She said I did well out there too. I thanked her and then burst out the question, "Will you train me?"

And she looked at me, smiled, and said, "Why should I train you?"

I answered, the only obvious answer, "Because I'm going to be a national champion someday."

Janice laughed and said, "Okay, Krista. I live in Cleveland; I'll give you a date and time and if you're there, I'll train you."

"I will teach you what you shall do" (Exodus 4:15 NKJV).

"I'll be there! Absolutely, I'll be there! For sure! Thank you!" I couldn't help myself and I hugged her.

The rest of the competition was for men, and it was incredible. I saw humongous lifts, massive attempts, and a few injuries. Throughout watching all of this was the reoccurring thought, *I'm going to train with a world champion, Janice Roge-Henderson.* I watched people lift amounts I had never even considered. These were the best of the best there that day, and it was unbelievable and so exciting for me to see what I had only read about in the magazines.

As I was wandering around the warm-up area, gathering up my equipment, I looked up and noticed a very big lifter was grinning at me. He was tall, maybe six four or six five, and I found out later he weighed in at 389 pounds. I think he was the biggest lifter at nationals that year. He had been watching me and said my lifts were very good. "Plus, I just had to meet the girl who has a pink squat suit," he continued, laughing. I thanked him and we started to talk, his name was Jim Voronin, and he was a math teacher. He'd been lifting most of his adult life and loved it—like Bob and I, and everyone else who ever got involved in powerlifting. Jim was one of those gentle giants, a genuinely kind person, and I liked him very much. We hit it off right away and he asked if I would assist his handlers. I was happy too, after all, I was done lifting and glad to be helping someone else. Little did I know at the time I would be one of Jim's handlers for the next fifteen years, an honor for me and a joy to have a friend like him.

After he was done lifting, and we continued talking, he said, "I saw you come in all wide-eyed and nervous. And then the next time I saw you, you were giving it all you had out there, really gutting it out, not just taking the guaranteed lifts. You're something, you know that? You're going to rock this sport someday, Krista. I know it." He gave me the biggest bear hug in the world, and we said goodbye.

I was sad to see the competition come to an end; it had been glorious. I met so many people, fellow powerlifters, coaches, and spouses, made some new friends, and I had a training date with the one and only Janice Roge-Henderson! Days just don't get too much better than this one. I was floating on a cloud for the rest of my time in Pittsburg and was already planning for next year. If I had any doubt this was my sport, I didn't any longer. Powerlifting was *it* for me. And I had all kinds of people along the way to thank, but deep in my heart, I knew who put all those people in my path. I nodded and said a quiet "Thank you" to the Man upstairs, who put this fire in my heart.

> **"TO EACH IS GIVEN THE MANIFESTATION OF THE SPIRIT"**
> **(1 CORINTHIANS 12:7 ESV).**

13

PURE AND UNCUT

My journey with God began before I can remember. As far back as my memory goes, He was there. He was there when I lived with other children who had no home, His picture on the wall. I was told His name was Jesus and He loved all little children, even us, and He answered our prayers. I felt Him, watching over me, wanting me to trust Him. I had no one else, except for a few kind ladies who took care of us. He was it, even though I didn't really know who He was, I knew He was there. And I did trust Him because He *was* always there. At least, His picture was. Other children had come and gone from the home and when I asked where they went, I found out families had adopted them—but Jesus stayed with us. I said to that picture of Jesus I wanted a family to belong to.

Almost a week later, *my* first miracle happened, and my trust became belief. John Ford (trailed by a rather unhappy Catherine) came to the house one day and as he looked down at me, and I looked up at him, that was it. I got adopted. My life became everything I could ever dream of. I had parents and a sister, good food, toys, and dolls. And to my amazement, He was still there. He didn't just usher me to my new family, He went with me. I was so thankful because He was my best friend and I wanted Him to be a part of my new life, my first miracle.

And I learned all about church. My parents always took Stacey, and I learned who Jesus was and why He came to earth. And He loved us so much, He laid down his life for us. That was the sad part of the story, but I had no doubt of how much He loved me, He made my miracle happen. I loved going to church, and it was my Aunt Bobbie (Barbara Huntley) I always wanted to sit next to as a young girl. She was warm, one of those big, gentle, soft women you can just melt into, and she loved Jesus. She sang each hymn like she was singing it just for Him. I would lean into her side and listen to her beautiful voice singing His praise. Aunt Bobbie loved me very much too. She said I was a gift from God.

One day before church, she told me, "Every child of God is so special in His eyes, that He gives each one of us our own personal gift." She smoothed my curly hair back and looked intently at me. "Since He created us, He knows how to pick the perfect gift for each of us. And someday, when we're ready, the gift will manifest." That meant it would happen, Aunt Bobbie said. "God has a special gift just for you, Krista, remember that." At my young age, I believed Aunt Bobbie was my special gift and I let God know just how much she meant to me and how much I loved her. And I thanked Him, especially on Sundays as I cuddled into her side, for my precious gift, my Aunt Bobbie. She always made me feel like I could do anything or be anyone I wanted. I didn't know what I was going to do with my life, but I always knew Aunt Bobbie believed in me. That was a monumental gift.

I loved Sunday school—hearing about all the stories in the Bible, those stories came alive in my mind. Noah's Ark was another favorite story. I could visualize the great ark with all the animals. If I were there, I would be feeding and taking care of them, two of every kind, a perfect place for a girl, having all the beautiful animals right with me to care for and love. And then after it stopped raining, God made the first rainbow. It meant God promised never to flood the earth again, and every time I saw a rainbow after that, I remembered God's promise. To this day, when I see a rainbow, I think of God.

Another favorite story was about Moses as a baby, being found at the water's edge and claimed by the pharaoh's daughter; then as an older man, leading his people close to the promised land. And, of course, there was the story of Daniel in the lion's den. Even though the lions were very hungry, they didn't eat Daniel—God protected him because of his faith.

All these stories had the endings they had because of God. He quickly became like an action hero to all of us kids, but even better, because He was real. God could do anything, *anything*. I grew up knowing this and believing this because it happened to me first-hand. I got adopted, just like Moses, and I had a family to call my own.

My parents had me baptized as a young child. I remember this with a sense of déjà vu because I had another memory of being baptized before I got adopted. I don't know how this was possible, I don't know how I can remember so far back, but I remember looking into the preacher's face as he put the water on my forehead. After the Fords baptized me my second time, I had no doubt God knew my life was dedicated to Him. Fast forward this wonderful news of God coming into my life, I was saved at eighteen years old when I lived in California at a nondenominational church, and again at thirty years old at New Birth Missionary Baptist Church in Decatur, Georgia.

During my years growing up, I had a bunch of friends. I loved to play any sport, climb trees, or do any other outdoor activity, and kids were constantly coming to our door asking if I could come out and play. Sometimes Stacey would come outside and play with me, but she usually preferred to read a good book or do something indoors.

One day, a bunch of us kids were out playing, and I got super hungry. Stacey and I were walking home by this time, and I spied a half-full jar of applesauce in a trash can as we were walking past. We were still a few blocks from home, and I was very hungry, so this applesauce seemed like a great idea and a time saver. Being a kid, I didn't know about food spoiling, so I grabbed up that jar and dumped a big dollop in my mouth. It tasted good, so I handed the jar to Stacey, and she took a small taste—smart girl. I took a few more big swallows, and it still wasn't too bad ... until it was, and then it was *bad*. I made it home, gagging and my mother was not too happy with me. Neither was I; I was sick for the rest of the day over that great idea. Of course, my mother wanted to know why I was sick, so I had to confess to her. The worst part was I got a hefty spanking from my mother for doing that—like I wasn't suffering enough, I got spanked for it too. That wouldn't have happened if my dad had been there, but by that time he wasn't there anymore. Regardless, with or without the spanking, that would be my first and last time eating out of a trash can. And God bless my sister, she never said a word. She acted like she had no idea why I was sick.

I ran everywhere I went. I was a bundle of energy and I never seemed to get tired. The only time I would quiet down and sit still was when either my Aunt Bobbie or my grandma would read to me. Mostly they read from the Bible. When either of them would read, their voice would take on a beautiful tone, like a violin maestro, the words so eloquently spoken, honor and reverence in each word. I hung on as long as I could, but the love and peace I felt while being held and read Bible verses to put me to sleep in the safest place on earth, the lap of my Aunt Bobbie or my grandma. And what better thought to go to sleep to every night, how much God loves Aunt Bobbie, Grandma (Florence Huntley), Stacey, and me.

The next morning I'd be right back at it again. There was a park close to our house, with a large version of a school playground, with swings, jungle gyms, teeter-totters, and monkey bars of all kinds. For me, it was my dreamland. I could do all kinds of tricks on the swings, watching what the big kids were doing, and then practicing until I could do it too. I could swing standing on my feet and then when I'm swinging high, lift one of my legs out the back and lean my body forward, like a swan, and swing like that for a few seconds. There were all sorts of tricks I dreamed up for the monkey bars and the jungle gym too. I could spend hours there. And I did.

As much as I loved doing acrobatics on the bars, I loved team sports just as much. At school, we played dodgeball and kickball. I could kick the ball past the kids guarding the bases and into the outfield almost every time it was my turn. I was also a fast runner, I usually got to the ball first when chasing them in the outfield. I was having so much fun, I didn't realize I was faster than most of the kids. I just thought I was trying harder because I loved to play so much. It wasn't until several years later when I started running track in junior high school that I realized I really *was* stronger and faster than almost all the other girls. Track meets were my time to shine. They were awesome—the competition, the camaraderie, and just seeing what you can do out there, made it the best part of high school. I was consistently stepping up onto a podium, mostly to the highest step, and receiving a ribbon or medal for my track efforts. Running fast was so easy for me. I prayed I would be a sprinter all the way to the Olympics, but unfortunately, my track days would end with high school.

I still dreamed of a podium, though, taking that big step up to the top level. Running had been easy for me. I was naturally strong and fast. We trained hard. Coach Ritter had us doing all kinds of drills, but everything came easy to me on the track. When I compared my old track days to my current powerlifting days, this training was a lot harder, and the results were slower. However, I was making progress one day at a time, one workout at a time.

Fourteen years later and still in the semi-infancy stages of my powerlifting career, I was led to two women in the powerlifting world that would change my life.

> "WHATEVER YOU HAVE LEARNED OR RECEIVED OR HEARD FROM ME, OR SEEN IN ME—PUT IT INTO PRACTICE" (PHILIPPIANS 4:9 NIV).

14

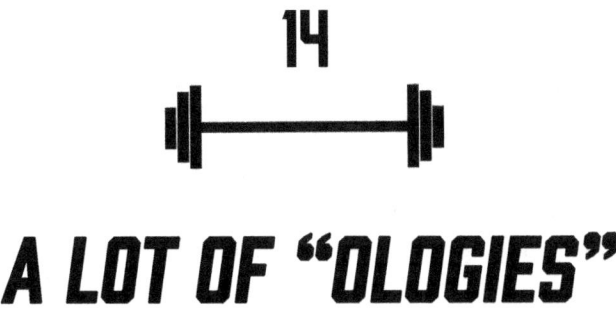

A LOT OF "OLOGIES"

In 1990, around October, I trained for a weekend with Janice Roge-Henderson and it was fantastic. I was twenty-four years old and ready to be coached by one of the strongest women in the world. Her first words to me were, "Krista, I'm going to tell you what you need to do, but I need to know first you won't question what I say. Because I'm already there. Can you do that?"

"Yep, I can do that," I said.

"Because I'm going to have you do some things you might wonder why, and I want you to know this works. Just trust me." And then we were off. When I left there, my squat stance was even wider, my grips adjusted, motions were more specific, and I did the motion over and over until I had it perfect. Motions had to be precise and exact.

She changed all kinds of stuff—I felt like I had a makeover. But, to my great relief, I felt stronger and more balanced under the weight. The better your form gets, the more balance you feel under the weight. I don't know if she taught me everything she knew, but she taught me enough to propel me into the next year of competition.

And propel I did! Bob and I still trained together, and I trained all year as hard as I could. I won the USPF Alabama Powerlifting State Championship, in June 1991, APF Senior nationals were in Pittsburg again. I saw a lot of the people I had met the year before.

Jim Voronin gave me a giant bear hug that, literally, swept me off my feet (the only guy to ever do that!), and of course, Janice was there, looking as formidable as ever. I set my sights on the numbers I wanted, and I turned to go get it done mode.

When it was all over, Janice stood on the top of the podium for the 148-pound class, as everyone expected. Competition was stiff and judging was as stringent as ever. Thankfully, I did get my numbers (319 in squat, 248 in bench, 429 in deadlift, for a total of 985)—fifty-six pounds more than the previous year—and I took a step up in the national standings that day, third place. I was thrilled, it was perfect. Third place at senior nationals! I was on my way in the sport I knew to be my true calling.

There were seven girls in our weight class. This year I truly was the third best in the nation. Thank you, God! So, I locked in on my focus to go home and start training with a new, upgraded version of what I've already learned thus far.

I continued to train as hard as I could, implementing everything Janice had taught me and everything was going great, training-wise. Financially, however, I was not doing as well. I still had my apartment, and although I was late on my rent almost every month for the three years I'd been there, thankfully my landlord was so kind, she always gave me a grace period. And of course, the second I had the rent money, I gave it to her. However, after working hard most of the year, I was caught up enough to sneak off to California for a Push/Pull (bench and deadlift) meet in Malibu on August 31 and September 1, 1991, and a bench-only meet in Fresno California, December 7, 1991. They weren't nationals, but the two first-place trophies I brought home took a little bit of the sting out of the year, and I could tell I was getting stronger—a lot stronger—especially on the bench. I went a little too deep in the hole a few times competing and traveling around, and it finally caught up with me in the summer of 1992.

Between the competitions and taking time off work to compete, and reduced hours at work due to seasonal changes, I found myself in a bit of a fix. Work and rent were not optional, so my competing had to take a hit that year for me to get caught up. This realization landed like a rock in the pit of my stomach, but I had to be responsible before things got too far out of hand. If I had any other landlord, I would've already been on the street again, a reality I did not want to repeat.

So, my year consisted of working, taking any extra shifts I could, and training as hard as I could. My only consolation for not competing that year was that I'd be a lot stronger the next year. That's not a lot of consolation, but it was all I had.

The 1992 nationals came and went, and I tried hard not to be disappointed—but I was. There's no feeling like not being able to compete when you're healthy, strong, and able. And to add insult to injury, if you can't afford to go compete, you can't even afford to go watch either. That broke my heart, not being able to be there at all.

At the last minute, I couldn't resist and entered a bench-only meet in Sherbrooke, Canada, where I benched a whopping 290, my best-ever to date. Oh, yeah, I would be ready next year.

I did secure a weekend with Dawn Reshel-Sharon (remember her, the best of the best, in all three disciplines). I drove six hours to Wisconsin, and she told me this was a one-time deal, no follow-ups, no phone calls. "I will teach you everything you need to know on how to master the techniques of powerlifting. *Really* master the sport." She said the word "master" in the full sense of the word. I got her message, "Don't just train your body how to do a motion. Do it, and feel it, until it feels like it is your own natural movement. That's mastery." She looked at me straight, and continued, "If you truly *master* everything, I tell you, you will be where I am."

So, as soon as we started training, I went into sponge mode, listening and filing every piece of information she gave into my brain. If I had a tape recorder, I would have recorded the whole weekend. We did form adjustments, positioning of feet and hands, several body positions, and in a whirlwind, we were done. Dawn was an incredibly smart woman, she had a lot of degrees ending in "ology," such as kinesiology, biology, zoology, and physiology—i.e., the title of this chapter.

I went home to put this into practice. I went over everything she told me, studying her technique and putting it into practice. In a few months, I could feel the benefits of these small changes. True mastery of the motions would take a little longer, years maybe, but I was up and ready for the challenge.

I began to wonder if I should look for a different job. I needed to make more money so I could keep competing. I wished I could find someone to fund my training, wouldn't that be awesome?! That was a great dream, but how does that even happen? So, back to reality. Soon I got a job at Walmart, restocking shelves. This was a full-time job, but it was nights, which were tough for me. I hung in there and began to regain some ground on my financial situation, but around the time of this job change and the rigorous training schedule, Anna and I broke up and went our separate ways. I must admit, I have always loved being in a relationship so I never gave the grass time to grow under my feet, and for the next thirty-five-plus years, I would find companionship with women only.

I spent as much free time with Aunt Bobbie and my grandma. I told Aunt Bobbie all about my competitions and she told me she would love to come see me compete—it would be my greatest honor to have her there, watching me. She was my biggest fan *and* the one who made me believe I could do anything I set my mind to. I wanted her to see what became of the little girl she bought the weight set for so many years ago. I wanted Aunt Bobbie to see me win nationals. And there it was, plain as day, my new goal.

I know it was kind of lofty, but what do they say in the gym? Go big or go home. So, I set my sights on the 1993 nationals, I was going to win for my Aunt Bobbie, and she was going to be there to see it.

Now I had everything I needed, training from Janice and Dawn, a new full-time job, and a date in August 1993. *And* I still had my beloved apartment. Everything was working out; I just needed to be patient, work as much as I could at my job, and train as hard as I could at the gym.

By the spring of 1993, I was chomping at the bit to compete again. I was big and strong, big enough I would not be competing in the 148-pound class again, ever. I was now comfortably in the 165-pound class. Bob was still my faithful training partner and Janice and I trained together whenever we could. It worked out for me to drive down every other month and train with her for a weekend. During one of our sessions, we decided to compete in a bench contest a month before nationals. This meet had prize money too, $3000 for the winner of each class. This was the first powerlifting meet ever to have prize money, which was why I wanted to do it. If I won, I would be, much more comfortable, and ready to travel and compete again. I had been benching heavy all winter and I knew I had a good chance of winning the 165-pound class.

The meet was at a high school in Baltimore. Outside, before the meet, Bert Wagner, the photographer for *Powerlifting USA*, was taking pictures by a big white limousine. He motioned Janice, me, and another lifter, Richie Creevy, to the side of the limousine. We were positioned to look like we were getting ready to climb in the limo. Richey was first getting in, with hundred-dollar bills coming out of his pockets, Janice was next, pointing at the bills, and I was behind her with two overflowing buckets of cash. In the foreground was Scott Werner, the meet director, in a suit with the pockets pulled out, like he had no money left—all his money was now prize money. Once we were all in place, Bert snapped what would be the cover picture for the August 1993 *Powerlifting USA* magazine, highlighting the powerlifting meet in Baltimore, and several of us lifters poised to win the prize money.

For some reason—maybe because I was so eager to get back into the game and I felt good and strong—I made the decision to open with a 265-pound bench. I could blow this weight away every bench workout for the past two months in the gym, no problem. Well, not today. I got that bar about two-thirds of the way up and then it stopped dead, and I could not lock it out for the life of me. This was a fluke—it had to be. I can get that weight any day in the gym, *any* day. It was a fluke lift. It just had to be. So, I made the dumb-dumb decision to go up to a 290-pound bench, which I could get in the gym more times than not. Well, this was not a day in the gym. That one went about halfway up and stopped dead. What in the world was going on? Why couldn't I lift what I knew I could lift? What was happening? I told the official I would stay at that weight for my final attempt, my one smart choice of the day. I was starting to get quite concerned. So many things were running through my head. I had never been in this position before, I'd always gotten my first lift, and usually my second. I was three red lights away from bombing out—bombing out! That's what rookies and dumb-dumb people do, and now here I sat, trying to bomb myself out. And with a $3000 check at stake, not just a trophy or a medal, but real cash I desperately need. I needed to dig deep for this final attempt. And I did. I dug as deep as it went, and that bar still didn't go up. I couldn't even look at the lightbox when I walked off the platform, I didn't want to see the three red lights I knew were blaring in the box. This was terrible. Now, not by sight would anyone have known about my ego lifting going on in my head, but by my numbers and jumps from weight to weight told the whole story of why I bombed out of my first powerlifting meet ever.

So, for the record, on June 26, 1993, I, Krista N. Ford, joined the ranks of arrogant-thinking people who bombed out of a critical competition. It was my own fault, absolutely, 100 percent. I was overconfident and overestimated my own strength. I wanted and needed that money so bad. It was the first time I competed for money and maybe my mind was more on the money and not what I was supposed to be doing out there. I'm not making excuses, there is no excuse for what I did that day, I'm just saying my bad choices made for a very expensive lesson in humility.

When the competition was over and the checks were handed out, all I could do was sit and watch, thinking about what I could have done with that $3000. I blew it. My dear friend Janice, never short on candid observation and always the straight shooter, had some choice words for me. "Krista, this could have been yours," as she snapped her $3000 check in front of my face. "When you bomb out, it's because you are either arrogant or stupid, and I know you're not stupid. This is on you, and you just embarrassed me as your coach." My gaze instantly fell to the floor. I was instructed to go home and think about what I did, and I wasn't to talk to her for at least two weeks. I felt about an inch tall. That day, I realized how much my lifting reflected Janice's coaching, and she was the last person I wanted to embarrass. Wow, I really messed up. I felt bad all the way around.

The following month, the *Powerlifting USA* issue came out with Janice and me on the cover. Perfect timing, this would be the issue everyone would be carrying around at nationals. Janice and I were on the cover, and the meet results were listed right inside, where everyone could see I bombed out. Lovely. Well, it was my own fault and I'm big enough to own it. (But just because I own it, doesn't mean I'm not embarrassed by it!) However, I was determined to put up some good numbers at nationals after that fiasco. Nationals were in Charlottesville, Virginia, that year and my Aunt Bobbie was planning to attend. No bombing out at nationals! That would be the ultimate lifting nightmare. I wanted to make my Aunt Bobbie proud, so a more conservative approach to my opening lifts was the new rule. All arrogance and stupidity will be left at the door from this day forward. I will *not* bomb out again.

In my mind, it was very clear to me there was no more room for mistakes like that. After all, I have total control of what amount of weights are being loaded onto the bar. I was told after I had this huge boo-boo happen. It is the fault of the lifter 100 percent of the time if she or he bombs out ever. The only exception to that rule is if the lifter gets hurt or injured during the lift, which is no one's fault.

> "TALK NO MORE SO EXCEEDING PROUDLY; LET NOT ARROGANCY COME OUT OF YOUR MOUTH" (1 SAMUEL 2:3 KJV).

My second powerlifting meet, 1989, the Canton Open Championships Canton, Ohio.

Jim Voronin and I at my first WPC World Powerlifting Championships in Macon, France, 1993.

Janice Roge-Henderson (my coach), Bob "Doc" Sidebottom, and myself.

Tower Club Central Indiana Powerlifting Championship (1989) my first ever powerlifting meet. Left–Right: Ron Hudson, myself, Bob "Doc" Sidebottom, and Marty Sheets. We all Lifted at GOLDS GYM west in Indianapolis, Indiana.

KRISTA FORD

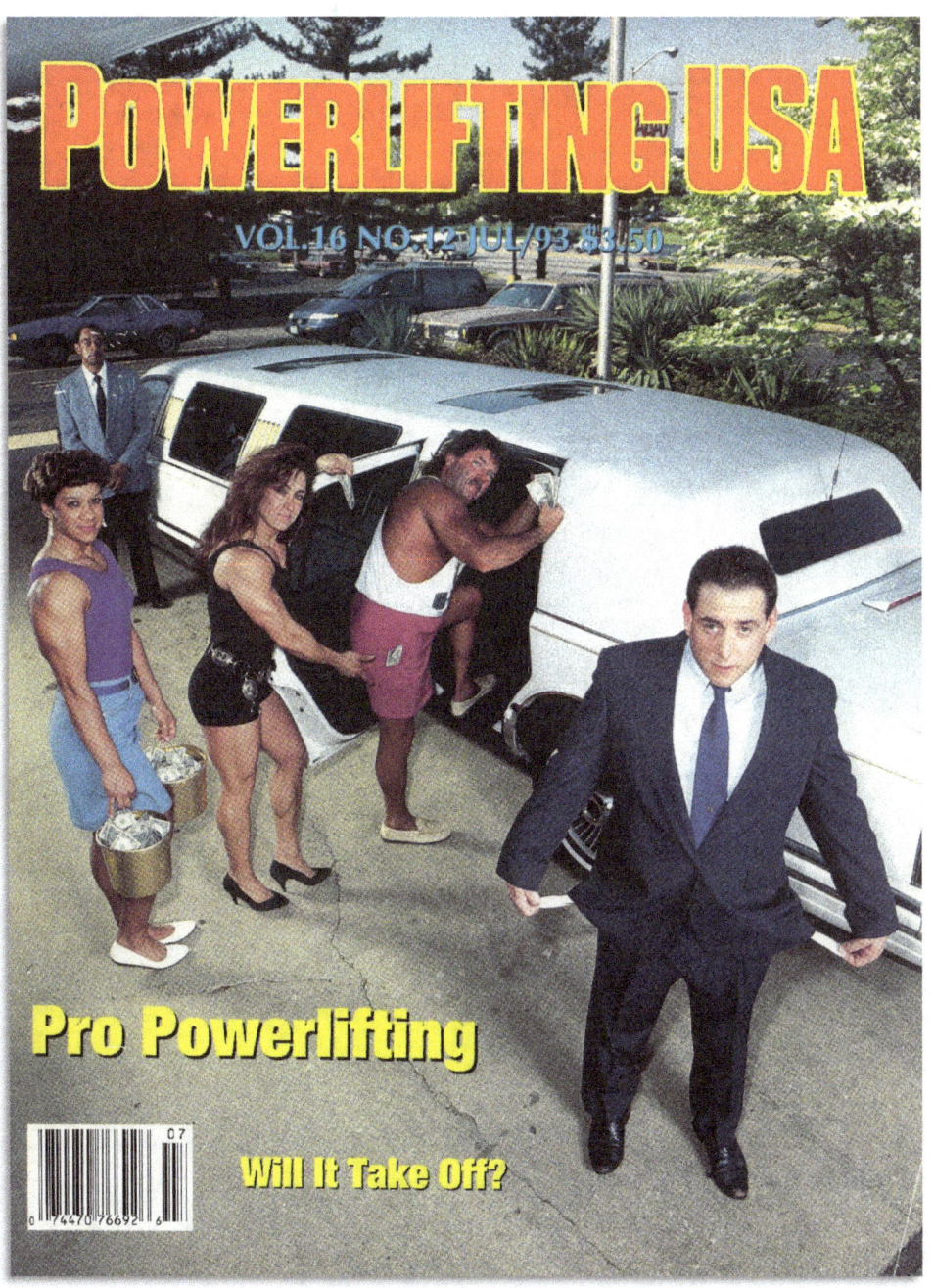

July, 1993. My first time being on the front cover of Powerlifting USA Magazine. *Benching for cash in Baltimore, Maryland, myself, Janice, Richey, Scott the promoter, and our cool limo driver.*

15

QUALIFIED SOLO

Nationals were just two weeks away when Bob and I decided to go our separate ways with our training together after nationals were done. Janice had suggested to me I might want to train solo going forward because Bob was not thinking past the level he was currently on in powerlifting while I was. "You must train with the best to be the best," she said. It wasn't personal at all; I still had the greatest respect for his knowledge of our sport and his training regimen. But, after that day, we did not train together, and I chose to lift on my own. Other than the times I trained with Janice, I trained by myself after that. This was difficult, to say the least, not having a spotter and training partner—not to mention Bob had always been my handler at competitions. But we parted ways, and that was that.

My Aunt Bobbie came through for me though. She was ready and excited to accompany me to nationals. This would be the first time she would see me compete in powerlifting. I don't know who was more excited, me, getting to share my sport with my favorite aunt; or her, getting to see her niece compete at the national level. We were both counting down the days until we left for Charlottesville.

The night before we left, I called Aunt Bobbie and made sure we were both ready to go. I was so excited, I wondered if I would be able to sleep. As it turned out, I didn't get much sleep that night anyway, but not from the excitement. At some point during the night, my grandmother had to be rushed to the hospital with some sort of intestinal problem. I learned of this in the wee hours of the morning when my Aunt Bobbie called me and let me know the situation. And in that instant, the nationals were off. I couldn't go with Grandma in the hospital, and Aunt Bobbie couldn't go. Grandma meant more than any competition. I was getting ready to go to the hospital, where Aunt Bobbie was calling from, but she would have none of it.

"Oh no, you're going to your competition. You've worked too hard for this, and Grandma would want you to go no matter what."

"No, no, I can't go, not with Grandma—" my voice trailed off and I couldn't get the rest of the sentence out. I felt my world crumbling around me. *Not my grandma, not my beautiful grandma.*

After a long pause, Aunt Bobbie said softly, "Then do it for me, sweet pea." I was terribly torn but when she spoke to me in that sweet and gentle tone, I would do anything she said. I would go. But my heart would remain in Indianapolis.

During the flight, I remembered something my grandma had told me when I was about seven or eight years old. One morning, I walked into her bedroom when she was awake and had a peculiar look on her face. I asked why are you still awake and she told me she had seen an angel at the foot of her bed.

Being as young as I was, my question was, "Wow, did the angel have wings and was the angel female or male? She said no wings and female.

"Well, why did she come here, Grandma? What does it mean?" I asked.

She had the sweetest smile on her face and said, it means I'm going to heaven." At the time, that was a good enough answer for me, and I don't remember if anything else was said. I hadn't thought of that memory in years, but it came back to me that day on the plane, and I prayed it wasn't happening right at that moment. I must have prayed all the way to Virginia, because the next thing I knew, the plane was landing.

August 7–8, 1993, APF Senior Nationals in Charlottesville, Virginia, I was only twenty-six years old and ready-Freddy I was.

Charlottesville was beautiful. I got a cab at the airport and took it to the city, where the storefronts were brick, emanating old southern charm and heritage. Nearing the hotel, we drove by a statue of a military man on horseback. My taxi driver told me the statue was of Confederate General Robert E. Lee. Well, that was something to think about, he certainly wasn't my favorite "war hero."

Once I got to the hotel where the competition was to be held, I began to feel the excitement, despite my heavy heart. I found Janice right away and told her what had happened.

To my amazement, my bombing out and the embarrassment I had just caused her a month before was instantly forgiven and she said, "Krista, I got you. I have some handlers with me, they will take care of you." Before I could even say thank you, I was wrapped up in a big bear hug from Jim Voronin, and I knew I would get through this.

When I got into the warm-up area, I saw something I had never seen before, a giant contraption with a group of lifters gathered around it. Janice and I went up to look at it as Ray and Mary Lou Madden were explaining the apparatus, their new creation, something that would revolutionize powerlifting forever. They called it the Monolift. It was supposed to allow the lifter to conserve energy and reduce injuries as many injuries happen when the lifter backs out of the squat stands or gets back into the stands. I wasn't quite sure how it worked and when my turn came to try it, I got under the bar, raised up, and instinctively backed out from under it, completely defeating its purpose. Laura Dodd and Mariah Liggett were right there and helped me understand it. Krista, you don't have to back out of the rack, just set yourself up, lift up on the bar, and the rack's arms come out from under the weight. It would take some getting used to, but I already liked it. The concept was brilliant.

Janice didn't compete that day. Her goal was to break the three-hundred-pound mark on the bench. A lot of people didn't think a woman could do it, but what other people think we can't do, fires us up even more—I think it's a powerlifting trait. Janice was no exception, and benched a perfect 308, breaking the three-hundred-pound barrier and setting a new WPC world record. It was poetry in motion, that girl could bench!

As for me, I would have my hands full. There was a newcomer to the national stage this year, in the 165-pound class, Stephanie Vandeweghe, she was a tough lifter. We went head-to-head and back-and-forth all day. I went three for three in the squat, lifting a personal best of 380 pounds, but Stephanie lifted more. On the bench, I put up 270 (I barely missed my final attempt of 281), and after the bench, I had the lead, but not by much. When the deadlifts were done, I had finally broken the four-hundred-pound mark, lifting 402 in the deadlift, another personal best, for a total of 1,052. Stephanie totaled 1,113 for the win, and I placed second. I must admit, I was a little disappointed, but the silver lining to it was the top two in each class qualified to represent the United States in the WPC World Championships, to be held three months from now, in Mâcon, France! I had qualified to go to Worlds! And it was going to be in France!

I remember the first day I met Janice. She had just come back from winning Worlds, and now I'd be going! I'm not even sure I knew second place qualified for Worlds, but now I did, and I was going! I was going to France!

After my lifting, I finished out the rest of the competition watching the remaining lifters, cheering on everyone. In the middle of the lifting, there was loud shouting backstage, and everything stopped. Loud shouting usually meant someone had gotten hurt. But not this time—two men were brawling it out. One of them, highly respected in the sport and my friend, Louie Simmons, and Terry Grimwood. There was blood coming from the faces of both and I heard later it was a dispute over excessive equipment. Apparently, someone said his wife, Tamara Grimwood, was trying to use equipment and wraps not authorized, giving her an unfair advantage. My friend called it and defended the established rules of the APF, and he was the unsung hero of the day. All of us compete hard but we do not disrespect the rules that are in place to protect every lifter.

To say the least, this was a very exciting competition. Janice benched 308, a WPC world record; the new Monolift; my personal bests in the squat and deadlift; a bloody battle backstage; and to top it off, I made the USA team, and I was going to France to compete with the best in the world! Suddenly I was overwhelmed and exhausted and I just wanted to go home. I was emotionally and physically spent.

The flight back home took forever it seemed. All I wanted to do was get home, go to the hospital, and see my grandmother. In fact, I went directly there from the airport. I rushed to Grandma's room as fast as I could. I'm not sure what I expected, but to see her lying there, looking so frail, I fell to my knees at her bedside. I couldn't say a word, I just touched her hand and sobbed. Next to Aunt Bobbie, Grandma was my rock. She loved me unconditionally, and I knew the value of that kind of love. It is rare, and it is powerful. Love like that is a gift from God. And I was blessed to have this grandmother, no other would do. This was my matriarch, my role model, the queen of my world. Hers were the arms that held me as a child when I got hurt, the arms that picked me up hundreds of times and told me to try again, whether it was learning to ride a bike, or when someone picked on me for being mixed-race. Hers were the arms who welcomed me home from California eight years prior, and the arms I would long for, and miss to the depths of my being so many times in my future. She was my world, and nothing else mattered. I would stand vigil and I was praying for Grandma's strength to return. Whatever it took, I would do it. I sat by her bedside until the staff told me I would have to leave and come back tomorrow.

A kind nurse helped me to my feet and told me, "Your grandma is a strong lady, she's not giving up." I had a hard time letting go of Grandma's hand, thinking I might not ever hold it again. I kissed her forehead and smoothed back her beautiful black hair, noticing for the first time the streaks of gray.

"I'll see you tomorrow, Granny. Goodnight, I love you." And with that, I was on my way home.

As soon as my eyes opened in the morning, I got dressed and rushed back to the hospital, I didn't even eat breakfast. Aunt Bobbie and Aunt Gloria were already there, and when I saw the two of them, tears began to fall from my eyes. Was she gone? I couldn't even ask the question.

Before I knew it, I was engulfed in Aunt Bobbie's arms, and she was whispering in my ear, "Child, child, Mama's going to be fine." Really? Was it true? I tried to stop the tears that were saturating Aunt Bobbie's blouse. "Krista, Krista, honey. Her signs are better this morning. The doctors are in with her now and I think she's awake. We'll get to see her soon." She patted my back and I held on tight to her. After a few moments, the door opened, and sunlight flooded into the hallway like a ray of hope. We rushed into her room, and it was true, she was awake. I was at her bedside in a flash. She turned her head and smiled at me as she raised her hand to touch my soggy, tear-streaked face.

"Krista, sweet pea, don't you cry now. I'm going to be just fine. I just needed a little rest. God's not done with me yet, I am pretty sure of that," and she let out a tiny giggle like she knew a secret. That giggle unleashed laughter in all three of us—probably more of an emotional release, not that it was so funny, but we all realized at that moment Grandma was going to make it. Then, suddenly, she turned to me and asked how it went at the competition. For a split second, I couldn't remember, it didn't matter compared to possibly losing her.

"Oh, fine, it was good," was about all I could say. Well, that wasn't good enough for Grandma, so she asked a question she knew would get me talking.

"Did you bomb out?" she asked with a sly grin on her face.

"No, Grandma, I didn't bomb out." I had to laugh; she knew how to get me to talk.

"Well, I hope not, because I was praying for you the whole time." I wasn't sure how that was possible since she was admitted to the hospital the day I left and just woke up this morning, but I believe, in her heart, she was praying for me. She knew Aunt Bobbie had canceled her plans to go with me, and I had to go by myself. "Come on, tell me, what did you lift?" I told her my numbers and that I had placed second. "Second is good, Krista. It's *very* good. And you'll be first someday, when God decides it's your time. I am sure of that. Grandmas know these things."

That got a smile from me and then I remembered to tell her about qualifying for worlds. "And it's in France, Grandma, I get to go to France to compete!" Her eyes lit up and I could tell she was genuinely happy for me.

She knew how badly I wanted to win at nationals, but what did she always say, "All in good time, all in God's time." I was going to worlds for the first time and Grandma was coming home. That was more than I could have ever hoped for or expected. Outside, the sun shined brighter than ever, and it felt like a hug from God. My assurance was that He was watching over us, Grandma, Aunt Bobbie, Aunt Gloria, and me. He had carried all of us through this whole traumatic ordeal. My words of thanks to God paled to the gratitude I felt in my heart. Thank you, thank you, thank you, God, for more time with my beautiful grandma. Florence Huntley (my granny) seemed to have God's cell phone number on speed dial, that's for sure.

> **"AFTER JOB HAD PRAYED FOR HIS FRIENDS, THE LORD RESTORED HIS FORTUNES AND GAVE HIM TWICE AS MUCH AS HE HAD BEFORE"**
> **[JOB 42:10 NIV].**

16

OVER THE WATER

With Grandma back home, things began to settle down and return to normal. Well, as much as could be expected with a world championship only a few months away. With each passing day, I began to wonder and worry how I was going to pay for this trip. It was all I could do to compete stateside, with airfare, hotel stays, entry fees, and taking time off work. Now I was hoping to go to France to compete with barely a dime to my name. My rent money wasn't going to pay for my plane fare this time. I had to have help. Back in those days, there was no such thing as a "GoFundMe" page, so I had to go old school. I would have to plead my case through the media somehow.

I called up an old friend, Stacia Matthews, who was a reporter for the local Channel 6 news station. Stacia did a feature story on me and my powerlifting accomplishments and how I had qualified for the world championships but needed help covering the airfare and expenses. The airing of my story on the news opened an opportunity with a local radio station. In a segment of *Operation Breadbasket*, a Christian show, I spoke about what I was trying to do. Fortunately for me, talking is something I enjoy—in fact, I love to talk. So, there it was, a ten-minute speaking engagement, where I told anyone and everyone listening how much I loved this sport and how hard I had trained, how hard I was currently training, and how much I desperately wanted to go to France to compete on the world level. People must have heard my plea because a few minutes into the segment, the phones began to light up. These were the sponsors that took me to France that year:

    Franklin Power Products—Larry and Maggie Light
    Golden Rule Insurance Company—Patrick Rooney, CEO
    Light of the World Church—Reverend T. Benjamin
    First Timothy Lutheran Church—Reverend Tom Brown
    Ebenezer Baptist Church
    Omega Psi Phi
    Kappa Alpha Psi
    Kiwanis Club—Al Scaife
    Gloria Jennings
    Barnes Methodist Church
    Rudy Hightower
    The Concerned Clergy
    Holy Angels School—Sister Mary Quinn
    Wanda Smith
    Pat Reeves
    Operation Breadbasket—Mr. and Mrs. Crawford
    Shirley Steward
    Mr. and Mrs. Donnie Young
    Arthur Jordon
    Stacey Ford
    Catherine Ford
    Shrum Manufactured Housing—Larry Fitzgerald
    Xerox—Donnell Hayes
    Camilla Spritz
    The Women's Sports Foundation—Traveling and Training Grant (Billy Jean King's Foundation)

All these generous people, most of whom didn't even know me, made my trip to France possible. It was going to happen! Some donations were ten dollars, and some were one hundred.

OVER THE WATER

The largest one was $1,200! That one was from Billy Jean King's Women's Sports Foundation Traveling and Training Grant. I was so thankful and appreciative of all these people. That's why I wrote down every single name as the donations came in and they are all listed here. If it hadn't been for every one of these people, this dream would not have happened to me. The kindness of these sponsors overwhelmed me, and I vowed to train as hard as I could, and then go lift as much as humanly possible. I wanted to do my best for every one of the people who believed in me. My lifting qualified me, but these generous sponsors were the ones who got me there. And I must admit, my rent money went into the pot too.

I went to the gym and trained like a woman on fire. There is no stopping me now! Mâcon, France, here I come! WPC World Championships, October 1993.

The day I left for France; I was electrified. My first international flight was on Air France out of JFK. I could barely sit for the long flight from New York to Paris. When I could feel the plane finally descending, I practically climbed over the kind gentleman in the seat next to me, just to see France! There was lots of water, and I could see a low bridge with what looked like cement arches underneath it, holding it up, and I think I even saw a small carousel by the bridge. There were other powerlifters on the plane, some I knew and some I could just tell. When the plane finally came to a stop, it was all I could do not to run right down the aisle and be the first one off. Other than my bench meets up in Sherbrooke, Canada, this was my first time out of the United States. And overseas! When I finally got off the plane, I was so excited, I ran to the taxi area. Fortunately for us lifters, most of the taxi drivers spoke enough English that we had no problem making our destination known. Several of us piled into a taxi and we were on our way. We got to our hotel, which was fancy and elegant. The competition was to be held about six miles down the street from the hotel at an indoor soccer field house. We passed by the field house on our way to the hotel and the taxi driver pointed it out to us, having been delivering powerlifters to the hotel for several days now. Once we all got settled in, a bunch of us sat around the hotel lobby and talked. Not much English was spoken by the hotel staff, and I regretted all the times I fell asleep and flunked out of French class in high school. Never in a million years did I think I would ever be in France, where I would've been able to speak this beautiful language with native French people. Not even in my dreams. But here I was, oh my!

    A lot of my friends were there. Big Jim Voronin, Scott and Mary Ellen Warman, Curtis Leslie, Nancy Dangerfield, Tony Myers, Tom Bauer, Larry McCauley, and a bunch more. Since we were there several days before the competition, we utilized what the hotel had to offer—the pool. There were all kinds of games we made up and played in that pool. We didn't really have anything else to do but get adjusted to the new time zone and get ready to compete. Later that first night, Mary Ellen Warman and I got into a pool game against Jim Voronin and John Neighbor, a nice lifter from England. We girls got beat royally by those big boys, and they had a fun time of it, and never let us forget it. I guess sometimes it does pay to be a nearly three-hundred-pound man, especially in pool games. All in good fun, however, it *really* would have been funny if us girls had won!

    The next morning, Jim and I and a few others went down to the meet site to get weighed in. I learned this meet would be under the World Powerlifting Congress and all the weights would be done in kilos. We met the meet director, Kieron Standley, a gracious man and a great meet director. I wasn't worried about the weights being in kilos, there were conversion charts all around so it would be easy to determine the weight we wanted. After weigh-ins, Jim and I went to breakfast. I was glad I already weighed in because I put some food away that morning! Maybe I was following Jim's lead, but I was voracious. Then I took a quick power nap, still having some trouble with the time change, but was up by evening for a tour scheduled for all the lifters.

We would be going to the home of the mayor of Mâcon, who turned out to be a female, which was very impressive to me. The tour was at her elegant home, and she was waiting for us with wine and food. It seemed like there was wine at every meal and almost all the rest of the day and evening too. This was a grape-growing region and wine was the main event. The mayor spoke a few words to the competitors and then our APF president, Ernie Frantz, spoke as well as leaders from the other countries present. Then we ate and drank and mingled and ate and drank some more. I barely remember the bus ride back to the hotel. I'm not much of a drinker, so my sips of fine French wine knocked me out good. I was asleep when my head hit the pillow.

Somewhere in the night, I heard a bunch of yelling and commotion. When I sat up, I didn't hear anything so I thought I must've been dreaming of the competition and must have lifted a big weight everyone was cheering for. So, I didn't give it another thought and fell right back to sleep. In the morning at breakfast, everyone was talking about "what happened" during the night. Larry McCauley had a heart attack and was rushed to the hospital. That was what the commotion was all about. Larry was a sixty-seven-year-old lifter who had been lifting for decades and was somewhat of a legend to all of us younger lifters. He had overcome physical problems, health problems, and the inevitable aging process. This news came as a terrible shock to everybody, and a feeling of worry came over us Americans. By evening we got word, Larry had passed away that day. My emotions had been at such a high this whole trip and then to hear this, I came crashing down and had to go to my room where I cried and cried over the loss of my friend. I felt so bad for Tom Bauer, a fellow lifter and Larry's best friend. I couldn't shake the sorrow and once again turned in early to sleep.

In the morning, the mood was still somber, at least for the Americans. We had lost one of our own. I was still in shock but my main handler, Curtis Leslie, kept me focused and moving forward. From the United States, it was me, Stephanie Vandeweghe,

Nancy Dangerfield from Illinois (she qualified in the 148-pound class, but she went up a class at this meet), Liz Allworth from South Africa, and a few others. I would have my hands full.

After the squat, I was in fourth place, but I was happy because I had squatted 175 kilos, or 385.75 pounds, 5.75 over my best squat to date. Then on to the bench, my favorite. I would have out-benched everyone if I had gotten my third and final attempt, but I just couldn't quite lock it out. So, my second bench was my official lift, 122.5 kilos, or 270 pounds, tying my best bench to date. But that lift allowed me to jump in the standings thirty-five pounds. All that remained was the deadlift and my first world championship would be in the books. I started out light, 352.5 pounds, and it went up easy enough. My second lift was 402.25, another one that went up easily enough. On my third attempt, I told Curtis to have them load 424.25 pounds, but Curtis pulled a bit of a fast one on me and had them load a little bit more. I didn't even notice and got that lift without too much trouble. I didn't hear them announce the weight as I had my headphones on till the last minute. The crowd cheered and Curtis whispered in my ear, that was 429.75 Krista. And with that lift, I captured third, the second-best American in the 165-pound class at worlds, passing up Stephanie in the process, the American national champion! I would have the honor of standing on the podium at my first worlds—I couldn't even believe it, but it was true. I won bronze! It was not a medal though, it was a goblet, a tiny one at that, but to this day, a most cherished award. My first worlds, and I competed well even after losing a friend and fellow American in the process. So, it was bittersweet, to say the least, but a beautiful victory.

One lifter that needs mentioning at this competition was my fellow pool-game partner, Mary Ellen Warman, who squatted 501.5 pounds at a body weight of 132, a phenomenal feat. *Someday I will squat five hundred pounds. Wow, wouldn't that be something!*

The next few days we all shopped and ate. I got what France is famous for, some fine perfume—no, it wasn't more wine! And the perfume was for Grandma, of course, I'm not much for the girly stuff. The French food was fabulous, and I probably gained ten pounds! When we finally flew home, all I could do was relive everything that had happened in the past week. I still couldn't believe the passing of Larry McCauley, a friend and fellow lifter. And the precious goblet I could feel in my carry-on luggage in front of my feet. I felt so honored to be included in this prestigious group of lifters, and the wonderful memory of standing on the podium—that was beyond my wildest dreams—and the support of all those generous sponsors, who were the ones who got me to France.

I couldn't have been more grateful to them, and for all the help I got along the way, Bob Sidebottom, Janice Roge-Henderson, Dawn Reshel-Sharon, and all my handlers. And of course, you know who I give all the credit to, God Almighty, who gave me the body and the spirit that made all this possible. Thank you, God! I think I found my true passion in life, and I will never ever squander this perfect gift from my Lord and Savior. It's fair to say some may never experience doing what they *love* to do versus what they *have* to do. I'm not one of them, I believe I've been highly favored. I love this sport and all it represents to all of us athletes involved. It represents discipline, determination, and perseverance, and in the end, you get back everything and much more. It is an objective and well-diverse sport that at the end of the day, the strongest woman and man win. That's it!

> "THE LORD IS MY ROCK, MY FORTRESS, AND MY DELIVERER" (2 SAMUEL 22:2 NIV).

17

RED LIGHT, GREEN LIGHT

The flight home from Mâcon, France, and the world championships seemed to take forever. I just wanted to get home and tell Grandma and Aunt Bobbie all about my trip. I told them play-by-play each lift, how it felt, how easy or hard each lift was, and the cheers and applause I got when my lifts were good. There were tears of joy in my grandma's eyes when I got to the part about them calling out my name to go up and stand on the podium.

"I knew you could do it, sweet pea, the Lord has found favor in you." Something Grandma would say, and her eyes twinkled even more, like she knew a secret. I think she knew a lot of God's little secrets. Well, I was just glad to be part of this one, that's for sure. Aunt Bobbie was just as happy and engulfed me in one of her famous hugs, which was like the hug of an ecstatic mother. She may as well have been, she loved me like a mother. And she was my biggest supporter.

My apartment manager was not quite so thrilled. This time I had been gone longer than usual and she knew what was about to happen. I would be short on my rent yet again. She was so sweet about it, but she told me I needed to figure out how to juggle my job and my competing and still be able to pay the rent. "On time, Krista, you need to be on time, from now on." I knew she was right. I needed to be more responsible and tighten up on all my spending, which other than lifting equipment, decent food, and rent, wasn't much. Once I realized this, I knew I needed to find a better-paying job. I would start looking the following day after I got off work.

Work went well and I told everyone I was looking for extra shifts. I got a few lined up right away and was very grateful. It was getting close to the holidays and people wanted to take time off to be with their families, but my priority was to make some money to catch myself back up.

Things were going according to my plan; I had gotten several extra shifts the first week I returned to work. In fact, I worked twelve days in a row, had one day off, and then did another six in a row and had one more to go. And I was keeping up with my training and was determined not to lose a step there. I had worked too hard to let that go to the back burner. On that sixth day in a row, driving home, I was practically falling asleep at the wheel. I knew I was pushing it, and I was really struggling to make it home. I must have crossed the center line a few times because suddenly, I saw red and blue flashing lights behind me. Okay, I'm awake now!

This was not good, not good at all. There I was, a good-sized muscular woman of color. It didn't matter that my mother was Italian white, my daddy was Black and that made me Black. The varying degrees of Black don't matter when you're getting pulled over, and gay too—oh, this was not good at all. Every group of people has their own fears about being pulled over by the police, and I was no exception—I fell into several of those groups that have not had the best treatment by law enforcement. The officer was professional enough, although things could take a turn for the worse at any moment. The officer asked if I had been drinking. I told him I hadn't, but I still got to do the sobriety test anyway, which I passed with flying colors. Then it was time for things to take a turn for the worse, but fortunately in my case, not physically. He asked for my license and insurance card. My stomach turned a flip over that request. I had let my insurance lapse almost three months prior. Same story, not enough money to pay for that and still compete. Oh, Lord. I prayed he would let me off with a warning. Apparently, this was not an offense that could be forgiven with a warning. Great, I was going to jail. Probably not, like, jail-jail, with the orange jumpsuit and all, but a holding cell at the minimum. Oh, this was going to be fabulous.

I was handcuffed and stuffed into the back seat of the police car. He made me leave my car on the side of the road, six blocks from my apartment. At least he let me lock it first. I should be glad for small favors. The ride to the local precinct took all of three minutes, I would have been home in less time than that, had I not been spotted weaving. At least I passed the sobriety test. But nonetheless, I was on my way to jail. First, I was locked in a little box of a cell, then fingerprints and all kinds of questions, and then I went into a large holding cell with a bunch of other women. There was some tension in the cell, it felt hostile as soon as I stepped in. My awareness was on full alert, even as tired as I was. A girl, a little bigger than myself, eyed me and started sauntering over toward me slowly, never taking her eyes off me. She was obviously the big fish in our little holding cell, and she had the other girls quietly intimidated. I was not hoping for a fight, but I would give it my best shot if I had to. I won't deny I was a little nervous, being my first time in jail, and she was big, threatening, and very tough-looking. I might have muscles but that doesn't mean I'm a good fighter.

When she got a few feet in front of me, she stopped, waited a long second, and then asked, "You lift?"

Her question changed my attitude right away. "Oh yeah. You?"

"A little, yeah."

"Hey. I'm Krista," and I held out my hand. She hesitated a second and then shook it and gave me just a hint of a smile.

"I'm Wanda." Once the subject of lifting was on the table, I began to talk about lifting and how I was working extra shifts to cover my competitions. I told them I had just gotten back from the world championships where I brought back the bronze medal. Just hearing that made me so happy, and I think the other girls caught my excitement and suddenly there was not much tension in the cell. I looked around at all us girls, in this predicament and I realized how, in one second, your whole life could change.

I finished by saying, "I was practically asleep at the wheel when I got pulled over."

Obviously, I wasn't intoxicated so Wanda asked, "What did they get you for then?"

"No insurance," I said. That got a laugh from her. She had a very infectious laugh, and a few of the other girls couldn't help themselves and started laughing too. Before long, I found myself sitting on one of the bunks talking about powerlifting and some of the girls wanted me to flex my biceps so they could feel them.

One girl giggled and said, "Wow, girl, you got more muscles than my man!" Another bout of laughter from us.

Then I asked, "What are you all in for?" There were various reasons, one girl said she got caught shoplifting; she slid a package of bacon down her pants in the grocery store, because she was tired of living on ramen noodles. Another girl got hauled in for resisting arrest (she said she resisted because she didn't do anything). Go figure. There was another girl who was totally passed out on one of the bunks brought in for the obvious, drunk and disorderly. She was still drunk but no longer very disorderly, occasionally snorting and coughing, but mostly just snoring happily. Then, I turned to Wanda, waiting for her to tell me her reason for being here. For a second, I thought our moment of comradery might be over, but she looked around and it seemed like she felt comfortable enough to spill it to all of us.

"I caught my man with another woman, really caught him, in my apartment, in *my* bed!" She was getting fired up by the end of her statement and the room quieted. She continued, "I yanked that MF out of my bed and beat his ass. Then he ran into my kitchen like a punk, and he grabbed a knife and called the cops on me. In *my* house! When I get out of here, he's going to pay for that, I am not even lying about that. He's going to pay good, mark my words." We all had no doubt, she was in no state of mind to be reasoned with, so no one said anything for a few minutes, and we let her simmer down. About that time, Linda, who had gotten picked up for solicitation, was being released. She was what I would call a little simple-minded and had locked herself out of her apartment. She had gone on a walk, waiting a few hours for her sister, who was her roommate, to get home. A man pulled over and wanted to know if she would go on a date with him. She said he looked nice, his car looked warm, and she was getting cold and hungry, so she said yes, then he said a bunch of other stuff she didn't understand. She didn't think most guys talked about how much they should pay for dinner before dinner even happened, but she said she agreed to something, and the next thing she knew she was here. Obviously not a street girl, so I was glad Linda was going home—this was no place for a sweet girl like her. But the rest of us, well, we should have known better.

I don't know how many hours passed but the ones who got released left one by one. By this time, we were like a bunch of friends going home from summer camp. As each one left, they called out, "Goodbye, Krista. Goodbye, Wanda," and those of us who were still there cheered them on their way. Wanda was still there when I got released. She was still visibly angry with her predicament, so I kept it short and to the point.

"Wanda, come to Gold's Gym West, ask for Krista Ford. I'll train with you, okay?" I wanted to give her something else a little more positive to think about besides her man.

"Okay," she said, showing me her beautiful smile. "Maybe I'll just do that." But she never did come to the gym and that was the last time I saw Wanda. I always hoped she would get away from the one who didn't treat her right.

By the time I finally got home, I had less than two hours to get to work again. Somehow, I made it through the day and home again that night, windows all down and singing at the top of my lungs just to stay awake. I did not want a repeat of the night before.

I didn't pick up any more additional shifts but spent my time looking for a better job. Since I was working nights, it was easy to look, fill out applications, and make it to interviews, if there were any on the horizon. Nothing happened for a week or so, and then I got called in for an interview with FedEx Express. I was super excited about this interview. And this was almost a full-time job. I knew they would see how hard-working and capable I was. I had such a positive eager outlook, and I tossed those packages up on the shelves like they were empty! They liked me immediately and I knew I had gotten the job before I left the building. I could feel it. And I was right. I got hired and would start in two weeks as a package handler, loading the containers that go on the aircraft for their destination.

I was so excited I could barely sleep that night. I called Grandma to tell her the good news. (She knew I was digging a hole every time I traveled to compete.) I was gently scolded for the hour, it was well past her bedtime, but she forgave me because of the great news I had. I'd been working nights for so long, I had forgotten to look at the time, I just picked up the phone and called her. I could hear in her voice she was smiling when she said goodnight.

Working nights had been difficult and I couldn't wait to start a day job. I figured my training would go better once I got on daytime hours as well—everything would be better. In hindsight, I should have done this sooner, but I was glad it was happening now. It doesn't help to beat yourself up for being a slow learner, I got there eventually.

The two weeks passed in a flash, and I was issued two sets of FedEx pants and shorts, four shirts, name tags, and even a sun visor. It was official now, I worked for FedEx and had the uniforms to prove it. My landlord raised her eyebrows in wonder the first time she saw me strutting by in my uniform. I was so anxious to pay my rent on time the next month, just so she would know I was getting my act together. I adjusted to the new hours instantly and everything fell into place, my training was going great, I was stronger, and more awake in the gym. I loved my new job, and was making more money than ever before, which meant I could compete more and get some new equipment. My mind was flying miles ahead of me as I loaded package after package. And you know talkative me, I was making all kinds of new friends and just enjoying my new life. One thing is for sure, I do have a gift to gab. I don't ever plan on pretending to be anyone other than my authentic self.

> "TAKE UP YOUR CROSS, AND FOLLOW ME" [MARK 8:34 NLT].

18

I CAN AND I AM

With a new job, more money, and perfect working hours, I was on my way. I got some much-needed new lifting equipment, and that pink squat suit finally got retired. In its place was a brand new red one. I couldn't wait to compete again. Every *Powerlifting USA* magazine I got, I read cover to cover, every article, every shred of lifting technique, every word—I wanted to learn everything I could. In the middle of each magazine was the "Upcoming Events" section, a listing of every meet on the calendar for all powerlifting federations, and I found a meet I wanted to compete in.

This was a WPA federation meet, the Can-Am International in Sherbrooke, Canada, on October 24–25, 1994—a full power meet this time. I did the bench meet there in 1992 and remembered the competition and the friends I made. There were two guy buddies, Louis and Clyde, lifters who had so much fun competing, they were just cracking jokes and doing funny voices the whole time—they had me laughing so hard. They told me they would take care of and handle me if I ever went back again. Wow, how nice was that! And I had met the meet director, Jean Marie Bergeron, who was a big brusque man but inside was as sweet as a teddy bear. He had such a strong accent for my young ears, I'm sure a few things got by me, but I really enjoyed talking with him. I mailed in my entry form the following day and planned out my ten-week countdown, my workouts, and numbers. I also saw that nationals would be in Pittsburg again that year at the beginning of July. Perfect.

Another thing I did to give myself a bit of a change was I started going to a different gym. I had been at Gold's West for almost ten years now, and I thought a change would be good. I joined the National Institute for Fitness and Strength, which was only a thirty-minute drive from home and that was fine by me. I started training with a friend named Rob. He was a good training partner, we both were feeling strong, and training was going great. The first four weeks of my countdown went according to plan, all my numbers were met, and I felt strong. Then the next week, on our bench day, I heard or felt (a very creepy sensation) a popping sound and something ripping inside of my right shoulder. *Oh no, please, not an injury, not when things are just starting to take off for me.* I went home and iced it immediately and didn't do anything heavy with that arm until I went to the doctor. Luckily, I got in within a week, and after the MRI results, I found out I had a full tear in my rotator cuff. I had to stop benching altogether but I did everything else I possibly could to keep my shoulders strong. The tear didn't seem to bother my squat or deadlift—well, it hurt a little on the squat bar, my arms were so far back, it felt like it was pulling and that was distracting as well as painful. However, I kept hitting my numbers in the squat and deadlift, so that's how I finished out my last six weeks of training for this meet, no benching. I had never done that before, and I didn't like it one bit.

When I got to Montreal, Louis and Clyde were there to pick me up at the airport, and it was like no time had passed. They were cracking jokes and talking in funny voices and just being so goofy, I think we laughed all the way to Sherbrooke. We eventually arrived at the Le Baron Hotel, where the meet would be held and where I would be staying. Jean Marie put me up in the hospitality suite free of charge. It was a beautiful suite and I felt like the guest of honor—I know I wasn't, but they made me feel like I was. I *was* the only female lifter from the United States, all the other females were Canadian. I weighed in at 164 and then had an early dinner. There was an awesome spaghetti place across the street from the hotel I remembered from last time and I took full advantage of it and then went early to bed.

In the morning, the lobby of the hotel was buzzing with energy. As I made my way into the grand ballroom where the lifting would take place, I felt the same energy and excitement well up in me as I always did before a big meet. The world of powerlifting holds such challenge and potential, and a little bit of risk, every time you approach the bar. You never knew how much you could lift until you're up there, the moment of truth, could you do it? You might have done it a hundred times in the gym, but if you can't do it at a meet, don't even say you can do it. Some people get to a meet and start doubting themselves. Not me, I get more and more excited, and I can't wait to lift. By the time I reached the warm-up area, I was already in the zone, seeing each lift in my head. My squats went well, three for three with my final lift being 410. My shoulder hurt a little holding the squat bar, but surprisingly when I got started on the bench, it wasn't as bad as I expected. I was able to get a 185 bench on my third attempt with a bench shirt on, of course, which gave me a lot of support. But I won't lie, it hurt, more than a little too; and I think that was all I could have gotten that day so I was good with that. Deadlifts went according to plan, and I pulled 440 on my final attempt. My total for the day was 1,035 pounds, which earned me a beautiful gold medal, and I even got Best Lifter! I couldn't believe it. What a day! If I had been able to lift my "pre-injury" bench weight, I might have made the Women's 1,100-pound club. Only the best of the best make that list and I wanted to be on it so bad.

One funny thing that happened at this meet was I tried on a new squat suit. It was one of those Inzer Z lock suits, size thirty, and when Louis and Clyde finally got me in it, to say I could barely walk was an understatement. I got under my bar okay but barely could get down far enough. That suit just wouldn't budge on me, almost like I was forcing myself down, while holding four hundred pounds on my back. I finally got it down but that was a weird feeling I didn't want to repeat in the future. The suit probably should have been a thirty-two or thirty-four!

Once I got home, there was not a lot of time to relax. Only thirteen weeks until nationals, and three weeks till the ten-week countdown began again. My body seemed a little tired of heavy training, I would normally like to have a few more weeks of maintenance training before diving into another competition cycle, but three weeks it was. Not having much of a break didn't slow me down though, I just kept training hard and heavy and, surprisingly enough, when it was nearly time for nationals, my shoulder had slowly gotten a little stronger. Or maybe it took more and more weight to get to the unbearable pain that told me I wasn't going any heavier. I was back in the mid-two hundreds, but with a big dose of pain for each lift so I could only push it as hard as I could bear the pain. But I was grateful I regained a lot of what I had lost, very much so—this was nationals!

The 1994 Senior Nationals were originally to be held in Pittsburg, but the location had suddenly been changed to Elmhurst, Illinois, due to the unexpected passing of the meet director, Jeff Wright. It was another huge loss to the powerlifting world, which is small enough as it is. He was a lifter-turned-promoter, and he had been very kind to me at nationals the year prior. Ernie Franz, our federation founder, moved the location to Elmhurst, Illinois, and he put on the meet himself that year. Elmhurst was about a four or five-hour drive from Indianapolis, which made me think, *maybe Grandma and Aunt Bobbie could come watch. Finally!*

As it turned out, they wouldn't be able to come watch me compete. This time it was Aunt Bobbie who was hospitalized two days before the competition due to complications from her type 1 diabetes. I'm not sure what happened, but I think this was the third time she had to be hospitalized for something related to her diabetes. It was scary as it always was, but so far, she had always made it through. So, once again, Grandma and Aunt Bobbie would miss seeing me at nationals, but I just wanted my Aunt Bobbie to get better, it didn't matter that they'd miss it.

So, I rented a car and asked my girlfriend at the time, Tami, to go with me. She took so much time getting ready to go, by the time we got there, weigh-ins were over for the day and would not resume until the following morning. So, I had to go the rest of that day and the whole night with barely anything to eat. I made sure she heard all about how hungry I was since it was her slowpoke butt that made us so late. By morning, I was first in line to be weighed and I weighed in at 161. My coach Janice was there, and we went straight out to get some breakfast. I really ate a lot, more than usual, but I couldn't help myself, I was starving.

Janice retired from competing in late 1993, but she came this year to support and help handle me and to run my numbers. Once again, Stephanie Vandeweghe and I would be in the same class, but I just lift for me, and try not to wonder who else lifted what.

That day was a great lifting day for me, I squatted 418.75 which was my best squat to date, I struggled painfully and got a 270 bench, and my deadlift was 451.75, also another personal best. However, once again, Stephanie got me good in the squats. I had the better bench and deadlift, but, because of the giant squat she did, she took home the gold, and I got the silver. It was okay, I was very pleased with how the lifts went, and best of all, my total was 1,135 so I officially was in the women's 1,100-pound club!

At most competitions, when I was done lifting, I tried to go back in the warmup area and help handle other lifters, but that day for some reason, I just stopped and watched the competition and talked to different people as we wandered around the ballroom. The big guys would compete the next day, so my friend Big Jim Voronin was out and about, observing the first day of the competition. He found me and sat down to talk with me.

He said, "Wow, Krista, I can't believe I caught up with you." This made me laugh because it's true, usually I am busy with the lifters in the warmup room. He continued, "Krista, you are like a quiet storm, you came to nationals and worlds last year all quiet, and you did your damage and then you were gone. "Just like a quiet storm, gone before we knew what hit us," and he laughed at his analogy. It's true, that is my lifting style, but most people don't use the word "quiet" to describe me in general. I would say that word would be *way* down the list. Quiet is about the last thing I am, but my nickname "Quiet Storm" came from Jim Voronin at nationals that year and I cherished it ever since.

There was a golf driving range behind our hotel and some of us went out to hit some balls after the competition. I played on my high school golf team and Janice played so we were hitting some balls. Tami said she would come too, so, we were all out on the driving range and then some of the super heavy-weight guys came out to hit too. A golf ball is not that big, but watching a three-hundred-plus pound guy hovering over this little bitty ball was so funny to see, soon Janice and I couldn't stop giggling watching them trying to hit the golf balls. We tried our best to hold it together, but the giggles kept escaping from us. We didn't want to offend anyone, so we figured we'd probably better go back inside, where we could laugh a bit louder. It was a lot of fun, to say the least, a good way to break up the monotony of the day.

The day after I returned, Aunt Bobbie was released from the hospital. Thank you, God! Aunt Bobbie and Grandma were my world.

At some point during training for these competitions, I got a letter from the AICEP (Association for International Cultural Exchange Program) in conjunction with the USPF (United States Powerlifting Federation) inviting me to represent the United States in an exhibition of powerlifting in the Goodwill Games in Russia next month, August 1994. Part of the exhibition would be a mass deadlift demonstration during the closing ceremonies of the games. Oh, and there was a follow-up trip to Finland to compete again there. This was the first time I was invited, by name, to represent my country. Of course, I would! Are you kidding me? I would be honored to represent the United States in my beloved sport, I couldn't wait to go, *Russia here I come!* One thing that always came to mind for me about Russia was the pictures of the Kremlin, something I hoped to see—after all it wasn't the eighth wonder of the world for nothing.

> **"YOU MAKE KNOWN TO ME THE PATH OF LIFE"**
> **(PSALMS 16:11 NIV).**

19

СПАСИБО = SPASIBA

The month flew by and before I knew it, the day to depart for Russia had arrived. The Goodwill Games were August 6–11, 1994 in St. Petersburg, Russia, when I was twenty-seven years old. My friend Stacia Matthews and her cameraman from Channel 6 were at the airport when I got there to cover my departure. She captured my feeling of excitement at representing our country again, just two months after competing at nationals. When I first got to the airport, I started walking around the terminal and I didn't see any "Powerlifters, this way" signs. Finally, I saw a group of people and I could tell I was in the right place. There's something about powerlifters, there's camaraderie, and kinship as soon as you meet. Our group grew as time passed until all the competitors arrived. The plane for Team USA for the flight was a huge Russian Aeroflot 747 wide-body plane, a good choice for a bunch of big powerlifters like us. Joining us was an American karate team, an arm-wrestling team, a gymnastics team, and one lone US fencer, Bob Hotchkiss.

We had a long delay before boarding and we were all getting hot and thirsty waiting and lugging our bags around. We were anxious to get on board, get seated, and get something to drink. However, as soon as we boarded for the thirteen-hour flight, we were told we couldn't drink the water in any way, shape, or form, which obviously included ice, so we had to settle for lukewarm soda. It didn't quench anyone's thirst for the next twelve days, where we still couldn't have anything with ice, nor did we ever get anything cold to drink. That was an unpleasant surprise, but we made the best of it.

Before we took off, I said a big prayer to get us all there safely, then spent the thirteen hours talking with the other lifters and sleeping. When we arrived in Moscow, we slowly made our way through customs and then boarded a bus about one hundred degrees that took us to another plane that flew us to St. Petersburg, Russia. By the time we got there, no one was concerned about making their weights, we all sweated off about five pounds each. Then there were three more (equally hot) buses to get us to our hotel. The word "hotel" was a bit of a stretch, it was more like a dorm or retirement home, not exactly a four-star place, but we were just happy to have arrived safely and have a bed.

I met the other female lifters and we all bonded. There was Lani Powell from Cali, Becky Steed from New Hampshire, April Mathias, Elizabeth Lester, and Wendy Hendrick—all from Virginia, Kelly Bergener from Alaska, Paige Clouatre and Elana Esposito from Texas, Griselle Ufret from Florida, and Teresita Frisbee from Washington. They paired us up according to weight class and I roomed with Wendy, and Lani and Teresita were next door. We checked out our facilities and found out our showers consisted of several showerheads with a few drain holes in the floor and not a shower curtain to be found. Also, there was a bucket next to the toilets for the toilet paper, which there was none of, but fortunately, we had been instructed to bring our own. This was a big eye-opener as to the things we took for granted back home—I didn't realize how blessed we are as a nation.

For the next three days, we were sightseeing, shopping, and practicing for the closing ceremonies while trying to get some training in. Shopping was great, and the exchange rate for the US dollar was in our favor: five dollars was worth ten thousand rubles, so our money went far. We had also been told that the local people would be interested in trading Russian items for USA things if we brought extras. Trading and bartering were fun. I traded a Nike windbreaker set for a beautiful chess set, and I got an authentic gray Russian military coat that had the soldier's name inside of it and the fury gray Russian hat I traded for three sets of my knee wraps and my powerlifting belt to one of the male Russian lifters. I was the only lifter on the USA powerlifting team out of eighty of us to obtain the Russian Military coat and hat. I even traded my Seiko watch for a giant Matryoshka nesting doll.

We had sightseeing trips almost every day. One day we went to Peter the Great's castle. It was amazing and there was this one ballroom where all the walls were covered with portraits of the royal family and no matter where you stood in the room, it seemed like all the eyes of all the portraits were looking at you. It was a little unnerving but intriguing at the same time. Another day we went to this cathedral where every surface visible was covered in gold. I have never seen anything like it in my life, I couldn't imagine how they did that.

The powerlifting competition was to be held at the training facility the gymnast Olga Korbut trained at for the 1972 Olympics, and her pictures lined the halls. We trained here with some Russian lifters and did our best to learn a few words in Russian. Most of the Russian lifters trained and competed raw, which meant they did not use lifting suits, or wraps, and they were very strong. This would be a great competition.

When the competition started, right off the rip there were problems. First, the warm-up area was two flights downstairs. Let's just say it was hilarious watching us go up and down those stairs in our suits and knee wraps. And then, the judges didn't know how to say our commands to us in English, so there was quite a delay. I was already suited up to lift, had struggled up the stairs, and then I had to be laid down on the floor so my legs wouldn't go to sleep while I waited for them to figure all of this out. Finally, my guys pulled me up to my feet and the competition began. I didn't feel my normal energy, the wait really zapped my strength, but I was able to squat 385.75. I attempted 402.25, but apparently, I wasn't low enough. I felt like I was, but the judges didn't think so. That was my first attempt ever over four hundred. Then on to the bench, and the problems just got worse. Since the bench rack was slightly behind the lifter, normally you have one of your guys lift the bar off to you and they know how you like it.

So, here was the first problem: they would only let the Russian men lift off to us. On my first lift-off, I almost fell off the bench, it was so quick and jerky, and he almost dropped the bar onto me. I was off balance and out of control for a second, not to mention it didn't feel very good when I already had some pain issues with my rotator cuff tear. I got the lift; thankfully, I went a little conservative in my attempt. Then I got my second lift of 270, and barely missed 281, I just couldn't quite lock it out. Deadlifts were going well, and I was psyched and ready to do a personal best (473.25) for my third and final attempt, but as I got up to the platform to lift, they told me to wait. The bar was misloaded, and they had to correct it. Misloading is incorrect weight on one or both sides of the bar. I tried to keep my focus, but all this chaos was getting to me. I didn't get the lift, it stuck hard at about three-fourths of the way up, so I had to settle for my second lift, which was 424.25. I ended up with a total of 1,080, despite only getting six of my nine lifts. I was not happy with my performance—I know I could have done better. However, with my total, I won the gold. Becky got silver and a Russian girl got bronze. A hard-fought battle for sure. After that, all of us girls stayed and cheered the guys on.

After the meet, we all went back to our hotel and everyone was socializing and talking about the meet, reliving the moments. One of the guys had a blowout during his squats which was scary. All of us girls were close to the front of the squat area, and we saw it firsthand. He was about halfway down, and his suit started to rip out in the crotch area, and as he continued down, it totally ripped out. He was a strong lifter and managed to come back up, despite the lack of support from his suit. It could have been disastrous. All the big lifts were talked about and analyzed, everyone hoping to glean any shred of technique to make us better.

I decided to turn in early so I told Wendy I would leave the door unlocked for her and she said she would be up momentarily. I must have been very tired because I was soon sleeping soundly. I vaguely remember hearing Wendy come back in the room and I turned over and mumbled hi or something like that. She didn't say anything right away and something made me open my eyes. Well, it wasn't Wendy at all, it was a small Russian woman, and her lips were about two inches from mine as she was puckering up to plant a kiss right on my mouth! This presented an unexpected problem for me. Before I got out of bed, I had a split second to reconsider why I slept naked, but as I yanked the covers off me and grabbed my T-shirt, I was asking her who she was and what in the world she was doing in my room, trying to kiss me. By the time I had yanked on my shorts, I was almost at the door. I was going to knock this girl out if she grabbed me.

I yelled, "Policea" at her, she obviously didn't understand my words up to that point so I figured she would understand that. She started yelling in Russian and then quick as a jackrabbit she pulled out the drawer under Wendy's bed and disappeared under it. I got out into the hall, as other lifters started coming out of their rooms due to the commotion. Two of the big guys went into our room and tried to pull her out from under the bed but she had attached herself to a metal leg of the bedframe, and they couldn't break her free. She had wedged herself in where the drawer had been, all the way to the back. Someone went downstairs to get Eugene, our translator, to see if he could coax her out. Nope. When the police got there, one of them flipped up the bed and this girl bit him on the hand, then the other one hit her on the head with a club so hard she screamed and instantly went unconscious, and they finally dragged her out of the room. No one wanted an international incident but wow, that was a hard blow to the head. I will never forget the sound the club made when it hit her. It almost made me sick to my stomach.

So much for my early night, as a bunch of us sat around and talked about the whole ordeal. From that point on, I got a lot of kisses blown at me by my teammates and they asked me if I checked under my bed before I got in it at night, they couldn't resist teasing me about it. All in good fun, but I always felt sorry for that girl and wondered what happened to her.

The next day was the final practice for the closing ceremonies, and we went through the whole program till we were positive we could do it perfectly.

The following morning, we headed over to Kirov stadium in three chartered buses and lined up in our assigned places. There were two tunnels leading into the stadium and half of the powerlifters were at the entrance of each tunnel. The other athletes, families, and friends made their way up into the stands to watch the final soccer match and closing ceremonies. This is what we came here to do, to be a part of the Goodwill Games Closing Ceremonies and attempt a world record. And then it was halftime in the soccer game, and we were running down the tunnels and into the stadium. The cheers of eighty-five thousand voices were cheering as Yanni's theme played in the background. This was the most exciting thing I had ever been a part of, and I was relishing every second of it. We stopped in the middle of the field in two lines, Russian lifters on one side and Americans on the other side, facing each other. We raised up our arms and made a tunnel as two little girls ran through the tunnel of arms, each with a handful of helium balloons. When they got through the tunnel, they let their balloons go, and the cheers of the crowd got louder. Then we all ran to our assigned bar.

The Olympic bars were loaded for what each of us and our Russian counterparts could lift on any given day. A Russian lifter and an American lifter would lift a bar attached together with some kind of flexible metal tubing. Once we were all in place, there was a lot of talking over the microphone and I think they were talking about our world record attempt. Every television station was there, including NBC Sports and TBS, and the flashing of cameras was nonstop. Then two huge barbells made from balloons were released into the air. A drum struck three times and then a massive cannon went off, that was our signal to pull. Everyone bent down over their bar, and we all pulled simultaneously. All those connected bars, loaded with 37,620 pounds, came off the ground and when we locked out the weight, we made *The Guinness Book of World Records* as the most weight deadlifted in one pull simultaneously. The crowd went crazy, screaming and jumping in the stands. We held it for a few seconds and then put it down with a thundering boom. We only had a few seconds to relish the moment, which we did with wide eyes and rapid heartbeats. The crowd was on their feet, cheering and clapping and they weren't stopping.

Then we turned and ran to our assigned spots in the center of the field. Each of us had either a green or a blue cape tucked in at our waist. We pulled those out as we ran and wrapped them around us and collectively, we gathered into a circle, making the world—the blue capes were the sea, and the green capes were the land. Once we all got in place, we swayed side to side to the Michael Jackson song, "We Are the World." We were all singing the song and I think the whole stadium was too. Everyone in the stands joined hands with their neighbors, and they were holding their hands up in the air and it made us all cry. I don't think I saw a dry eye on that field. It was very moving to see the unity between our two countries that had not been possible a decade prior. It was the greatest feeling I ever had, and I was so proud to be a part of it. When the song was finished, we ran out of the stadium and back down our tunnels, the crowd still on their feet and cheering for us. Once outside of the stadium area, we hugged and savored the moment.

In no time at all, the soccer game was over, and the closing ceremonies began. All the athletes lined up and made their way down the tunnels. When it was our turn, we were each given a bunch of small American flags on little wooden sticks, as many as we could hold. We didn't quite know what this was for, but when we got into the stadium, people were screaming and leaning over the rails with their hands out, begging for one. We walked around the entire stadium and as we got to a section and waved to the crowd, they cheered and got louder and louder as we waved enthusiastically at them. It was the highest honor for us, to feel this much admiration from these fans. At one point there was a camera close to us, off to the side a little, and several of us jumped in front of it and flexed our biceps in front of the camera. It just happened to be ABC Sports, and that shot was aired back in the States and all over the world. By the time we got around the stadium, none of us had a single flag left.

Now that everything was over, some of us girls really needed to use the restroom. Lani and I headed over to the door that said "Toilets for Women" and went through the door but stopped dead in our tracks. There were a bunch of holes in the ground, with places to put your feet, and there was an array of ladies, skirts and dresses hiked up, or slacks pulled down and, once again, no toilet paper to be found. As bad as we had to go, we decided we could wait till we got back to our hotel, and we turned around and got on the bus. We thought we would leave right away, and we'd be back in our rooms soon, so we wouldn't have to wait very long. But that was not to be the case. A headcount was taken, and we were one short. It was the fencer's wife, Grace, who was missing. She had been up in the stands with the other Americans that had come with us. A few people who knew where she was went back to get her, but she wasn't there. So, believe it or not, Stella, one of our directors, decided we would leave anyway. We were all shouting and having a fit about this, one of our own—a female at that—was going to be left behind in a country where she didn't speak the language. This did not sit well and dampened the elation we had been feeling. The fencer, Bob, got off the bus and stayed behind to look for his wife, and the buses took off with the rest of us. Once we got back to the hotel, we waited around for word of Grace.

Finally, they both returned to our hotel at around three a. m. and she looked like she had been roughed up. We didn't get the whole story but apparently, the police had been holding her and questioned her relentlessly for hours before Bob found out where she was. We all hugged her and let her know we had been praying for her safe return and that's why we were all still up at that hour.

A few hours later, we all boarded buses again. This time some of the lifters got on a bus that would go to Moscow and then back to the States, while some of us lifters, including Lani and I, got on a bus headed for Finland. To our great surprise, the bus had air-conditioning, a television, and restrooms complete with toilet paper. It was about an eight-hour drive to Finland, and we enjoyed the air-conditioned coolness for the first time in over a week. Most of us fell asleep on the ride there since we had been up most of the night before.

Our Finland destination was Järvenpää, where there was to be a friendly bench press contest. Lani and I roomed together, and the rooms were gorgeous, all decorated in white (my favorite color), with fluffy bedding and all kinds of fancy contraptions in the bathroom. We finally figured out which one was the hair dryer, but there were a few things we never figured out. But we didn't care, we were being treated like royalty. Tons of food was placed out buffet style in the dining hall and we ate and ate, the food was so delicious.

When it came time to lift, I had a problem. Well, dummy me ate so much, I was overweight, and I had to do something quick to make my weight class. So, I starved myself for the rest of the day and the next morning, didn't drink anything, spit, and all that ridiculous stuff people do to make a weight class and I finally made it. When it came time for me to lift, I was really exhausted and weak and (I'm so sorry, Janice) I bombed out. Again! Honestly, I didn't really care, this was a bonus competition. Lani did well and won her class, so I was happy for her.

When the competition was over, we played the slot machines in the lobby and then went on a local shopping tour. The next morning, we took a very fast ferry ride back to Helsinki and toured a famous church, the Temppeliaukio church. It had a pure brass ceiling, and we learned a lot about the history of Finland and Helsinki. There were many Volvo's, Mercedes-Benz, Saabs, and BMWs being driven around town. We saw three or four Afghan hound dogs being walked by their owners and people wore leather and really dressed to the hilt.

From there, we took another bus back to Moscow and got on our Aeroflot plane bound for New York. We mostly slept on the way home; we were all so tired. Somehow, I made it back to Indianapolis in a few short hours after landing in New York and I called my girlfriend and told her I was home and went directly to bed. I was exhausted, but I couldn't sleep. Wow, what an awesome experience that was!

I am proud to say I learned some keywords in Russian, one of which is the name of this chapter. "Спасибо" is how it's written in Russian (pronounced "Spasiba") meaning "thank you."

> **"REJOICE ALWAYS, PRAY CONTINUALLY, GIVE THANKS IN ALL CIRCUMSTANCES"**
> **(1 THESSALONIANS 5:16-18 NIV).**

20

PUMPMAMA4U

After returning from Russia, I allowed myself a few days of rest before I started training for worlds. This competition would be held in Columbus, Ohio, on November 3–6, 1994. That was about two and a half hours away from Indianapolis. This was a blessing for me because money was so tight, I was not sure I could have made another long trip. I was still training at the National Institute of Fitness and Strength, but I was looking for a change of training sites. Not only was I exhausted from training so hard and competing already three times that year, but I also just wasn't feeling it at that gym anymore, but I powered through with the help of my training partner and handler, Ron Riley.

I prayed Aunt Bobbie and my grandmother would be able to come to Columbus, but I tried not to hope too hard as we had tried this several times before and they couldn't make it either time before due to health issues. Maybe this time would be different, God willing. I was still working at FedEx, and my competitions made the newsletter that came out for all the employees every month. A lot of my FedEx friends had learned of the upcoming competition and wanted to come watch what this obscure sport was all about and see their coworker compete. By the time the meet came around, there were at least five friends coming from work to watch. Of course, I invited Aunt Bobbie, Grandma, and my sister. Timing is everything and wouldn't you know it, my car started acting up just before the trip to Ohio. My friend Lori Miller, from the gym, lent me her car for the trip as we were both pretty sure mine wouldn't make it. That was a huge and unexpected gift.

By the time I got to Columbus, I had nine people coming to watch me, and Janice came to handle me. Grandma wasn't well enough to make the trip, but Aunt Bobbie and my sister, Stacey, were on their way! (With none other than my mother, unbelievable to me as she had never supported my athletic endeavors whatsoever.) Aunt Bobbie can be persuasive when she wants to be, and it was okay by me. I preferred just to go with my handlers, but I was honored by the support of my friends and family, especially Aunt Bobbie, my biggest supporter.

I weighed in at 160 and I was happy for that because I had just gotten a new custom pink squat suit, an Inzer Z suit, which was cut differently than the regular squat suits and much tighter in the legs. Once again, it was Stephanie and I battling for the top spot in the 165-pound class. After I was partially warmed up for the squats, Brian Meeks, a friend, and Janice worked on getting that suit on me. They yanked and pulled and were covered in sweat by the time they got it on me, and it was so tight, it just didn't set right, and my last warmups felt a little off. When I got on the platform it still didn't feel right, and these were the slowest squats I've ever done. I got the first two (380.25 and 418.75) and missed the last one, 429.75, even though I had gotten it before and should have been able to get it then. I was disappointed but I just wanted that suit off. We headed back to the warmup area, and it came off my shoulders okay, but it was stuck tight around my thighs. When you have a suit on, your quads swell up anyway and this was no exception, but there must have been no room at all for blood to get back up into my torso, as the suit was so tight. Janice worked for about five minutes with no luck. Eventually, every big guy in the warmup area pulled and yanked on the suit, and it would not come off. My legs at this point were going numb. Someone suggested we should cut the suit off. My brand-new, forty-dollar, custom-pink squat suit—no way! Keep pulling, guys! I was flat on my back, holding on to some chair legs (with the biggest guy in the gym sitting in the chair) and I was yanked and pulled for another ten minutes. By this time, as painful as the decision was, I told them to go ahead and cut the suit off. First and last time I ever had to do that. After it was off, I had to go straight over to a massage therapist who worked on getting the blood flowing again and then I went to the chiropractic table to get me back to my normal size again. I think I must have been almost six feet tall after all that pulling. Eventually, I was five six again and it was on to the bench.

The bench went great, and I did the most I had done up to this point, a whopping 275.5 pounds. I was stoked! Then the battle began. Stephanie and I were within fifty pounds of each other. I got my first deadlift easily enough, 402.25, and then I got 451.75. My final lift of 462.75 but I just couldn't quite lock out. Stephanie, once again, out lifted me by seventy pounds. One thing I do remember specifically about this competition was the crowd cheering. Usually, the crowd yelling and cheering for you just sounds like background noise, but when there's a voice within that crowd you've known all your life, you can hear that voice over every other voice, and I heard my Aunt Bobbie screaming her lungs out for me. That is probably why I did as well as I did. After the squat suit fiasco, and my body being fatigued from all my competitions that year, I think her cheering gave me just a little extra strength. She was always my God-given rock.

As we received our medals, mine was silver again this year, I saw my Aunt Bobbie making her way to the front of the crowd, camera in hand. I could read her lips as she passed everyone, "That's my niece! That's my niece! That's my niece!" She was so proud, snapping pictures through her tears of joy. I nearly lost it on the platform just seeing her so happy. I had been excited for Aunt Bobbie to see me lift, but I never thought she would be that overjoyed. And then I remembered why it was so personal for her. She was the one who gave me the weight set when I was ten years old, and she just got to see where that gift took me. I couldn't have loved her more than I did at that moment. Then as I made my way off the platform, I was engulfed by my FedEx friends who were patting me on the back and clapping, saying how awesome the competition was. It was a bit overwhelming; I had never had that many people come and support me before, but it was fabulous.

I saw Janice out of the corner of my eye, smiling, and she nodded her head at me once, and I knew she was saying, "Well done, my friend, well done."

The evening passed quickly and lots of food was eaten, especially by me, I was so hungry after that long day. The following morning, all my supporters left for home, and Aunt Bobbie gave me the longest hug I think I've ever gotten from her, telling me in my ear how proud she was of me, her little sweet pea all grown up and strong like Wonder Woman! That left Janice and me to watch the big guy's lift. Most of our guys did well and had a great day lifting.

In our time together, Janice told me I had put a very hard load on my body this year and, for my body's health, please not to do that again. "Don't do back-to-back world-class meets in one year, just do nationals and worlds, Krista, that's enough. Doing that many meets is how you get yourself hurt." I had to agree, my body was exhausted. That's one thing I liked about Janice though, she always told me the truth, without too much sugarcoating. She always was the voice of reason.

Our federation president, Ernie Franz, saw us talking and came up to me and said he was amazed I could get those two squats in that suit. He laughed when we told him we had to cut it off, but he wasn't surprised. I assured him I wouldn't do that again. At the end of the day, Janice and I said our goodbyes to everyone and headed for home.

After being home for a week or two, I bid on a job in Connecticut, still with FedEx, but this job was a courier position driving around and delivering the packages, not working in the hub loading the airplane containers. It was more money and after the financial struggle that year, I was anxious to make a positive move forward in my life. My current girlfriend and I spent our last night together and we would say our goodbyes with no regrets. Our relationship was solid as she whispered in my ear, "Baby, I would never get in the way of your dreams." From 1985–1995, I would reflect on the other four relationships I had with some amazing women. I got the job. I moved to New Haven, Connecticut, in February of '95, and I lived in the apartment building George W. Bush lived in when he went to Yale. I stayed there a few months and ended up in Bridgeport, which was closer to the FedEx station that was in Stratford Connecticut.

I found a good gym called Southside Gym, owned by Joe and Donna Silva. I felt right at home there and the lifters welcomed me into their powerlifting circle, and I loved every minute of training there. Before long I had a girlfriend named Therese and she would be the first woman to slip a diamond commitment ring on my finger when we were sleeping. She beat me to the punch on that one and we just laughed at that sneaky maneuver. The following month, *Powerlifting USA* magazine came out with the "Top 20 Lifters" in every weight class. This year, I ranked fourth in the squat with 418.75, fifth in the bench with 275.5, and second in the deadlift with 479.5—and an overall ranking of fifth with 1,146 pounds. I was very pleased with these rankings, every year I was getting stronger and stronger.

I settled into my new routine and by early summer I had built up some vacation time and enough extra money that I decided to go back to Indy and visit my family and friends. The day of my flight out, there was a big delay at the Newark airport, and by the time we got going, I wasn't sure I would make my connecting flight at O'Hare. When I deboarded the plane, I dumped my bags by a row of chairs, and went directly to the counter to see what gate my connecting flight was at and if I still had time to make it. The agent told me I could make it if I ran, so I took off and sprinted to where I had left my bags, hurdled the row of chairs (kind of like those old O. J. Simpson commercials), and when I came down there was a sickening pop that came from my left knee. I went down in a heap, intense pain shooting up and down my leg. Hoping this was just a sprain, I tried to get up and almost collapsed again. Finally, I made it to my feet and got to my gate as fast as I could. So much for running, but I made it. Once I boarded and got to my seat, I looked down at my knee and it was about the size of a small basketball. This was not good, not good at all. When my friend picked me up in Indy, she got me a wheelchair to get me out of the terminal. She took me to a twenty-four-hour emergency care facility and the tentative diagnosis was an ACL tear. They said I'd need to get back home and get an MRI to verify the diagnosis. I was devastated. The timing couldn't be worse, three weeks until the '95 nationals.

The next three weeks were miserable. The diagnosis was confirmed and since I was so close to the competition, we decided to try intense physical therapy for the three weeks, putting off the surgery until sometime after the meet. It didn't feel like it was doing much good, but I did my best to complete all the physical therapy exercises.

The nationals were in Dallas, Texas, that year and Janice met me there. She knew what happened and watched me warm up in the squats. I tried 135, which was painful, and then I tried 185 but I couldn't even get down to parallel. When she saw my face on that attempt, she made the call I should just do a token lift. That means the bar, the two little 2.5-pound plates, and the collars—not exactly my idea of a national-level lift. I saw Jim Voronin off to the side, sitting there watching me. I made my way over to him and put my head on his giant shoulder. He put his arm around me, and my tears started to fall, I was so disappointed.

He let me cry a little and then he said to me, "An ACL tear is something you can come back from, Krista, it's not the end for you. Don't be sad, Krista. If anyone can come back from this injury, it's you." I tried to take heart. He said he wouldn't be competing this year at all due to some back issues he was having, and then, I felt sad for him. We had a few quiet moments and then I had to go do my token lift.

Only three women qualified for nationals this year in the 165-pound class. Of course, Stephanie Vandeweghe would win the competition for the third year in a row, and the newcomer, A. D. Gordon, would place second, and yours truly, well, I would be coming in last. I was the first lifter up. There's nothing like having the bar loaded with 2.5-pound plates to humble a person. And it did, but I just wanted to get it over with. The squat went off with no problems, but I did scratch my next two attempts. It wasn't like I could do much more than that token lift anyway.

Bench was next and I got my first and second lifts (253.5 and 275.5) which were tough as my knee hurt when I tried to get my legs as far underneath me as possible. I still hadn't gotten my rotator cuff repaired so I was still dealing with the pain of that. But I was greatly relieved my strength had come back so well on the bench. However, my final attempt of 281 just wouldn't lock out so I had to settle for my second lift.

Deadlifts went well despite my knee being swollen substantially and getting quite painful by this time. I got all three lifts, 303, 341.5, and then 363.75. I thanked God this competition was over and for getting me through it. And yeah, a whopping 694 pounds total.

One nice thing that happened that day was a new competitor joined the ranks, a 132-pound girl named Vanessa Schwenker. Now I wasn't the only Black female in our Federation at this level. It was about time!

An unexpected bomb out on the bench by A. D. Gordon left me unexpectedly in second place. I almost wished I would have gotten third, second qualified me for worlds and I was not feeling like I could perform at 100 percent, not with my bad knee and shoulder. But, oh, how I still wanted to go.

Jim Voronin gave me a hug, and said, "Next year will be your year, Krista, just take it easy and get yourself healthy now." Janice concurred and urged me to take some time off and rest and get my knee and my shoulder repaired and not push it anymore this year. With a heavy heart, I knew they were right. So, this began the first time I had to take time off lifting due to injuries.

> "PRAISE THE LORD, MY SOUL, AND FORGET NOT ALL HIS BENEFITS— WHO FORGIVES ALL YOUR SINS AND WHO HEALS ALL YOUR DISEASES" [PSALMS 103:2–4 NIV].

21

RUN, SKIP, HOP, JUMP

Let me go back for a minute. Right before I moved from Indianapolis to Connecticut, I was invited to an awards banquet ceremony to honor some of the top athletes in the city of Indianapolis. I was being honored for my powerlifting accomplishments, having placed second at senior nationals recently. I sat with a girl named Crista, *Same name, just spelled differently, interesting*, I thought. She was a speedskater and she was telling me about the US women's bobsledding team and how they were looking for strong women to try out for the team. She said she thought I would be a good bobsledder, because I had been a sprinter, and I was very strong. It could be interesting, although I didn't know the first thing about bobsledding, let alone any other winter sport, but I did remember how many people told me I would be a good weightlifter, and how true that proved to be. So, I listened, and I took her seriously, even though I couldn't even imagine bobsledding. She gave me the coach's phone number, and when I got up the nerve to call him the following week, he informed me the tryouts were over for the year, but they would love for me to try out the following year, 1995.

So, back to today in Connecticut, still delivering packages for FedEx and having a torn rotator cuff, a torn ACL, and taking time off from competing because I'm injured. What an excellent time to try out a new sport! I figured I could do it though; the movements were different than I did for lifting. For the rest of the year, I did every physical therapy exercise I knew and worked as hard as I could to get as strong and healthy as I could. Then I made the phone call to Steve Maiorca, the coach for the women's bobsledding team. He remembered me from my phone call the previous year and invited me to come try out for the team. I was nervous but excited, I told him I didn't know the first thing about bobsledding, and he assured me they would teach me everything I needed to know, just come try it out. *Okay, I can do that.*

In September 1995, I took a train to Lake Placid, New York. It was an eight-hour ride, just long enough for me to get good and nervous. Visions of the movie *Cool Runnings* ran and reran through my mind, crash after crash after crash while they were learning. Was that how it was going to be? Hopefully not, but what was I getting myself into in my (slightly) compromised state? The following day I would find out. When I got off the train, I met up with another girl who was trying out, Amy Bawyer, and we rode the shuttle to the Olympic Training Center together. We got checked in and got our room assignments. My roommate was Joyce Pusehaus, a wife and mother of two. The remainder of the day was spent getting acquainted with the other girls, our new surroundings, finding the track, and where the cafeteria was. We would all be meeting at the track in the morning, and I couldn't wait. I met all the girls who were trying out that year for the first time, fourteen of us. One more girl had already tried out, so there were fifteen of us newbies trying out total.

When we got out on the track in the morning, I was so ready. Being on a track again, felt good. They had six physical tests for us and a point system to rank us. To make the team, we had to get 425 points. The first three of the tests were sprints. No problem you might think, I was a sprinter in high school, right? Well, I haven't used my sprinting muscles for several years, eleven to be exact, *and* I was tipping the scales at 170 these days, not my high school sprinting weight of 135, so I was not sure what might happen, but apparently my sprinting muscles remembered what they were supposed to do. I sprinted a 4.21 in the thirty-meter dash, 7.82 in the sixty-meters, and 12.78 in the hundred-meters. All of us completed the sprints and then went on to the bunny hop. I'm not sure what this skill measures in relation to bobsledding but we all had to squat down, put our laced fingers behind our neck, and do five bunny hops right in a row, no break to reposition. This was so hard to do without laughing (or falling over), it looked hilarious. I worried about my knee during this event, but it was stable, and I got through it. Then we did a vertical jump and a shotput throw, not the normal way to throw the shot though, the shot had to be tossed underhanded like a granny basketball shot, swinging it between your legs before letting it go.

When we were done, we all hung around and waited for our scores. Everyone had their fingers crossed for a score over 425. When Steve came back and read off our scores, he announced that seven of the fourteen of us had made the team. Amazingly, I got the most points, 766, with the next closest score being 580 (that was Elena Primerano, the one who tested earlier). I had broken the records in each of the six events. *Maybe I will be good at this sport* as well as my powerlifting, I smiled to myself. Huh, I did not see that coming. What an unexpected blessing. Now I would be training for and competing in two sports. I was very excited, even though I still knew nothing about bobsledding. Six of us remained at the training center and the other seven left for home. The ones who remained were Laurie Miller, Liz Parr, Amy Bowyer, Michelle Powe, Courtney O'Neil, and of course, me.

For the next three days, we practiced pushing a sled with wheels on a track. On the third day of practicing that, we did a timed run with it. We drew numbers to see who went first. I drew number seven, so I would go last. When it was my turn, I put my weight into that sled and sprinted, pushing it as hard as I could past all three electrical timers. When I passed the final timer, the girls all cheered—I had just broken that record too with a 5.93. Steve pulled me to the side and congratulated me and said he hoped to see me heavily involved in this sport. I assured him I would be, absolutely.

For the next month and a half, I did my physical therapy for my knee and shoulder, I trained in the gym as hard as I could (and with great care around my knee and shoulder, so as not to aggravate those injuries), and I mentally practiced bobsledding, even though the only thing I had ever done was push the land sled with wheels. And, of course, I delivered packages for FedEx. Then, I got the call! Our first race would be the following month in Calgary, Canada. Oh boy, here we go! This competition would be my first time on actual ice. The US had two female teams going that would compete, Jill Bakken and I were USA Team 1 and Chrissy and Liz Parr would be USA Team 2.

After a few delays with the airlines, I made it to Calgary and Jill was there waiting for me. Liz and Chrissy would be flying in the next day. We made our way to our hotel, chatting nonstop about the upcoming race.

The next morning, I would find out what it felt like to race down the ice in a sled. To take off, Jill, the driver, was on the left side of the sled with a bar in front of her she'd push. I was directly behind the sled, with my hands in the "hooks" (openings in the top back end of the sled), and I was to pull the sled toward me up tight, lean forward, and take off. My head would be almost inside the sled, driving hard like sprinting out of the starting blocks, my arms behind me as I was almost pulling the sled with my arms while driving with my legs. Then I would push the sled out in front of me, and Jill would jump in, then I would push the sled *and* Jill. Another sixty yards of sprinting my hardest and then I would jump in. As I jump in, I'd piggyback right in behind Jill, and my feet would reach my blocks. My hand grips were down by my midcalf, and with my knees slightly bent, I grabbed the handles. Finally, I'd tuck my head in behind Jill, and would be in this position for the duration of the race. I leaned when she leaned, and I copied her every move. I had to study and memorize the course beforehand so I would know what turns were coming up.

The driver could see, but the brakeman needed to have each turn in the course memorized because she couldn't see anything. Simple enough in theory, but let's see what happened when we put it to the test on real ice!

As our teams came onto the practice area, all heads turned to look at me—and then I got it, there's a Black woman on *our* team. As I looked around, I saw I was the only Black person there, including coaches, staff, and everyone else. I thought of Jackie Robinson and all he went through to play baseball, and Althea Gibson being the first Black woman of tennis to win Wimbledon in 1957. I held my head up and was determined to show these gawkers what a strong Black woman could do.

Practice runs down actual ice began at one hundred meters. Two runs at that distance and then two more runs at two hundred meters. The actual racecourse was 1,600 meters long so I had a good idea of how long I would be crunched down in that sled. Being tucked inside was very uncomfortable and gave me a headache—so far, not liking this too much.

Then it was our turn to race. I was understandably nervous; this was the first sport for me where I was not 100 percent under my own control. Running on a track or lifting a weight, I was under my own power. This was an altogether different experience. A crash could be catastrophic, to say the least, and our sled was not considered top-of-the-line either, more like a Pinto compared to a Mercedes. This didn't make me feel super confident. Looking at it, I couldn't help but think it looked like a glorified trash can. Well, no turning back now.

From the starting line to the first timer, we were perfect. In our first run, we had the second-best start time of the day with 6.11 seconds. We started out fast and were in a great position. However, I'll have to say that was the last time we were good. We didn't gain much speed going down the course and we were both fine with that, nearing eighty miles per hour in a little metal ice rocket was slightly outside of my comfort zone anyway. We weren't expecting a miracle run either. It was our first race as a team and my first race ever. We scraped the sides a little coming down, but we held on and made it all the way down the course without crashing. Both times. Apparently, that is quite a feat when you are a new team. Chrissy and Liz crashed on both of their runs, fortunately, neither of them got hurt. I wasn't sure I liked this sport; I was trying to decide if it was more fun or scary. I think it was scarier, as my shaking hands confirmed this. It was fun though too, scary fun, thrilling for sure.

For some reason, or reasons, a few of the girls on our team started getting an attitude toward me. I wasn't sure why, maybe because I didn't crash or because I didn't equal their economic status. I don't know. I had made friends with the team members from other countries and when they all said hi to me in passing, it was genuine. But when I was around my own USA teammates, I felt hostility and jealousy from them. I thought that was how athletic competition was supposed to be, with tough competition and good sportsmanship. Regardless, I felt it and decided I would just rise above it and let it go. I was good at this sport and was not stepping aside because of some petty jealousy.

Or was it something else? The longer I spent in this sport, I realized that my skin color was another thing affecting some of my teammates. This had been a white-only sport, as were most of the winter sports. Most of the girls were awesome, just a few bad apples in the group; it was eloquently subtle, but it was there. This was the first time I experienced prejudice in a sport. If I was lousy at this sport, I could understand why they wouldn't want me on the team, but I was the best brakeman this team ever had. What the HELL does my skin color have to do with that, I don't know. I couldn't believe it, some of my own teammates! Wow. Racist assholes! And some of the staff of coaches and the president of the USBSF weren't any better.

You know what though? I was good at this, so I was going to do it anyway. I will say some of the athletes are merely competitors. I basically ignored the other few and hung with the girls who accepted me as an equal teammate. These are the ones I would come back to compete with for the next six years. And I came back with a vengeance and would become the best bobsledder I could be.

Besides, I already made history, along with the greats like Althea Gibson and Jackie Robinson, it was an honor being the first Black female bobsledder ever in the history of this sport. I didn't even realize it at the time, but I am a pioneer and trailblazer for future strong Black women to shine in bobsledding and other winter sports.

> **"IN HIS HAND IS THE LIFE OF EVERY CREATURE"**
> **[JOB 12:10 NIV].**

WPC World Championships Macon, France, 1993. My First Worlds.

WPA World Championship in Sherbrooke, Quebec, Canada, 1994.

Goodwill Games in St. Petersburg, Russia, 1994.

Goodwill Games in St. Petersburg, Russia. 1994. Closing Ceremonies.

22

KRUGERRAND

After that first bobsled season, I went back to the gym and started training for powerlifting again. Nationals were coming up and I wanted to be as ready as I could. I still didn't have my ACL surgery nor my rotator cuff surgery. I guess I was putting it off as I just couldn't bear the thought of being out of commission for the length of time the rehab would take. Not to mention I couldn't afford to take time off work; I was already barely making ends meet. I did so much training in the gym, my supporting muscles helped to take the load off the injured parts and my numbers began to climb back up to where they were. This was a most exciting surprise, and I was looking forward to competing in powerlifting again. There was the issue of my knee buckling under me periodically for no reason (well other than the torn ACL), so I had to be extra careful and pay constant attention to it so as not to fall when I squatted. That was really the only time it bothered me, when I was squatting. I just didn't fully trust it.

Training was going great. I felt strong and I was so happy to be back doing my favorite thing, training in the gym. And I was still getting bigger. At twenty-nine years old, I took another weight class jump and went up to the 181-pound class. Currently, I was about 175. Janice helped me make this decision and it was the right one. I liked the extra weight on my five-foot-six frame and I felt strong. During my ten weeks of training prior to nationals, I squatted the most I'd ever done in the gym, 490 pounds, and benched the most ever, three hundred pounds, and then deadlifted the most I'd ever done, 470 pounds. The ten weeks flew by, and I was on my way to Atlanta, Georgia, for nationals. It was 1996 and this was the year the Summer Olympics were held in Atlanta, Georgia. *How cool is that*, I thought.

Janice met me in Atlanta so she could do my numbers and expedite for me. Expediters are the ones who tell the officials what weight the lifter's next attempt will be, while the lifter is getting her belt off and knees unwrapped by her handler. Janice also arranged my handler for the day, as usual, and it would be Mark Krug. Since Janice knew me so well, she could choose my next weight based on her observation of my strength during my current lift, and, also after the lift, she would ask me how it felt. Based on those two things, she would decide what the weight would be for my next lift. We had been doing this for several years and had a good system down. I felt blessed to have someone as knowledgeable as Janice in my corner. If I didn't tell her that enough, I'm telling the whole world now. If you have a great expediter, someone who really knows you and your capabilities, that is a straight-up blessing. That was what Janice was for me, besides being my coach and mentor. Thank you, from the bottom of my heart, for everything, Janice Roge-Henderson.

Competition day started like always; breakfast, rules briefing, and then warmups. I weighed in the night before at 174 so I was right in the middle of the weight class, which was fine. I felt strong during my warmups; actually, I felt *strong*, I think I'm going to have a good day. My first attempt was 402 pounds (the most I had ever opened with), and I went down and came up like I was lifting 135! Kind of even surprised me.

The announcer said, "Let's put some weight on the bar next time!" I had made it look so easy. A smile from me and chuckles from the audience let me know it wasn't just me who thought the weight was easy. I was smiling when I got over to Janice and Mark.

"How'd that feel?" Janice asked me.

"Light, like 135," I said. I was feeling so good I told Janice, "Just put on whatever you think I can do." That's how much I trusted Janice. My next attempt was easy enough, 451, and I saw three white lights confirming it. The crowd was cheering, and I waved at them for their support. And then, my final attempt, 485. I got under the bar and lifted it off the rack and for a split second, I was not in control. My knee had started to do one of its buckling stunts at the absolute worst moment. I prayed a quick prayer for balance and got myself steady again. I took a breath and went down slow enough, and then blasted that one right back up just like the first two. The crowd cheered and I knew, even before looking, there were three white lights in the box above me. I pointed upward, smiled, and waved my hand to the crowd. This was the most I had ever done in a competition, I was psyched!

Then it was onto the bench. Just like in the squat, my first lift was more than I ever had opened with before, 270. My day was going great, and I blasted that one right back up for three white lights. My second attempt, 292, was not quite so great. It went down fine but, on the way up, pain or weakness in my rotator cuff made my right arm trail behind the left, the bar rising unevenly as it went up. The bar can go up slightly uneven, that's okay, as long as neither of your arms comes back down at all. I finally got it locked out. After that awkward lift, Janice and I had to have a serious talk.

"How did that feel? And how does your shoulder feel now? And what should our next move be?" Janice asked. We decided I would go for 303. Go big or go home, right? This would be a PR (personal record) if I got it. I had done three hundred in the gym, so I thought I could do it if my rotator cuff didn't act up again. I got set up on the bench and took the bar down slowly and then blasted that 303 right back up to the top, no uneven bar, no sticking points, no pain, just down, stop (wait for the command, Krista), and then right back up. The crowd went crazy. I think since my last lift was so awkward-looking, they didn't know if I could get this one. But I did, and the crowd was behind me. Again, I smiled and waved at them, thanking them for their support. Then I ran over to Janice and Mark, beaming. Janice was trying to control my excitement, I was starting to jump up and down, so happy and excited. I had just done a PR (personal record) in both lifts *and* at Nationals! I might've even been in first place!

"Calm down, Krista, you still have your deadlifts to do," Janice told me sternly.

"I know, I know, I know," I said, and I knew it, but I was having trouble containing myself. This was the APF 1996 Senior Nationals, and I was spot on!

My first deadlift was 402 pounds, and I was so excited I ripped that bar off the floor so hard, I thought I might go over backward—that bar was on my thighs so fast!

The announcer once again said, "Put some weight on that bar now, will you?" The crowd really laughed this time; it was the third time he had said it to me. I had to laugh as well. If it looked as light as it felt, I could understand why he said that. What they didn't know was that I just lifted more than I ever had before on my first lift. The second lift was good, 462, but I was starting to feel tired. When I returned to Janice after my lift, she wanted to know how that felt.

"I'm getting tired, Janice. Just put on whatever you think. I trust you." With a nod, she was off to give the number for my last lift. She decided on 479.5. Once on the platform, I took a few deep breaths and gathered all the strength, heart, and faith I had in the world for this last lift. I hadn't come this far to give up, so I grabbed that bar and pulled and pulled and finally (seriously, my eyeballs were ready to pop out) got it all the way up and locked out, waited for the "down" command, and that was that. I stood there on the platform for a second, not quite believing what had just happened. I heard the click of the lights and from the sound of the crowd, I knew they were white. It was a perfect day. I went nine for nine and PRs in all three disciplines. And later that day, for the first time in my life, I stood on the top of a national championship podium. After twelve years of training, I was the national champion! It didn't even seem real, but it was. I just kept saying, "Thank you, God," over and over. I jumped up and down a lot more too. This was my biggest lifelong dream, honestly my heart's desire, and it just came true. There were some tears of joy, and I'm sure a lot more jumping. *National champion, national champion, national champion, unbelievable.* I thought of the verse, "The joy of the Lord is my strength" (Nehemiah 8:10).

The following month our picture was in *Powerlifting USA* magazine. "Mighty Ladies" we were called.

After I finally wrapped my head around the fact, I was the national champion, I realized I would be the frontrunner for the United States when we went to worlds in five months, and my next goal was right in front of me—world champion. But first things first, I needed to get funding. Worlds was in Durban, South Africa, that year, and it was going to be a spendy trip. But I must go!

I was thankful I could get a discount on my flight from Federal Express (since I worked for them), a huge blessing. As usual, I squeaked in under the wire, money-wise, and was able to pay for my ticket and had just a little bit of spending money, but I was in the hole and had people to pay back upon my return.

Another goal I had for worlds was to squat five hundred. I remembered when I saw Mary Ellen Warman do it and now, I was almost there. I remember it seemed so insurmountable when I saw her do it, just a faraway dream, but now I was getting very close. Five months passed in a flash, I was so busy with work, training, and making calls for sponsorships, when the day arrived to leave for South Africa, I was buzzing with excitement. I was probably packed two days in advance, I was so excited. When I got to the gate at the airport, my friend Jim Voronin was already there. A smile broke out on my face; this was going to be a great trip.

When we finally arrived in South Africa, we were bussed to this five-star hotel overlooking the Indian Ocean. It was breathtaking. There were three days until the women competed, so I mostly just hung around the hotel. I could have spent hours looking out over the ocean. The food was great too and by the second evening when we had to weigh in, I was tipping the scales at 180. Wait, what? (That sure didn't take long.) But my weight was the least of my concerns. I still felt sluggish, and jet-lagged from the flight, with two days to go! Hopefully that would be over by the next day.

When I woke up on the day of the competition, I felt okay but still a little sluggish. I was a little better after warmups, rules briefing, and all that, but I still wasn't sure how the day would go. I was more nervous about my knee; it had been buckling more often lately it seemed. My nerves were on edge too, this being my first time as the frontrunner for the US. Thank goodness Jim Voronin was there. He always had a calming effect on me. He was a gentle giant if there ever was one.

And then it was show time. From the start, things did not go right. First, there was a mix-up in the handler situation and for a few minutes, I was running around trying to find my handler. I never did find him, and I was getting stressed. At the last minute, two guys came up to me and said they would be my handlers, but by this time, I was getting kind of cranky. I like to lift when I'm happy, not stressed. Regardless, the problem was solved, so I had to concentrate on what I needed to do.

My opening lift in the squat was 418.75, usually an easy enough lift, but that day it felt heavy. I got my second attempt, 462.75, but that felt heavy too. I should have gone with 485 for my final lift, but I just had to try for that 490, which did not go too well, needless to say. Bench was the same story. I got my first two, 264.5 and 292. You would think I would go a little more conservative after that third squat but no, I went for 308.5. Nope, that was not happening either. Oh my, not the great showing I was hoping for. So, it was on to the deadlifts I hoped would get better. I opened with 418.75 and that went up steadily. My second lift was 462.75 and I got that one as well, but it was hard. For my final attempt, once again, I wanted to hit one PR so bad, I told them to load 485. This would be the final lift of the day. The cameras were aimed at the loaded bar on the platform. The crowd was waiting with anticipation. I got into position and gave it everything I had. Slowly but surely that bar kept coming up, my form solid all the way to the top and it was done. I got the "down" command and by the time I let the bar down, the crowd was already cheering because there were three white lights in the box! I was super happy to get a PR in the deadlift. That lift redeemed me a little bit.

All in all, I lifted enough for the win! I was thrilled to be the world champion; I just wish I had done better in the squat and bench. You always wish for a perfect day, nine for nine, like I did at nationals, however, perfection is the goal, not generally the rule. I felt blessed I lifted well enough for the win, I was the world champion! And again, unbelievable! I felt so blessed. I thought of the verse, "Delight in the Lord, and He will grant you the desires of your heart" (Psalm 37:4).

I was always Jim Voronin's handler, so I spent the next day with my buddy, getting him ready for his lifts. He had a great day and placed second to Pete Tregloan. After the competition was over, we took in the local sights and bought our souvenirs. That evening, we all went to a local bar called the Red Dog. Inside, they had one of those mechanical bulls and some of the locals were riding it. It didn't look that hard, but I was happy to stay with my feet firmly planted on the ground. Well, until I had an adult beverage, which I don't do very often. Somehow, I got talked into riding that stupid thing. I got on and was riding it just fine until it went into a major bucking fit, and I went sailing away. When I finally landed in a heap in the sawdust below, I looked up and saw Jim's worried face, and I burst out laughing. It was funny to see a 389-pound man looking so helpless and horrified. Once my teammates knew I wasn't hurt, everyone else started laughing too. I was glad to provide entertainment, but I think I won't be riding one of those bulls again. At least it didn't come over and gore me after it bucked me off. Mercy.

I went home as the world champion in 1996 and I would defend that title for the next several years. How many, I won't say yet, I don't want to get ahead of the story.

In March of 1997, the "Top 20s" came out and, I was ranked third in the squat with 485, second in the bench with 303, second in the deadlift with 485, and second in total weight, 1,267—my total from nationals. I know my gift of strength is from God. I felt blessed beyond my wildest dreams. I was on top of the world, and I couldn't have asked God for more. For this day alone, I will be grateful for the rest of my life. I needed nothing more. I thanked God for making my dreams come true. What a blessing, beyond measure.

However, I could barely make ends meet for one sport, and now I was going to be competing in two. That meant twice as much traveling, twice as much time off work (which equates to not as much income), and I can barely make it financially doing one. Plus, I needed two surgeries, which meant even *more* time off work. What was I going to do? I couldn't begin to think how I would do all of this; I'd cut every possible expense and was living as frugally as I could, and still was in the hole more times than not. Bottom line, I needed a miracle. Seriously, God, no joke. "If you want me to use the strength you blessed me with, I'm going to need some help. I'm going to need an honest-to-goodness big-time miracle. I spoke to God and said I don't know how else to ask you but to pray." And pray I did. I prayed and prayed and prayed.

And when He answered, oh my, did He answer! I don't know why I was worried; I've seen God do this with me time and time again.

In case anyone was wondering what the meaning of this chapter's title, Krugerrand, is it's a gold coin in South Africa first minted in 1967 to help market South African gold, produced by

Rand Refinery; the South African mint name is from Paul Kruger, the former president of the South African Republic.

> "WHAT IS IMPOSSIBLE WITH MAN IS POSSIBLE WITH GOD" [LUKE 18:27 NIV].

23

HOPSCOTCH

God doesn't always answer right away, but I kept praying and praying. When I was alone in my FedEx truck for eight hours a day, I would talk to God, a lot, and He got a steady stream of chatter. It was the same discussion in varying forms. I told Him every idea I had to make more money so I could compete in both of my sports. While driving around all day it would give me the opportunity to plead my case, not to mention God is great company to have all day long. I'm pretty determined if you didn't already know that about me. I kept my eye out for any possible job God might put in front of me. I knew this was the way my prayers would be answered, a great-paying job, with lots of paid time off, travel benefits, medical coverage, and good hours. I followed every lead; I just knew this job was out there for me. My faith was unshakable, and I knew it was coming. God would bless me with this great job and all my struggles to make ends meet would be over. I would be able to compete in both of my sports, without having to put my job and apartment at risk each time. With my perfect job, I could go to all my competitions and have enough money to cover my expenses. I wasn't asking to be a millionaire, just to be able to compete. "And whatever you ask in prayer, you will receive, if you have faith" (Matthew 21:22).

I don't mean ten minutes of faith or until the crisis is over. Undying faith, the never-give-up kind, no matter how long it takes or how many setbacks happen. Whatever happens, you don't give up, you don't stop believing. That is the kind of faith that's needed to step out in faith. And that's exactly the kind of faith I had, and still do.

So, the next two years were spent running around like a chicken with its head cut off, rushing to work, rushing to the gym, or rushing to a plane to get to a competition. My schedule was insane; I remember flying into the States from competing at the 1997 Worlds (Powerlifting) in Blackpool, England, exiting that plane and going directly to another gate, and getting on a flight to Calgary, Canada, for a bobsled race. All that competing and working was starting to wear me down. How much longer, God? I couldn't keep this up forever.

And then *finally* the golden opportunity presented itself, and I was so grateful my answer had come at last! A friend of mine, Curtis, was opening a new gym in Atlanta and he wanted me to manage it! I had been wanting to move to Atlanta for some time now but didn't know how I could ever manage to save up for the first and last month's rent on an apartment, as I was almost always in the hole—either to myself or to someone else. But I trusted God, and I believed this was the answer I had been praying for, so I made the choice to move to Atlanta. I had a dear friend there, Shana, and she found an apartment and had it reserved for me. I just had to pay the balance owed once I got there. The pieces were falling into place, and I knew my days of struggling were coming to an end. The word "relief" does not begin to scratch the surface of how I felt; I was exhausted.

So, I gave notice at FedEx, and once again, Therese and I said our goodbyes after a two-year relationship, I packed up my things from our apartment (we lived together for about eight months after I moved to New York from Connecticut) and headed south. It was so exciting, moving to Atlanta for my dream job, working, training, and coaching other lifters in the gym. It was perfect. I said thank you a million times to God for this opportunity. This was my life's purpose, to be a full-time athlete in my beloved sport.

I got on the road and told God, "Okay, I'm doing it, I'm stepping out on faith." Once that was said, it seemed like all the bad forces in the world were not going to let me get out of New York. No sooner than I got on I-95 heading south, the U-Haul trailer I had rented got a flat tire. I pulled over and called them for a new tire, then I called my friend and former girlfriend, Therese, and talked to her while I waited. She got me calmed down and I was ready to go again when the U-Haul guy came. He put on a new tire, and I was back on my way. I got back on the freeway; traffic was light, and I was making good time. And then the bad forces caught up with me again and (believe it or not) *another* flat tire! Are you kidding me? So, I pulled over and called U-Haul, *again*, and then called Therese back, *again*, and she calmed me down, *again*, while I waited. Another U-Haul guy came and replaced this tire after an hour and a half wait. All this was making me get the impression something didn't want me to leave New York. I got back in my car, and I said out loud, "Well, enemy, you can sabotage my trip all you want, but I'm following God, right down this freeway to Atlanta." The heaviness left the car, and the rest of the trip was beautiful. From then on, I think I smiled all the way to Atlanta.

Once I got to Atlanta, things suddenly changed for the worse. Curtis told me the gym deal had fallen through, and he wasn't going to be able to get the new gym. When I heard this news, my stomach turned over and I thought I might get sick. I had just given up everything for this opportunity and now it was gone. The gym deal falling through was not entirely Curtis's fault, there were other people involved, first and foremost his current girlfriend Jean was the real con artist here. and this was my first experience getting caught up in a scam. It was an eye-opener as to how some people can be, and how they don't even care who they hurt, deceive, or betray. But now with no job, memories of my experience in Tracy started to resurface, including the same sinking feelings that came with that time in my life.

My prayers escalated to pleads.

And still no answer.

I must admit, at this point, my faith was being tested. I always tried to do the right things and make the right choices. I reflected on everything; and took a hard look at my life. I always went to work, didn't smoke or drink (well, occasionally I drank a little), didn't do drugs, tried to eat right, and took care of the body God gave me. What else could I do? I couldn't think of a thing, so, I opened my Bible and read the book of Job and all he went through. I thought of losing Aunt Bobbie and my grandmother. That put things in better perspective, all I have lost so far was my job and apartment (replaceable things), but I was still in a very tight spot. *Come on, God, please hurry. I don't know how long I can go on like this.*

The apartment Shana found me was a blessing, but once again I was short money-wise. I called Therese and she sent me $200 so I wouldn't lose the apartment. By the grace of God, and help from friends, I was squeaking by. It was the second time in my life I was somewhat hungry most days. I wasn't starving but I would have loved to eat a whole lot more.

To make matters worse, I had difficulty doing something as simple as opening a bank account. Apparently, a credit check must be run for a bank account to be opened in this area. Well, you could imagine my credit was not so great, in fact, it was bad, but finally South Trust Bank agreed to let me open an account. (After they made me take a class on financial responsibility.)

On the upside, I did acquire work through a temporary service, packing Amway orders in a warehouse on the graveyard shift, paying just a bit over minimum wage. These hours were once again tough, but I held on until I got another job, which was loading *USA Today* newspapers in the boxes on street corners outside grocery stores etc. . . . and I learned how to fix the broken newspaper machines. At least I was outside, and I was working daytime hours. This job also allowed me to learn about the city of Atlanta.

Three great things happened during the first few months in Atlanta. First, I met a wonderful woman and we soon started hanging out, doing lots of cool things together and getting to know one another which would lead us into a two-and-a-half-year relationship. And the second was finding the Main Event gym, owned by Lex Lugar and Sting, popular WWF wrestlers on television. Because I was a world-class athlete, they comped my membership. In return, I would represent their gym in my competitions. This was a giant blessing as I couldn't even begin to afford a gym membership. It was a tiny slice of heaven for me, with a powerlifting room complete with platforms, squat stands, a regulation bench—everything a powerlifter could want. This was the place I could come to every day and *almost* forget my cares. Six months later, God blessed me to be fully sponsored. Now I'm living my dream.

A letter came to me during one especially hard week. It was good news, something I really needed right then. I had been invited to the annual dinner put on by the Women's Sports Foundation (Billy Jean King's Foundation). It was in New York and the foundation would fly me there and put me up at the Waldorf Astoria as one of seventy elite female athletes in their prospective sport to be honored at the dinner. Wow! I felt so humbled and honored at the same time the sport of powerlifting was a nonmainstream sport, to say the least, and bobsledding was not yet an Olympic sport for women. I felt sincerely blessed by this honor. In my situation, this was a real boost for me. I couldn't wait to go.

I arrived in New York for dinner, anticipating eating like a horse for the slim times I was having, but my excitement got the better of me and I'm not sure I ate anything. The first person to greet me was Yolanda Jackson, a famed basketball player and the previous director of the Women's Sports Foundation. She made a funny comment about my big biceps and we both laughed.

Yolanda took me around to introduce me to the other athletes and show me where my table was. In this event, there were seventy tables, each athlete being assigned to their own. The other people at the table had paid a hefty price for their seat, to support women athletes and the foundation. I heard each table brought in ten thousand dollars. The first lady Yolanda introduced me to was her roommate, Willye White, a five-time Olympian in track and field (1956, '60, '64, '68, and '72). She was one of the first Black female track and field athletes, and a member of the famous Tennessee Tiger Belles. She was an honorary guest and had her own table.

Right before the dinner some of the athletes were introduced. My name was called, and I stood with Jackie Joyner Kersey, Tauna Vandewegh, and one other girl, and we were introduced as dual athletes. What a moment!

There were other honorary guests present, including Venus and Serena Williams, who were still quite young at the time, but they were already making headlines in the tennis world. This was incredible and I loved every minute of it.

Then we all sat down at our tables and prepared our meals. The main sponsors for my table were John and Deborah Larkins. John was a prominent lawyer in New York. I began to talk to Deborah and tell her about my sports, especially powerlifting.

At some point, there was a pause in the conversation and Deborah said, "Is everything okay? You look perplexed, what's on your mind?"

"I'm fine, I'm just so tired," I said, and I explained how hard I was working at a minimum-wage job and still trying to train and travel for competitions in two sports.

Her face lit up and she said, "Come with me, I want you to meet someone." I obediently followed her to another table which happened to be Anita DeFrantz's table. Anita was one of the first Black women on the US row team and the current president of the International Olympic Committee. Deborah introduced me to a man at Anita's table. "Krista, this is Richard Ader." We shook hands and before I could say anything more than a greeting, Deborah continued, "Krista needs your help."

Richard turned back to me and said, "How much money do you need?" My mouth dropped open, and I was speechless. Was he really asking me this? My mind started to spin, and I just stood there, frozen. When he realized I was shocked speechless, he turned to Deborah and said, "Give Krista my number and have her call me Monday morning at nine a.m." Deborah nodded in understanding. Then he turned to me and asked if I had a proposed budget plan. All I could do was nod. I had been discussing it daily with God for the past two years.

We returned to our table, and I sat in stunned silence for a few minutes when a man approached our table.

"Hi, I'm Herb Weinstein, and my wife would like to meet you," he said to me. I extended my hand, we shook, and then I followed him to his table, which happened to be Willye White's table, and she gave me a huge smile when we approached. Herb introduced me to his wife, Wendy, and I sat down next to her, and their daughter Jordon. Herb wandered off for a few moments.

Wendy began by saying, "My husband is a powerlifting enthusiast and I'm wondering if you could train him."

My heart leaped at the opportunity. This is what I wanted to do more than anything, train other athletes and share all I had learned. "I would love to, I really would, but I live in Atlanta. I'm not in the New York area."

"Are you serious, you would train him?" she asked, excitedly. I nodded, not sure if she heard what I just said. "Great, then he'll fly you up here for his training sessions. He'll take care of everything." And once again my mouth fell open.

Herb returned at that time and said to me, "Were you just talking to Richard Ader?"

"Yes," I said.

"Did he offer to help you?"

Again, "Yes," and I was wondering where this was going.

"Well, I want to help you too. Call Richard and he will call me and then I'll get back to you." Could this really be happening? Pretty sure my mouth fell open once again. I was in la-la land, I could not believe this. A thousand no's and this one yes! *OMG*, I thought, *My dream is finally coming to fruition*.

Deborah and I made our way back to our table, me on somewhat shaky legs, I was so overwhelmed. As soon as we sat down, fitness guru Donna Richardson came up to me and said, "Tom Joyner would like to interview you." He had a national radio talk show, *The Tom Joyner Morning Show*, and he chose a few of the athletes to interview—and I was one of them. This was blowing my mind. Could all this really be happening?

I don't remember the interview very well, but at the end of it, he asked if I would be on his talk show. The night was getting better and better. Apparently, I regained my ability to speak at some point and, before long, people were coming up to me and wanting to talk to me. By the end of the night, I had made about twenty contacts, including Jean Zimmerman, a writer. Jean was working on a book titled *Raising Our Athletic Daughters*, and she wanted to interview and include me in her book.

After the dinner was over, everyone was mingling, and I saw Billy Jean King had joined the event. I walked over to her to thank her for inviting me. She made a comment about my big biceps and asked with a sly smile if I would train her so she could have big biceps too. I said absolutely and we laughed. She had a very pure and natural spirit, she made me feel comfortable, and we talked for a few moments. Meeting her was like the icing on the cake, the younger pioneer meeting the elder pioneer.

That night was one of the most magical nights of my life. I had been praying for a great job, and that was what I was so sure God would bless me with. But God must have been in the gym when we say, "Go big or go home," because He went big for me that night. He had something so much bigger for me than a job, actual sponsorship! That meant no more money worries; I would be able to train and compete in both of my sports with all my travel expenses covered, the rent for my apartment would be taken care of, I would be able to buy healthy food again, and—best of all—sleep, glorious sleep, so I could finally rest and get stronger, faster, and better.

I barely made it out of the dinner before the tears of gratitude began to fall. When I got to my hotel room, I fell to my knees, cried my eyes out, and praised God with all the strength I had left. The desire of my heart was a great job, but I guess that wasn't big enough for my mighty God. He gave me full sponsorship! Go big or go home, right, God? Oh yeah, He went big! He went *really* big for me. That following Monday morning, Richard Ader's secretary called, and I spoke to Richard. He had received my proposal of my budget for living, traveling, and training. Richard then said, "Herb and I have come to a decision to sponsor you three/fourths of your proposed amount."

I was so elated with this because this would be more than I have ever earned in my life. I then asked Richard, "What can I do for you guys in return for this wonderful gift?"

He said, "You just take care of training Herb in the gym as his personal trainer and we'll take care of you."

All I could do was say thank you, thank you, thank you, from the bottom of my heart. Thank you, God! I thought, *you can get a thousand no's and the one yes is all it takes for you to believe!*

> **"THOSE WHO SOW IN TEARS SHALL REAP WITH SHOUTS OF JOY!" [PSALMS 126:5 ESV].**

Women's Sports Foundation Annual Dinner, 1997, Martina Navratilova and I.

WSF Annual Dinner, Jackie Joyner-Kersee and I.

WSF Annual Dinner, Billie Jean King and I.

Patrice Arrington (volleyball), myself, v-teer Dawn Ellerbe (hammer).

Christine Leslie (mother of Lisa Leslie), myself, and Lisa Leslie in Washington DC.

Myself, Dominique Dawes (gymnastics), and Lillian Greene-Chamberlain (track and field).

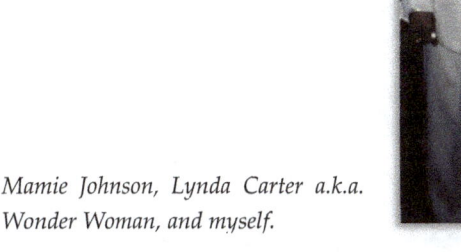

Mamie Johnson, Lynda Carter a.k.a. Wonder Woman, and myself.

WSF, Billie Jean King' Women's Sports Foundation Dinner, held at the Waldorf in Astoria New York, New York, 1997. Seventy of the best female athletes in their prospective sports are honored. I am in the first row on the far right at the end.

24

MY PIT CREW

On November 10, 1997, I received my first sponsorship check. I gave notice at the temporary service and my new life began. I must have slept the entire first week, I was so exhausted, then I proceeded to get my ACL repaired and my rotator cuff surgery. Once my body was healthy and strong again, I began to hit the weights hard, real hard. And my lifts started to increase, slowly but surely.

It was around this time that my "pit crew" evolved into a core group of guys and some women who trained with me, loaded up the weights on the bar for me, etc. These guys were instrumental in my climb to higher weights. They wrapped my knees, got my suits on and off, tightened my belt, spotted me, and kept me safe. Bob Sidebottom was my first handler; he was amazing while I started lifting heavier and heavier. He set the standard for those first few years. Think of my pit crew like this, if I were a boxer, they would be in my corner while I was fighting a match.

Over the years, a lot of guys were my handlers but there were some very special, loyal ones I want to acknowledge. From back in the early days, Monty Adams was always special to me because I also trained him in powerlifting and watched him compete. Mark Generight was a quiet man and a great listener. He's also an educator which makes me happy because he was an excellent role model for youngsters. Then there's Fredrick (Derrick) Riley, an accountant—who doesn't need an accountant? I know I do! Darrin Barnes, a bodybuilder and supervisor at FedEx Ground. Darrin was a bodybuilder for many years and finally tried his hand at powerlifting. He got a three-hundred-pound bench that set him on fire, he was so excited. I got invited to the Arnold Classic in 2014 and I squatted six hundred like it was nothing. Yeah! Darrin was one of my handlers there and he introduced me to Joe Williams who's from New York and had also competed under my tutelage in powerlifting.

Squatting is the discipline that requires the most spotters, and they are in various spotting positions. To be a back spotter, for example, you need to be tall. My first back spotter was Joseph Kennedy, six five, and we called him Big Joe. He would drive up to my house on Sundays, coming directly from church, and would get out and spot me in his church clothes. Now that's loyalty. His kids were always lined up in the car, watching from the windows. Big Joe loved some fancy cars, like Lamborghini, Phantom Rolls-Royce, Benzos, and BMWs—which I've seen four or five of over the years. Sometimes, his friend Ozzie Anderson would come to help spot me or just come with Joe and hang out while training was going on. Big Joe and Ozzie would come rolling up in a flashy new car and everyone had to go check it out. Unfortunately, Big Joe ended up losing his life in one of those beautiful cars. He crashed his Lamborghini in 2015. He was only thirty-four years of age. A beautiful person was cut down so young, it was heartbreaking and tragic. I miss him so much.

With Big Joe gone, my next back spotter was Lacy Coleman, six five, who worked with me at Delta Airlines. Lacy Coleman handled me solo at APF Senior Nationals in Salt Lake City, Utah, 2015, where I received my second-overall best lifters award. It was a cool belt that looked like what the WWF wrestlers would come into the ring with around their waist. Mine was pink and the best overall guy's belt was blue—seemed appropriate. Then came Courtney Cohen. He was also six five, and about 230 then (now, he's 270 pounds). He was deadlifting when we met at the gym, and I invited him to start training with me at my house on Sundays. He was studying to be a firefighter and when he came on Sundays, he brought a book with him that had to be five inches thick. I don't think I've ever seen a book that big. Between sets, he studied—that's some serious determination, and he made it too. I admired how he was able to help me and not lose his own focus.

Then there was Robert Davis, a bodybuilder, and despite how I tease bodybuilders, he was an excellent handler, knew how to wrap good and tight, and totally understood the sport of powerlifting. He's retired from AT&T now and owns a roller rink (Golden Glide) in Atlanta. How fun is that?

I don't know how I got all these bodybuilder handlers. Maybe I'm trying to convert them to the powerlifting side—and it has worked a few times. Gene Johnson is a national-level bodybuilder and has been very successful at it. This year, though, he told me he was ready to try a powerlifting competition. I'm winning them over, one by one! Gene was also an educator, teaching health at Jonesboro High School, where he's also the wrestling and track and field coach. Gene competed in his first powerlifting competition on April 1, 2023, and he not only won his age and weight class, but he also went nine for nine lifts, which was a perfect day! All his attempts were passed, and I was so proud of him.

Sam Garr, a former professional boxer for Don King (the promoter), lived right around the corner from me. Sam Bam Bam Garr was his boxing name, and he was very good. He let me watch a tape of one of his fights, and his movements reminded me of Sugar Ray Leonard, he was quick and light on his feet. He now owns a lawn service that keeps him busy.

Another one of my guys was Matt Baker, he's six three and 260 pounds of good solid muscle. He's also an exotic dancer, stage name Romeo (we call him Rome), and he danced with the original Black Chippendales, and then they left the group and started their own group called ATLANTA HOT Boyz. When Sam and Rome get together in my garage, Rome's busy showing Sam how to do some nice dance moves and Sam is busy showing Rome how to do a perfect left jab. It's comical as I can't really see them doing each other's events.

Then there's Curtis Gibson, retired Army, John Jones ("Jonesy"), retired Navy—Jones is the comic relief for the group; I don't have to work abdominals if Jonesy is around, he'll have me laughing till my belly hurts—and Shy Darious Slaughter, retired Marine. When those three get together, oh boy, anything goes. My garage becomes the man cave and military trash talk fills the air. And if Sam and Rome are there, doing their thing, it gets wild at times, but all in good fun. Shy Darious has got his sites on going after John Inzer's record in the deadlift of 728 pounds at 165 body weight. I just have to get him to do his first powerlifting meet, first—a joke amongst all of us. Newcomer Nate Hollis is an MMA fighter who also is around six two, and 258 pounds. He's learning the ropes from me and the other guys.

And finally, Savoy Curtis, another person I consider a blessing from God. I met Savoy shortly after I moved to Atlanta, and he was also from the same church as Joe Williams and Darrin Barnes. Savoy was more than a handler, and more than just a friend, he was my God-given solace. He could calm me down when no one else could. He got me in a way nobody else ever did. I can't say enough about Savoy, he was a good man, salt-of-the-earth type, a good husband to Gregoryia, and a loving father to his four children. I met Savoy when my powerlifting career started to really take off and he was there through all the climbing of the ranks, the injuries, the setbacks, and the challenges; he never lost hope, and he was always positive. I think that's what I liked most about him, and he displayed the quiet strength of a man who is secure in himself. Savoy Curtis went on to be with God on August 16, 2021, after a semi-long battle with his heart. He was only forty-six years old. I feel Savoy's spirit all the time, especially when I start training. God broke the mold with him. He will always be in my heart.

I wish I could do more for all these guys, to give them all compensation for all their years of dedication and loyalty to me. They are a big part of me, like a family, and I love each one of them. So, guys, here's your shout-out. You're the best "pit crew" ever, and I truly could not have done it without you all. I am forever indebted to all of you. A million thanks for all your time, dedication, friendship, and hard work.

> **"GREATER LOVE HAS NO ONE THAN THIS: TO LAY DOWN ONE'S LIFE FOR ONE'S FRIEND" (JOHN 15:13 NIV).**

25

GOOD NATURE

Where I go to recharge or calm my spirit is out in nature. Ever since I could remember, nature, animals, really anything alive or growing, fascinated me, and gave me great joy and a sense of rejuvenation. I watched Dr. Jane Goodall's study of chimpanzees on television when I was a teenager and I thought she had the greatest job in the world, studying animals in their own habitat, in Africa no less. Studying animals was one of the first career interests I had. At that time, Africa was a million miles away, but somehow—maybe not by the chimpanzee route—I would get there. Someday. Also, Africa was the land of some of my roots.

When I did finally get to Africa—remember worlds was in Durban, South Africa, in 1996—I was determined to explore it as much as I could, languish in its beauty, and learn everything I could. So, I signed up for several excursions that were offered to us. The first was a trip to a rainforest. This was an overnight trip and I made friends with a girl from Germany, and we ended up being cabin mates. In our encampment, there was a big cabin in the center where we ate and gathered for our outings. Then, encircling the big cabin were a bunch of smaller cabins where we slept. The best part of being in this rainforest was the air. It had an extremely high oxygen level, and it was moist and soothing. It felt like perfect air to me. I loved taking deep breaths of it.

On one hiking trip, the tour guide bent down and picked up something that was about the size of his hand, seriously, about eight inches long. I hesitate to call it a bug, it could have weighed upward of a pound. It was huge! I asked him what it was, and he smiled and thought for a second and said, "Well, in America, you would call it a grasshopper."

"Nope, grasshoppers don't look like that," was all I could say. This thing was bigger than most rodents. I looked closer and its structure was pretty much like a grasshopper, but on a mutant, *Jurassic Park* scale. I still remember that big bug whenever I see a grasshopper. I wish I could have seen it hop, it would have set a new long jump record, I'm sure.

On another excursion, about twenty of us hiked up some cliffs. The unobstructed view of the Indian Ocean was spectacular from our viewpoint. What a place to have the opportunity to learn how to rappel! And that's exactly what I did. There was a small cliff we all got to practice on, and the instructors told us just how to place our feet and work the ropes. I got the hang of it quickly and it was game on. Once we were all done at the little cliff, it was on to the big cliff, all the way down to the ocean. We could do it if we were brave enough. The little cliff was not too bad. I'm not afraid of heights, but that's what stopped a few of the people from wanting to try, or the fear of falling—that was a thought that went through everybody's mind, it positively went through mine. Then we were on to the big cliff, and the line shortened quickly, in fact, there were only six of us in line. The others were backed up far enough not to be mistaken for being in line. Right about then, the ocean looked a whole lot farther away than it did before and, I won't lie, I was scared. In fact, I was scared to death, but I wasn't going to pass up this opportunity because of it. For me, fear is not a legitimate reason not to do something. So, of course, I was first in line to go, and I wasn't sure if that was a good thing or not, but I was already committed. As they were getting me all harnessed up, I said a prayer for safety, like I get the opportunity to do a lot in my life. Then I got myself backed up to the edge of the cliff, took the first and hardest step, and I was rappelling. Down and down, looking over my shoulder at the ocean, until I got all the way down. Hanging over the cliff like that, the ocean looked huge and formidable. My hands were still trembling when I finally reached the sand below. But wow, it was exhilarating, and I would do it again in a heartbeat. Thrilling for sure, off the chart. Even down at the water's edge, the ocean was still spectacular.

Then, another day, a bunch of us powerlifters went on a safari. We were in big safari jeeps, and we saw some lions off in the distance, and a white rhino mama and baby standing side by side just taking a rest. Our jeep approached them from the rear, and I was amazed at how wide their rumps were, even the baby. I had to laugh at how thick they were, I didn't realize they were so massive. We also saw leopards, cheetahs, and hyenas and I couldn't take my eyes off any of them. I studied them, each one, mesmerized. These were the animals I watched on television for so many years and now I was seeing them alive in their habitat.

Next, we went on to view an indigenous tribe. We were told not to take pictures of them as they believed if you took a picture of them, it would take a piece of their soul. No problem, so we drove up to their village and were just observing them. I noticed the men had a lot of piercings all over their bodies, and wore heavy rings in their ears, stretching the lobes an inch or more downward, and their hair was braided or in dreads. The women wore colorful clothes and had bright head wraps to match, and most wore sandals, while some were barefoot. The women were elegant, with high cheekbones and long oval faces. Their skin was very dark, and they were beautiful. About the time I was taking all of this in, some idiot in our group couldn't stand it any longer and tried to sneak a photo. Well, he was spotted by a tribal leader who began to walk toward our jeep and then the rest of the tribe joined in behind him. This was not good, not good at all. Our tour guide said we needed to leave, like right then—as in throw the jeep in reverse and get out of there! So, that observation was cut short, but I'll never forget how natural they looked, living so close to the earth like that. I could have watched them a lot longer. They seemed very peaceful and content.

My second time in Africa, in 2001, a friend I made the first time I was there, Ian Morris, remembered me and wanted to show me something special. He was a native South African and he knew I loved animals. I was excited and he drove me over to Cape Town, then proceeded to drive up a mountain. He kept looking at his watch and I didn't understand. Were we late? I didn't even know where we were going, he wouldn't tell me. Then, about halfway up this mountain, he pulled over and did something crazy; he rolled up all the windows. It was hot outside, so this did not make any sense at all, until I saw it just moments later; a group of baboons came around the corner of the mountain, walking right down the middle of the road, coming close to investigate the car as they walked by. A mama, with a baby on her back who looked asleep, walked right under my window. Wow! The males were looking aggressive and maybe challenging each other to a show of strength, and Ian told me that if we had an antenna on our car, it would get ripped off by one of the males showing his might. As they were getting past us, the colorful part of them was apparent, they really do have funny colorful butts. They didn't care, tails and butts up in the air as they made their way down the mountain road. All I could do was shake my head. It was unbelievable. What a great surprise.

I also love the ocean, and anything associated with it, beaches, beachfront homes, and of course, the ocean wildlife. On a trip to the Dominican Republic I took in 2006, I got to do another fun thing. They had this underwater motorcycle-type craft called a Scuba Doo, and it was attached to the side of the boat, submerged just below the water level. First, I had to get a wet suit on and then I climbed onto the Scuba Doo. Then they lowered it down into the water about twenty to twenty-five feet down, where I could drive it around just like a motorcycle, while it was connected to the boat by a cable. There was a clear bubble for my head, and I had to put it on just right, so I could see all around, but the water didn't come into the bubble. I thought I must look a lot like the great Gazoo (the Martian on *The Flintstones*, minus the antennas). All I had to do now was ride around and call everyone dumb dumbs. Obviously, I didn't do that. It was like another world down there, underwater, looking at coral, vibrant plants, and all the bright fish. There was so much vivid color, it looked like some crazed artist had gone down there and just flung paint everywhere. Dots of color all over, dancing and shimmering in the sun's rays. It really was like a different world. We were also given water bottles filled with fish food. Once we reached for our bottles, the fish knew what was coming, so they started gathering around us. When we squeezed the bottle and some food would come out, there was a feeding frenzy right in front of us. These were not large fish, so none of us were in danger of falling off our Scuba Doos, but it got intense for smaller fish. This was twenty minutes of my life I will never forget. The water here was beautiful, turquoise green up by the shore and Mediterranean blue farther out.

Nature to me is God's salve for all our pains and hurts. Just spend some time in nature and bathe in the beauty and peacefulness of it, you will be refreshed and renewed every time. Try standing under a big tree in your bare feet, wiggling your toes into the grass, then placing your hands on the trunk of the tree, closing your eyes and just feeling the tree's energy, like that of an ancient warrior. It's a very powerful experience for me.

I had a long-standing bucket list item, and that was to swim with dolphins. Well, it just came true for me recently on my birthday, August 30, 2022, on a trip down to Playa del Carmen, Mexico. It was a two-part excursion. First, I got to get into the water with some manatees, also called sea cows—they are massive but so very gentle. One of them came up to me in the water, it was a young female. They gave me a head of lettuce and said, "Tear off a few pieces and give it to her." So, I tore a few pieces off and held it out to her, and she took it from my hand, gently too, for such a big mouth, and then touched my back with her flipper as if she were prompting me, "Come on already, I can eat faster than that!"

I ripped off a few more pieces and she ate those right up. She ate about two and a half heads of lettuce by the time we had to leave there. She was so relaxed and chilled out, just snacking on her lettuce. I was able to touch her skin and it was slimy. We were told that algae grows on their skin and helps protect them from too much sunlight. I wouldn't have thought so, but their skin is very delicate.

Then it was on to the dolphins. This was what I was here for! They were sleek and smooth, and I was able to touch them and feel their strength as they moved around in the water. They were so eager to play, I could just see their playful nature radiating from their whole body. First, I was in the shallow water with them, and I got to throw a beachball for one and he would bring the ball right back for me to do it again. We did that a dozen or so times and then the real fun began. I went out into deeper water, my life vest keeping me afloat, and when I was in position, two dolphins came swimming up, one on either side of me, and I was instructed to grab their dorsal fins in my hands as they swam by me. They were perfectly in unison and my hands felt the fins at the exact same moment, and I grabbed onto them. Talk about power! Those two dolphins swam across the water, me in tow, with no more effort than swimming by themselves. They were so strong! A more challenging trick was next. They told me to swing my arm over my head a certain way and the dolphins came swimming up behind me, then they dove down a little deeper, and both swam up under my feet and then pushed their noses right into the arches of my feet. Then they pushed me up almost out of the water and I was balancing on two speeding dolphins, and I felt like I was flying! I'm not sure how far we went, maybe forty or fifty yards and, let me tell you, it was thrilling being on such powerful animals and going along that fast, balancing on the noses of two dolphins. I felt like a Greek goddess, being brought into my court by my ever-faithful dolphins. That day ranks among one of the top ten days of my life, for sure.

There is a place called Stone Mountain Park, close to where I live, and I go there almost weekly to get some exercise, spend some time in nature, and get recharged. I am currently blessed to be accompanied by my little dog, Narita. She is a Morkie (a Maltese and Yorkshire terrier), and she is quite the athlete herself. She's a whopping nine pounds, stands about ten inches high, and that little girl can do a five-mile jog with me and she's still ready for more. It would be ten miles if she was in charge. She goes to the gym with me and waits patiently until it's time for cardio, then we go for our walk around the gym. Sometimes she insists on doing it twice. She takes our exercise time very seriously; she knows it's part of our lifestyle. She's a good little buddy, and I'm very proud of her. After all, Narita must get her cardio in too, so she can live a long healthy life like her ma'am.

I've had a small variety of pets over the years. Meshach, a male AKC Siberian Huskey (red and white); Snap, a female dwarf rabbit that was three and a half pounds, and lived with me in four states, Indiana, Connecticut, New York, and Georgia. She was nine years old when she went to be with Bugs Bunny in the sky. Toni and Teddy were two small, half-dollar-sized turtles that lived with me in two states, New York and Georgia. They both grew to sizes of small grapefruits, and I released them in a big pond in Georgia. Baby was a male, six-pound rabbit (who was by my side after I had my pelvic surgery). And finally, Narita, my female Morkie (I mentioned her above already)—these dogs are called designer dogs because they take 2 AKC registered breeds and mate them together.

> "LET THE FIELDS BE JUBILANT, AND EVERYTHING IN THEM; LET ALL THE TREES OF THE FOREST SING FOR JOY" [PSALMS 96:12 NIV].

26

BLUEPRINT

By 2004, I had been living in the Bishop's Gates apartments for four years. I loved the area because it was so close to Stone Mountain, my favorite nature park, and I was always hoping to buy a house in the area but was currently in an apartment, which was fine, I was grateful to have a place to call my own. And I was in the area I like so, all in all, a good place to be. My goal was to have my own house by the time I was twenty-five years old. Maybe that's a little lofty, but I was now almost thirty-seven years old, working a job paying less than ten dollars per hour, and with competition costs, along with rent, food, and all that, I wondered how I would ever be able to afford to buy a house.

One day at the gym, Savoy and I were training, and I'm not even sure how the subject came up, but we started talking about houses. I must have said something about wanting to buy a house, but I wasn't even close to having the downpayment. Savoy told me of a program for first-time home buyers called the Nehemiah Program (which later became the Acorn Program) and he suggested I check it out, they might be able to help me. I thanked him for the information. And then I prayed on it, hard. I wanted to put my hard-earned money into creating some equity for me, not just making my landlords richer. So, I prayed and asked that I would qualify for this program.

An appointment was made, and I went in with my hopes high. I filled out all the paperwork and after a credit check was run on me, I came back qualified, and the ball started rolling. This program offered credit repair assistance, but my credit was much better by this time, so I didn't have to spend any time doing credit repair. I got to bypass that delay. I had a full-time job working for AirTran Airways and even though it didn't pay great, it was a solid income, and with that, I was qualified! I couldn't believe it; I was going to be able to buy my own home! This was huge for me. The cool thing here is that I took the job with the airline so I could defray the cost of airfare for my sponsors. I would now be able to fly for free, and they would no longer have to pay for me to get to my competitions.

Not wanting to waste any time, I quickly secured a real estate agent named Rhetta Williams. "Here's my perfect outcome: three bedrooms, two baths, two-car garage, in a nice neighborhood. And it must be a ranch, I am not doing stairs." That sounded simple enough, and she said there were numerous listings that fit those parameters. Once I heard that, I immediately gave my thirty-day notice at my apartment. And yes, I know, I'm a hundred miles down the road already. I knew this was going to be a huge blessing, and I really couldn't wait. And obviously, I didn't.

So, we started to look. And we looked almost every day that whole month, sometimes up to ten homes in a day. There was always something not up to specs for me, it was mostly the fact that most garages were only one car that was often the deal breaker. I wanted a nice garage where I could keep two cars. If the garage was dark, dingy, spider-webby, or creepy in any way, it was an absolute "nope," and we were on to the next house.

As you can guess, my thirty-day notice came and went, and I still had no house. I had a moment of anxiety and then I just had to give that to God. I knew He was making this happen for me. I was not going to be homeless again, ever, was my vow to GOD.

He did come through for me via my apartment manager, who suggested I do a month-to-month rent until I find my house since I had been such a good tenant and always paid my rent on time. I was so grateful, and the tightness in my chest eased up right then. I wasn't on a deadline now, and that was a huge relief. Thank you, God, that was stressful.

For the next four months, we searched far and wide for my perfect home. We went neighborhood after neighborhood, and still, we could not find it. It was getting frustrating, but I was on a mission and of the mindset, as I often am, "I am not quitting until this is done." And on and on it went. Day after day, where eventually we would go into a house and go straight to the garage, and many times didn't have to go any farther.

One day, Rhetta was driving me home and, for some reason, she turned into a neighborhood we were close to, on our way back from searching that day. I was just gazing out the window, and it almost got past me but at the last minute, I saw it. There was a house, with a "For Sale" sign in front of it and it just called me. I screeched "Stop! Stop! Look, look, look, that one right there," as I pointed frantically. She stopped and backed up the few feet we had gone past the house and then we were parked in front of it. I jumped out of the car, and walked up the driveway—and I could just tell the garage would be just like I envisioned it. I held my breath as I waited for her to put the code in. As she was working on it, I was just staring at the house. Then I looked at the yard and the neighboring houses. The neighborhood was nice, and I felt comfortable, but what I felt most was excitement, like the kind that makes your body almost vibrate, energy surging all over at once.

When the door was opened, I walked in, and the most incredible sensation came over me. I'm not kidding when I say, the moment I stepped over the threshold and touched the floor of the entryway, I knew. I knew this was the one. I hadn't even seen the listing to know if it had three bedrooms and two bathrooms. It was weird, I just knew in my spirit, I felt it, I knew this was going to be my home. And, no surprises, three bedrooms, two full bathrooms, a two-car garage, and a 1,299 square-foot, ranch-style home. It was clean and bright, priced at $103,000—perfect, like God made it just for me. And how incredible, Stone Mountain Park was only twenty to twenty-five minutes away now, I would still be close to the nature area I love so much. Rhetta said, "Slow down, Krista, you haven't even made an offer yet!" But I knew it was already a done deal between God and me.

I qualified for $180,000, a much higher amount than the house was listed at, but I was looking at the low end of what I qualified for. I didn't want to get ahead of myself or any of life's events, maybe an unforeseen injury in my case, might render me unable to pay my mortgage payment. I wanted a house I could afford if I had to work at McDonalds, I didn't want to buy the absolute maximum I could afford. That just didn't seem smart, as you're banking on a perfect world, and things happen, injuries, job changes, accidents, anything can rock your financial boat. And usually, the things that rock your boat are things you don't see coming. I wanted to do this right.

By the end of the day, the documents had been signed around and I was poised to be a first-time homebuyer. I couldn't wait. We closed in a few short weeks as my paperwork had already been completed. The appraisal and the inspections went without a hitch and on March 27, 2004, I got the keys. I was a homeowner! I couldn't believe it. When I went inside my home for the first night, I walked around it probably a hundred times, looking at everything and just loving my home. I looked out the windows into the backyard and it was huge. I looked in the garage at least a dozen times, turning the light on, seeing my old hooptie 1993 Toyota Celica parked neatly on one side, perfect. I remember I was getting ready to leave the house and as I was backing out of my driveway, I stopped in front of my mailbox. God and I had a moment together. I just looked at this beautiful house and said to him, "I don't want for anything else," and I cried tears of happiness and joy. God always keeps His promise to His children.

It took a few nights to calm down enough to sleep. I was so excited. I couldn't stop thanking God. Every time I came home to my very own home, I thanked Him, over and over. I also said to God, Wow! *You made sure to manifest this house just for me off a job that only was paying nine dollars an hour. How amazing is that! Who soever believes RIGHT!*

About a month after I bought my home, I got a letter from my grandmother, who had been getting well along in her years by this time, but she took the time and effort to write me a letter of congratulations. Her words dissolved me into tears when I read them. My precious grandmother's words, something I will always cherish. The letter holds a place of honor on my refrigerator.

> April 3rd, 04
>
> Dear Kris, I thank about you so very much, and my prayers are all ways with you. I am so proud you, just think you have your own have good things happen when you put God in the plan you be good, dont let no one take you money, just keep on praying, God will all ways help you, with love and best wishes
>
> Grandmother Hunter

All I can say about my home is this: Thank you, God, for providing for all my needs in such a wonderful way. Thank you, thank you, thank you. This was the only thing I really needed, and You have blessed me with this home, and I am eternally grateful.

> **"EVERY GOOD GIFT AND EVERY PERFECT GIFT IS FROM ABOVE"**
> **(JAMES 1:17 ESV)**

27

MONOPOLY GAME

I didn't always make the right choices in my life. This is probably true for most of us, but a few main boo-boos are part of my story and should be mentioned. I have learned some lessons in life, the hard way. Sometimes there's just no other way. The first time I really lost my temper was in ninth grade at Broad Ripple High School. I had some candy and this older girl, probably a senior, said she was going to take it from me. Her hand snaked out so fast for my candy, a few pieces went flying as I wrapped my fingers around the pieces I could, and she scratched me on the back of my hand as she was grabbing for it—and that did it. We got into a fistfight, at school in the lunchroom no less. Not exactly the thing to do when you're trying to fly under the radar with your mother. I was getting the better of her and then Stacey was there. She jumped into the mix and that girl slapped the glasses right off Stacey's face. That sent me into ballistic mode, and I was really getting after it when several teachers jumped in and ended the fight. I think the candy thief was glad because I was kicking her butt. None of the girls ever bothered me again at that school and all three of us got suspended, not just me. When we got home, Stacey got in trouble for taking up for me and jeopardizing her education, and not to ever do that again. Later she told me, "I will always take up for you, Krista, I would do it again," and we smiled. Stacey's tough.

Another time, I was in the auditorium, playing backgammon with a beautiful marble set my cousin Gloria West in New York had given me. This guy, a thug by reputation, decided he was going to take it from me. And he grabbed up a piece, a bishop, I think. I had to stand up to get it back. While I was standing up, he hit me so hard in the face, he knocked my two front teeth out. They were hanging there in my mouth. I was full-on pissed, that hurt bad. I don't think he was expecting what happened next. I hit that guy with everything I had, I'm surprised I didn't break my hand. He staggered back with the most dumbfounded look on his face, then he dropped the bishop, grabbed his bleeding nose, turned, and ran from the auditorium. He was done. Just like that, and that was the end of it. Well, until I got home. I got in big trouble for getting hurt. Now I needed major dental work and that cost a lot of money. I told Mommy I was sorry, but I didn't start the fight. What was I supposed to do, just let someone take my stuff? I had to stand up for myself. I just didn't expect to get my teeth knocked out while I was standing up. That was a tough day.

My two front teeth had to be pulled the rest of the way out, and they made me a bridge. Many years later I was able to afford dental implants.

When I got back to school, after my dental work, some of my friends got me out of class and into the hallway. They had that thug (James) in tow and asked me if that was him. I nodded yes, and those four boys kicked his butt right there. Chivalry is not dead. Three of my guy friends, fellow athletes—football I think—and another big guy, showed that creep that guys shouldn't hit girls. That should be the rule, and I hope he learned it that day.

Then there was this other time, however, this time it was my fault, big time. When I was living in Indy, in my apartment alone, I decided to get a gun for protection. I never got jumped or anything, it just seemed like a good idea at the time.

Meanwhile, I was dating a girl named Debbie. Things were good for a while and then we started to have problems again. We had broken up once or twice before, but I was always able to win her back. This time, we broke up and I went over to her house to see if I could make up with her and get her back. I walked up to her front door and knocked, and she came to the door. Unfortunately for me, she was already moving on and had some new love interest in her house already. She kept telling me to leave and I started escalating, being as how we were together just days before and now, she's already talking to someone else. That hurt and I was getting mad—not a good combination. I went back to my car, not sure if I was going to leave or not, when I remembered what I put under my car seat, the gun! That'll scare her!

I wish I had gone home that night, but I didn't. I should have had more self-control than that, but I pulled that gun out from under the seat and walked right back up to the front door. I tapped the glass with the gun and Debbie came to the door, wide-eyed, but didn't open it. The love interest was right behind her on the phone, calling 911 that there was a crazed woman with a gun at their front door and she was scared for her life. The fact that Debbie didn't open the door was satisfaction enough for me, I scared her and that was the point. She yelled through the glass that the cops were on their way, and I better get out of there. I stayed about thirty more seconds, which was exactly thirty seconds too long, which I would find out later. I got in my car and started driving out the back way, through the corn fields. Within sight of the road, yep, about thirty seconds ahead, red and blue lights were flashing in my rearview mirror. Three sets of them! And with all three sirens, you could hear it from the next county. *Good Lord, I've done it this time*, I thought. Why did I do that, flash that gun, why? The first officer came up by my window and ordered me to turn off the engine and get out of the car. I did, and immediately I was handcuffed, frisked, and arrested, and I was on my way to jail. Again. Great. Almost like:

> "Go to Jail
> Go Directly to Jail,
> Do Not Pass Go,
> Do Not Collect $200."

The strangest thoughts go through my head sometimes. My car was towed, and I didn't even get a phone call. But, being in that neighborhood, I did not utter a single word, other than yes or no to their initial questions, and then I didn't say another word all the way to jail. This was one of those towns, white, racist, and KKK territory. If you're Black, you don't want to have an altercation with the police. I was in enough trouble already, so I just kept quiet. For one of the few times in my life, I was quiet, believe it or not!

Processing was about like I remembered, pictures, fingerprints, and this time I *was* issued the dreaded orange jumpsuit, a toothbrush, and just enough items for a hoe bath. I was all set for my long weekend, because *of course* this was Friday! My cellmate was already in our cell when I got there. Great, I get to be the newbie, invading her territory. She was cool though, and we made friends. She had a deck of cards, and we played all kinds of card games for the next three days since there was no television. I told her I would have gone nutso if she didn't have those cards, she laughed and said this wasn't her first rodeo. We had a good laugh over that.

Monday morning, bright and early, my lawyer and I went to see the judge. When it was all said and done, I got my gun back, since I had a permit for it and no priors. And I was enrolled in a forty-hour course on anger management. I was not looking forward to it, but it turned out to be a very interesting class, and I enjoyed it. I learned a lot, especially about people who have a hard time containing themselves when they're angry. I'm glad I took the class; it was informative and helpful to me. And yeah, this was the last time I went to jail.

Debbie didn't press charges, which was gracious of her, and I was grateful, but I was still on probation. I was never so surprised when my probation officer turned out to be Debbie's aunt, who I already knew! That was a blessing, she knew me and understood our gay relationship. She knew I wasn't a bad person; I just did a stupid thing. I wrote an apology letter to Debbie and gave it to her aunt. She said she would give it to Debbie. What I did was a terrible thing to do, and I was ashamed of myself for doing it, and I was sincerely sorry. I wanted her to know that.

Anger management class really got me thinking about my emotions and temper and from that day forward I have worked on keeping my temper under control and not letting my anger inspire me to make stupid choices. I'm not saying I haven't lost my temper since then, but never in a way that would land me in jail again. I learned my lesson.

The other aspect of my life that has been kind of crazy but true is prior to moving to Atlanta, Georgia, in 1997, I had twenty-seven jobs in my career. I think that's mainly because I've always been striving to better myself and my situation in life. From 1997 to 2022, I can add five more jobs to that list, making a total of thirty-two jobs my entire life.

> "ANYONE WHO HAS BEEN STEALING MUST STEAL NO LONGER, BUT MUST WORK, DOING SOMETHING USEFUL WITH THEIR OWN HANDS"
> [EPHESIANS 4:28 NIV].

28

BLACK COOL RUNNINGS

It should be noted that I almost didn't graduate from high school. It wasn't because of bad grades or lack of credits. I graduated with a good solid C, maybe even a B-, and I liked school and most subjects I found interesting enough. But about a month before graduation, something happened that almost got me expelled. Let me give you the background for this event.

I went from Broad Ripple High School, a 98 percent Black school, to Ben Davis High School, a 98 percent white school. I think my coping skills were not quite prepared for what I encountered at my new school. There were the stares, the whispers, whatever. That didn't bother me, I thought it was stupid really. If you can't tell somebody to their face what you're thinking, what's the point? If you think something that strongly, come tell me to my face. Up until this incident, I had not gotten in trouble for fighting all three years of attending Ben Davis. But a month before graduation, this girl who sat directly behind me in history class, was saying stupid things just loud enough I couldn't tune it out. It was obvious she was trying to get a reaction out of me. I was doing my best to ignore her, and she was getting a little closer, and a little louder, and a little meaner with what she was saying, until ultimately flat out calling me a nigga. Well, that crossed the line, inexcusable, and I spun around in my seat, leaped out of it and across her desk, and my hands wrapped around her neck and tried to choke her. I was yanked off her by the teacher, who deposited me on the other side of the room and stood there, guarding me against going after her again. Surprise, surprise, nothing happened to the "victim." Everyone was asking her over and over if she was okay, and of course, since I was the "attacker," I got suspended. Many teachers, coaches, and classmates pleaded my case to the principal not to expel me, which was the original plan apparently. No one even asked me why I "attacked" her. No one cared, I guess. And that was my first experience with blatant prejudice. It's interesting because I was super popular in school with everyone, the rich kids, jocks, Einsteins, etc.

To my surprise, I later found my original birth certificate from being adopted by the Fords, and guess what box was checked under the race? White not Black. Growing up, I used to hear this phrase, "light, bright, damn near white," even though I'm biracial my skin color is so light, and back in the '60s they must have thought I was white.

In the powerlifting world, there is every type of person, size, shape, and color. I never experienced prejudice in the gyms. Another reason I love this sport is that everyone is welcome, accepted, and encouraged. God created our skin tones with beautiful variety, but all our souls are the same color. During the years of being sponsored, I was living my dream, training myself and teaching others about this great sport of powerlifting.

Probably my biggest supporter was Herb Weinstein, one of my sponsors. Several times a month, Herb would fly me to New York and put me up at the Renaissance Times Square, which was a luxurious hotel, and room rates were a whopping $530 a night. I worked with Herb and his local trainer, Paul, and we would have intense training sessions. Herb was progressing, learning the disciplines and getting into shape. His only downfall was he never got more than about four hours of sleep each night. He kept telling us he would do better.

We started talking about him taking part in a powerlifting competition. He was game and we were keeping an eye open for a good meet for him. When I came to New York, it was great. I didn't realize Herb was a senior partner for one of the biggest law firms in New York City (Proskauer Rose), and whenever we would go to eat, he was always greeted by the staff, "Hello, Mr. Weinstein," he would smile, and they would seat us. I realized he was a very respected man in New York. Everywhere we went, it was "Hi, Mr. Weinstein." He was adored by his colleagues and acquaintances. And me too, he made my dream come true, he was my angel. And I think, even though he had it all, I was making a dream of his come true, something no one else could do—teach him how to powerlift. And he loved it. I couldn't wait to see him compete. He was going to do great for a first-timer. All the times I hung out with Herb, I never felt he had a prejudice bone in his body. He was an extremely wealthy Jewish man, and I was a sponsored Black female athlete, and he was proud to take me around with him. No one acted prejudice or unkind in any way, color and finances didn't matter to Herb, he was a genuinely good and fair man.

Equality was not the case in the bobsled world, as I soon found out. Since I had never experienced much prejudice in sports, I was a little blind to it at first, but by the second year of competing in bobsledding, I got a good healthy dose of it. At the beginning of the season, we were all at the Olympic training center, and I overheard some of the other girls talking about the schedule of races. I realized they all knew the schedule and I hadn't been given the information. This did not sit well at all, as I was an integral part of the team. Why wouldn't they give me the schedule? I stewed on this for about a day and then I called a meeting with our coach, our trainer, and the president of the bobsled federation, Matt Roy. I thought I better get this all on tape, so I took a mini recorder with me, tucked it in my parka side pocket, and pushed record. When we were all assembled, I asked the obvious question, "When are the athletes supposed to be notified of the season's schedule?"

The three of them agreed that all members of the team should have a schedule prior to leaving the tryouts. "Well, tryouts were in the summer and now it's November and I'm just now hearing about the schedule, and from the other girls no less," I said and looked at them all levelly. Some lame comment was made like it must have been an oversight. Oh please! "I hope that is the case because it better not be because of this." And I ran my palm across the back of my other hand, indicating my skin color. "Because Johnny Cochran is only a phone call away." There was a bit of scrambling and back peddling and an assurance that the color of my skin was not it. Well, what was it then? Come on now. They told me I would have the schedule within the hour. Having made my point, I rose and said, "Have a great day, gentlemen," and I walked out. And I did have the schedule within the hour. After that day, I was the first one with the schedule. How unfortunate I had to raise a fit and threaten to call Johnny Cochran just to get equal treatment, but sometimes you must stand up and fight. I can do that, any day of the week, for equality. And I will, every time.

On my way to the bobsled tryouts in 1998, I called Herb from the airport, and we talked while I waited for my connecting flight. He was catching me up on his training and was getting excited for his competition. We had a great talk, and I was anxious to see him after the tryouts.

Once all the bobsledders got to the Olympic Training Center, tryouts began. I had already completed the initial six timed tests and was getting ready to do the dry sled push, that's all I had left, when I got a phone call. This was not the phone call you ever wanted to get. When the first question out of the caller's mouth is if you're sitting down, you know it is not going to be a good phone call. I sat down and braced for the news. You hear the words, but they don't quite make sense.

I was told Herb had passed away. I couldn't believe it. I just talked to him! This couldn't be happening. Apparently, Herb had had a massive heart attack and barely had time to say but a few words to Wendy, his wife of over thirty years. He was only fifty-four years old.

I didn't even do the timed push; I don't even remember changing my clothes. I was instantly on my way. Nothing mattered but getting to the city. I was upstate in Lake Placid, New York, at the Olympic Training Center. I got there safely and when I arrived for the funeral, I couldn't believe the number of people in attendance. It was packed with hundreds of people there to pay their respects. I went in with Paul and we walked right up behind Richard Ader, my other sponsor. He was sure I was still at the tryouts, but when I tapped him on the shoulder and he saw me, he gathered me in his arms and said, "You will sit with me and my family." So, there I was, in a whole pew of Aders, up near the front. It was a very long funeral. Toward the end, people started getting up to talk about Herb, funny things he did, and the good memories that had been shared. There were about eight people who spoke. No less than four of them spoke almost exclusively of his love for powerlifting and how he was really having fun learning the sport and he was even going to compete soon; my name wasn't mentioned but Richard and his family knew it was me and they all just looked down my way and smiled at the one who gave him a new sense of excitement and hope in his life. I went into tunnel vision at about this time, knowing full well what my sponsors were doing for me, but I had no idea how much I mattered to Herb. Instantly, I was having a moment. My tears fell, and I almost had to gasp for breath. I knew God had sent him to be my angel, but I had no idea I was more to him than his trainer—I was his friend. That was a humbling moment for me, to be that important to someone as successful as Herb. After the funeral, people found out who I was to Herb and I was thronged by people wanting to catch a moment with this world-class powerlifter Herb had bragged about to all of them. It was a lot to handle, but I stayed strong and talked with Herb's friends. They all made me feel like I was worth my weight in gold. Wow, I had no idea.

When I got back to my hotel, I had a long talk with God about all of this. I thanked him for my sponsorship, it was a fabulous blessing. I was able to train and compete in two sports. I made a real bond with Herb; we were truly friends. He was more like a father to me. Herb and Richard were put in my life right at the perfect moment. A million thanks to God, for the opportunity these two men gave me, and the gift of Herb's friendship.

During my years of bobsledding, I had another sponsor who gave me two generous donations. He was Lenita's first cousin, Erroll "Doug" Woods. His wife had a clothing shop in Atlanta, and I wore the shop's emblem on my helmet when I competed—that was my end of the deal. His gifts included two substantial checks with a little note that said, "Go slide." That support was invaluable and allowed me to stretch out my sponsorship a little longer.

By my third season, I was really getting good, and I was liking it more and more. Our coach was Pat Brown, the original man who coached the Jamaicans in the movie *Cool Runnings*, played by actor John Candy. The first race of the season was always in Calgary, Canada. This year, in our first run of the season, I pushed that sled for a track push record, which is from the starting gate to the first sixty-meter mark. I pushed my driver, Jill, and our sled sixty meters in 5.85 seconds, for the record. And we won that race, hands down. That was the first time a US women's team had ever won a race in Calgary. And Jill and I won the $3,000 first place prize money, that was $1,500 a piece! When I received my check, I had to laugh; for a split second, I wished Janice could be there so I could snap my check in her face, like she did me when I bombed out in Baltimore. It was six years later, and I had just won my first prize money for athletics. Later that same season, Jill and I competed in Utah, and I pushed again for another track push record of 5.46. Maybe the records are still standing, I honestly don't know. Later, still in the same season, I pushed again, with Jean Racine, my driver for this race, and we were the first women's team to place in a bobsled race in Germany, capturing the silver medal. I finally quit bobsledding after the 1999/2000 season, but from late 1995 to 2000, I was the best brakeman for the US team. By the end of 1999, the Olympic committee inducted bobsledding to be an Olympic sport for women, to begin in 2002 in Salt Lake City.

Being a brakeman, I had to know each course by heart and know exactly when to start braking. Too soon and you will ruin the end of the course, and too late and you'll plow into the snowbank. It takes about three to four good pulls to stop the sled, kind of like pumping the brakes on a car. And it's about as manual as it gets too. When you pull up on the brake, the teeth on the other end of the brake go down. However hard you pull up is how hard the teeth on the bottom dig into the ice. If you pull like a wimp, you'll end up in the snowbank. That is an embarrassment I'm glad to say I never experienced. I don't pull like no wimp!

I can't talk about bobsledding without covering the subject of crashes. Some people think bobsledding is like a roller coaster, a ride. Not even close! It's a lot more like a racecar driving on ice. Crashes are inevitable and can be dangerous, even life threatening. My most memorable crash happened in Calgary. The course had twelve turns. I was pushing with my driver and on our first run, we crashed at turn ten. Instantly, the sled was on its side, and I was sliding along on the ice, getting a friction burn on my shoulder as it scraped over the ice. It was scary and I was a little rattled after this, but I got myself calmed down and ready for our next run. I talked to a teammate who told me how to avoid getting friction burns on my shoulders. She said to place my helmet onto the ice and put your weight on your head, then lift your shoulder off the ice. This piece of information was vital as our next run would turn out to be epic. We crashed at turn five this time, so we had to go through seven turns to get to the end of the course. So, we're not only speeding at eighty miles per hour, but now we are completely out of control! On the initial left-hand turn where we crashed, we flipped onto the sled's right side. When you're going down a course in a bobsled you hear the whooshing of the ice constantly, it's loud. You can tune it out, but it's still there, always. Well, the second we crashed, there was total silence! Eerie silence! I couldn't understand what happened, we didn't come to an instant stop, so why was it silent? I was confused. I don't know how long it was actually silent for, probably just a second, but it was one of those slow-motion moments that happen in life that seem to take forever. And then, as we crashed back down onto the course on our right side, I realized we had been airborne! We slid like that until we got to a right-hand turn, and that turn flipped us over the other way, onto the left side of the sled, going airborne once again. By the time we slid to a stop, near the end of the course, we had flipped from one side to the other four times, I think. All I could think of was, *We must have looked like Chitty Chitty Bang Bang coming down that course.* We were all over that track. I can laugh about it now but at the time I was not laughing at all. I was scared. But at least I didn't fall out. That happens to brakemen when they crash sometimes. I believe my powerlifting had a lot to do with that not happening to me. Consistently deadlifting five hundred pounds, I had a very strong grip.

It takes a good grip to be a brakeman anyway, but once you crash, you go into death grip mode. That sled is flipping around and yanking at your hands, threatening to break your grip. You can only hold a death grip for so long and then your hands start to fatigue. If the crash lasts long enough, you will eventually lose your grip. Then you come spitting out the back end of the sled to slide down the track in your suit, with no control whatsoever, friction burning all the way down, all over your body. Fortunately, I did not have the experience of finding out how that felt. Airborne was enough for me! It was way worse than any carnival ride I had ever been on, not for the faint of heart. I almost threw in the towel that day, it was awful!

Shortly after my crash, but not because of it, women were finally issued Kevlar vests, like the men wore, to combat the ice friction burns that are inevitable when you crash or come out the back end of the sled.

I finished out the season, but once Herb had passed, Richard could not sponsor me on his own indefinitely, so at the end of that year, my sponsorship was over. I got a job at AirTran and was able to fly to the rest of the competitions in the season free because of my employee flying pass privileges, but I knew I couldn't do both sports without sponsorship. I was able to stretch out my funding for one more year, thanks to Erroll, but the 1999/2000 season was the last year for me. So, unfortunately, that was the end of my bobsledding career. I was back on the forty-hour work week rat race and trying to train after work.

And of course, when it came to choosing which sport to keep and which one to drop, not much of a dilemma there, powerlifting wins in my book any day of the week.

One notable female bobsledding fact: Katheryn Dewey was the driver on the 1936 US national championship Team. She and her three male counterparts captured the gold medal. Women were banned from bobsledding after that, as bobsledding was deemed "too dangerous for women." Something about bobsledding makes ladies unable to bear children. Seriously? Yes, seriously, and bobsledding was banned to women for the next forty-six years.

> "OLDER WOMEN LIKEWISE ARE TO BE REVERENT IN BEHAVIOR" [TITUS 2:3 NIV].

*Olympic training center, Lake Placid, New York, 1985.
Six item test to secure a spot on the US women's bobsled team.*

APF Senior Nationals, Atlanta, Georgia, 1996. My first national champion title.

USA Women's Bobsled team.

*That's me lying down low in
the back of the sled with USA showing on my speed suit.*

World Cup bobsled race in Calgary, Alberta, Canada, 1999. I'm the brakeman or back pusher. We took first place and set new push track record of 5.46 seconds.

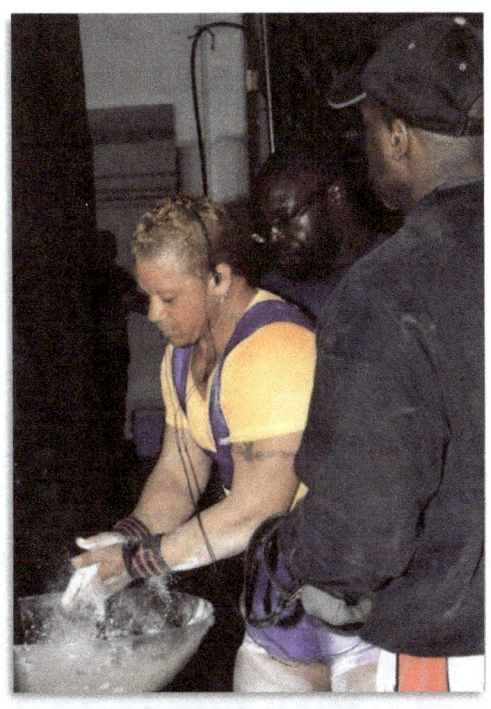

At the Arnold Classic in 2014 with Savoy Curtis and Darrin Barnes.

APF Senior National Championships, 2011. Derrick, Floyd, and Joe. I set a world squat record 628.2 lbs. at 181 lbs. in the open women's class.

29

DISCIPLINE IS MY DESTINY

By 2008, I was squatting in the high five hundred. I had been looking at the world record in the squat for a few years now, and the current record was 623 pounds. This record is for the open class, all ages, whoever is the very best, no matter what age. Deb Widdis set this record in 2006. When you break a record, you must break it by a minimum of five pounds. I wanted that record, which would mean a minimum of a 628-pound squat. By this time, I had been the national champion seven times, and world champion four times, so that record was my next goal. I was getting close too. Just the year before, at nationals, I squatted 584. I was hoping to break the six-hundred-pound mark this year and try for the record in a few more years. My squat poundage increases had been about thirty pounds per year for the last three years. If I could keep up that rate of increase, I would be right near the record in a few years.

This is my source of love, passion, and power. No discipline, no destiny. You don't fight backward, you fight forward. Step by step, trust in the process, trust in the universe, sometimes it's just the action merged with the right intention, which is going to bring the difference.

Training leading up to nationals that year went just as planned. I was squatting right at 585 on my final day of squat training before the competition. Bench and deadlifts were good, I was strong and ready. Nationals was at Virginia Beach, Virginia, this year, and my handlers, Joe Williams and Savoy Curtis went with me. I was very disappointed I couldn't make weight. I did everything I could think of (you don't want to know) to shed the last three pounds and I just couldn't do it. I weighed in at 184 for my final weigh-in, so I would be competing in the 198-pound class. This was totally on me. I always wait too long to start the weight making process. I was disappointed in myself, but that's beside the point, I was here to squat six hundred pounds.

Savoy was the one who got me calmed down, reset, and refocused.

He said, "Let's just do what we came here to do. One lift at a time." So, my first squat, 529 pounds, was hard for me and I came up slow. I wasn't set up quite right, I didn't get underneath it right. Surprisingly, I got three white lights. My second lift went a lot better, 573 pounds, I paid a lot more attention to my set up and stance, and I blasted that one up like it was light. Three white lights again. That felt good so I made the decision to go for it, six hundred pounds. At first, I couldn't even get the bar off the hooks, it was so heavy. But then somehow, I got it off the racks, backed up, and got set up. I went down, my eyes never leaving the head judge. When I got down past parallel, I blasted it up and it didn't feel quite as heavy as I was expecting. I knew I had it when I started powering back up, I knew it, and I smiled just as I locked it out. This was the first time I had ever felt six hundred pounds on my back. I was so excited, partly because I had finally broken the six-hundred-pound barrier and partly because I knew I could do more. I was on cloud nine and really had to work hard at putting that on the back burner until after the meet. I still had to bench and deadlift.

Bench went well, 225 pounds, 242, and 253, all white lights. Then it was on to the deadlift. My first attempt was 501 pounds. That felt heavy, so I decided to skip my last two attempts. I totaled 1,355 pounds, my best total ever, even with passing up my last two deadlifts. And the funny thing, I had been so upset I couldn't make my weight class, and when it was all over, I started laughing because I had just broken nine American records, between my master class (age group) and the open 198-pound class, *and* I won two gold medals that day. So, all in all, quite a glorious day. I couldn't have been happier.

Looking back before this glorious day, I remember Janice telling me, "Krista, I need you to just put six hundred pounds on the bar, unrack it, but don't squat it. And each week, start descending two to three inches and come back up." This technique proved to be most effective in my training. Baby steps toward adult steps is how you master your thoughts in reaching any goal. It doesn't matter how slow you go as long as you never stop. Consistency and hard work are also key to anything you would like to obtain in life no matter how crazy it might sound. It's never too late for you to be great. Look back and thank God, look forward and trust God!

I heard someone say this and it really resonated with me, I hope it can do the same for you. We can relax on a bus going somewhere and don't know the driver, we can relax on a plane when we don't know the pilot, we can even relax on a ship when we don't know the captain, so, why don't we relax in life knowing God is in control? (Think about that.)

Life goes on with or without whoever and whatever, and whatever makes you feel bad, leave it! Whatever makes you smile, keep it.

I saw this on a reel, and I thought, *Wow, this is so true*. It said, "Faith is like Wi-Fi, it's invisible, but it has the power to connect you to what you need."

F=FOCUSED
O=OPTIMISTIC
R=RESILIENT
D=DISCIPLINED

God is cultivating my tribe called Team Marvel to be a positive influence on and in my life. On this amazing God-purpose journey with book, movie, and documentary, I only need and want to be around people who want me to be the best version of myself and I want the same for them. I am about to be the happiest, most healed version of myself. I am walking in my purpose. I am so proud of how far I've come, and I can't wait to see how far I go from here.

> "DO NOT BE MISLEAD: 'BAD COMPANY CORRUPTS GOOD CHARACTER'" [CORINTHIANS 15:33 NIV].

30

NOT ALONE

Worlds was just two weeks away and I was determined to squat six hundred in my normal weight class of 181-pound versus the 198-pound class. Training was right on schedule, and I felt confident I could do it.

The day started out great. First, I had an appointment at the barber shop to get my hair cut, then I met up with my girlfriend, Nee, and we had sushi for lunch and went to a park where we walked around and looked at the beauty of the grounds. We were in separate cars as she was coming from a doctor's appointment. When we were done at the park, we said our goodbyes, and got into our cars to leave. I pulled out first, and she was right behind me. We headed down Evans Mill Road and I remember seeing a few nice estates as I drove down the road and then, a quick flash of yellow and everything went black.

When I woke up, I was in my car, shattered glass all over me. The front bumper of a school bus was lodged inside my car, trapping my left leg. I tried to pull my leg free and horrendous pain shot up through my entire body. A groan escaped my lips at the realization of what just happened. I just got T-boned by a school bus! When trauma happens, time takes on a whole new dimension. It seemed like an hour before the ambulance came and people ran up to help me. But in the first moment of that hour, literally instantly, there was a young woman in the car with me.

She told me to keep still, that help was on the way. I was starting to panic, my left leg being trapped like that, and I started to wiggle and pull on my leg. She was beautiful and almost glowed with kindness; I just wanted to get over to her. Finally, I was able to pull my leg free and move myself up a little bit and I started to inch toward her. The pain was unbearable, it felt like my guts were falling out of me. I was able to move a few more inches to the center console before I had to rest. She reached out and held my head.

I was in and out of consciousness, but every time I was conscious, I would scoot closer to her, and she held me to her chest and smoothed my hair saying, "You're doing great, keep talking to me. Stay with me." Her voice was so soft and sweet, it kept me calm and relaxed. By the time the emergency team arrived, apparently, I was half in and half out of the passenger seat door, which was still a mystery to me. The way I remember it, I was barely halfway over the center console, lying against her. When the emergency people arrived, she began to let me go.

I grabbed at her arm and pleaded, "Don't go, please don't leave me."

She reached for my hand and said, "I won't leave you, I am right here," but then I didn't see her anymore. The medical team did their best to gently pull me the rest of the way out of the car and onto the gurney. I screamed and yelled in pain, then I was out for a few minutes, and then woke up from the pain again.

I thanked God I had health insurance at the time through my job at AirTran Airways. The ambulance took me to Grady Memorial Hospital, which is ranked in the top five best trauma hospitals in the nation, I was rushed there because of the amount of trauma my body had just gone through. It was about a twenty- to twenty-five-minute drive, and I think I was conscious of every bump in the road. I was in excruciating pain, and very confused, I was not entirely sure what was going on, but I knew I was on my way to a hospital.

Once we got there, I had to be transferred to a hospital gurney. When they picked me up, my left hip popped, like it had popped out of its socket, and it just popped back in. I don't know if that's what happened, but it set me off on another screaming fit. Once I got through that, they took several vials of blood, and then I was rolled out to get a CAT scan.

The nurses, or somebody in the room, began to cut my clothes off. I wished I had the strength to protest but they were so fast, it was over before I could say a word. I do like my nice clothes. Once they got my shirt off and saw my muscles, they asked if I was a bodybuilder. I told them, no, a powerlifter. A lot of people don't know the difference so sometimes you need to clarify, but one of them said, "Like how much you can lift, not posing on a stage, right?" I nodded. When the doctor came in to look at me, he observed my physique, and the nurse informed him that I was a powerlifter. He knew what that meant, and he pressed on a few spots on my body. Nothing he did hurt so, I thought maybe I wasn't injured that bad after all. But he was not poking to see if something was hurt, he was poking uninjured areas, feeling the density of my muscles.

I didn't realize this until he said, "Well, two things saved your life today. God, and your muscles. They absorbed so much of the impact; the fender recoiled off you like a rubber band. Don't get me wrong, you are bruised substantially, but that impact would have killed an average person, absolutely. It is a miracle you are alive."

I was still out of it, but that was scary. I knew I was hurt, and something was broken, but I didn't realize how close I had come to dying. I looked up at the nurse who was down at the foot of my bed, a cross hanging from her neck. She looked familiar and the recognition must have shown on my face because she said, "Krista, I train at Gold's too." Then I knew who she was. She touched my ankle and said, "I got you, okay, I got you." Her face was so calm and reassuring, I relaxed a little, knowing I was not alone.

During the scan, they realized I was bleeding internally, so I was rushed downstairs, and two doctors came in and cauterized arteries on each side of my lower groin area. *This* was God and those doctors saving my life, because I could have bled out internally and died if this procedure was delayed by even a minute, but that didn't happen on God's watch. Or theirs for that matter. They gave me some local anesthetic, otherwise I would have been yelling and screaming a lot more.

After all that, I was wheeled back to my spot in the ER.

There was a young man in a bed close to mine with a gunshot wound to his leg. Whenever the hospital people touched him or moved him, he yelled, and then so did I. When they touched me and I yelled, he yelled too. We didn't know each other but we were united in our pain. Yelling, yowling really, was about all we could do at the time.

Finally, the doctor came in and informed me, "You have a broken pelvis, a bruised kidney, and a bruised spleen. And," he continued, "a lacerated head with contusions. But your spine is uninjured." That was a lot to take in, but nothing sounded life-altering. Well, maybe a broken pelvis. I didn't know much about a break like that.

I asked about my eye, realizing I was only seeing out of my right eye.

"Your eye is fine; it's just matted with blood, and we need to get all the glass shards out of your scalp and forehead before we can clean off your eye." Relief flooded through me. Both of my eyes were still intact. Thank you, God! There was a big piece of glass lodged right below my left eyebrow, I could feel that one for sure, probably where all the blood was coming from. That one left a scar I still see to this day when I look in the mirror.

The bus driver was uninjured. And she had one child left on her bus in the very back when the accident occurred. She had come to the hospital to check on me, which was kind, but I didn't see her, I was off getting scanned or scoped.

Then I was off to get the glass shards removed. They numbed my head and two people with tweezers picked every piece of glass out of me—it took about half an hour. Then they gently washed the blood off my face and eye and, sure enough, thank you, Jesus, I could see out of both eyes again.

After all of that, I was wheeled up to a room in the ICU, which meant I'd be staying for a while. I kept thinking anxiously that worlds was only two weeks away. Later that evening, after receiving the long-awaited pain meds, I realized I would miss worlds this year. This was just about as painful a realization as the injuries I just sustained. So, November 10, 2008, eleven years to the date of my first sponsorship check that changed my life, once again my life changed.

My trauma team arrived in my ICU room the next morning to check in on me, and the head trauma doctor sat next to my bed, and just looked at me. I know doctors rely on medicine and facts, but I know they see things that don't fall squarely into those categories. He was looking at me like that. He told me, "You are a living miracle, young lady, do you know that?"

I shook my head and smiled at him. I was smiling inside too because I realized that it was thanks to the physique God gave me, which I had trained and developed so well, that saved my life. I was so grateful God spared me. And I realized for certain this was the path God made for me, my lifting—I'd be dead now if I hadn't chosen this path. And some peace came over me about my injury and missing worlds. I knew God wasn't done with me yet, I would recover. And I believed I would compete again. In fact, I was positive I would.

When my friends were allowed to come into my room, they were telling me that the crash was on the news and my car looked like a crushed Coke can. The news reporters were saying the driver of the car, me, had somehow miraculously survived. Miraculous was right, an honest-to-goodness full-blown miracle straight from God. That's what I believe. And that lady, she had to have been an angel. Nobody else saw her, except my girlfriend and me. I was in and out of consciousness, but I wasn't delusional. She was there, right there in the car with me, holding my head the whole time until the paramedics came. And I love the fact that she said she wouldn't leave me. To this day, I believe she was an angel sent to protect me because when I was in the ICU, I asked my girlfriend if she got that lady's number so I could call her and thank her, she said, "Yes, I have it right here in my purse." She emptied that whole purse out onto the bed. Nothing, absolutely no card, and she swore she got that from her. Well, I have always believed there are angels walking around this earth cloaked as humans!

So, worlds went on without me. I got the whole story from Amy Jackson, from APF, who told me all the highlights and what I missed. Yes, I would be back next year, I vowed to myself.

The time between the accident and December 15th—my surgery date and thirty-five days to be exact—were the most painful, awful days of my life. I couldn't sit, stand, or lay down without terrible pain. If I coughed or sneezed, it felt like my guts were coming out again. Nothing gave me relief. I had pain medicine, morphine—the heavy-duty stuff, but that only gave me partial relief for about forty-five minutes and then it was agonizing pain again. Sleep was impossible, the only way I could get a few minutes here and there was to sit at my dining room table and put my head down on my hands. Ten minutes was about as long as I could nap sitting. It was a miserable five weeks I never want to repeat. I went through the gamut of emotions. I was mad and angry, sad, lonely, grouchy, and I felt sorry for myself, having to endure all this pain, and the question that never has an answer, "Why did this happen to me?" I didn't want to talk to anybody most of the time, but I did ask God that question, several times. He didn't give me an answer I could hear, maybe I wasn't listening very hard, I just couldn't understand why this terrible accident happened, and it happens just two weeks before worlds was just adding insult to injury, literally.

My pelvic repair surgery was on December 15, 2008. I was so ready to begin the road to recovery after. My surgeon, Dr. Lundy, got the whole run-down on me.

I told him, "I am a competitive powerlifter and I want to be right back where I was before this injury. I want to squat six hundred pounds at worlds next year."

He looked at me closely and finally said, "Krista, I believe you *will* squat that six hundred pound next year. If anyone has the heart and soul to do it, it's you. And I will do the best repair I can possibly do." He looked at me with the sincerest eyes I've ever seen. Then he smiled at me. "Okay?"

"Okay," I mumbled as I went under the anesthesia.

The surgery went perfectly. Not to say I wasn't in pain, it was a different kind of pain though now, and it was a great improvement. In fact, I could sleep for several hours at a time. Every day, there was a little less pain and a little more sleep. I realized how I had always taken sleep for granted before. I never had insomnia, I used to lie down, and I was out. This accident gave me a new appreciation for sleep, being as I missed it terribly for thirty-five nights. I never considered sleep a blessing, but now I do.

After about a week, I was released to go home. My girlfriend picked me up and drove me home, and others would call or come by and see how I was doing, they all took good care of me. It was so humbling to me how many people called and stopped by. I felt blessed to have so many good friends.

The days turned into weeks, and I recovered enough to start training lightly by the following month, January, and my healing was miraculous. When I started doing my heavier normal training in the gym, there was no pain in my pelvic area, and I felt back to normal, a little weaker from all the down time, but it was all coming back. I was on my way. Next stop, God willing, a six-hundred-pound squat in the 181-pound class. Nationals was only six months away; I wouldn't be ready for that. But worlds was exactly eleven months from my surgery date, I thought I could be ready for that, God willing. I saw an affirmation that was spot on with my car accident, "God delays you in order to display you!"

> "THEN JESUS TOLD HIS DISCIPLES A PARABLE TO SHOW THEM THAT THEY SHOULD ALWAYS PRAY AND NOT GIVE UP" [LUKE 18:1 NIV].

31

628.2 LBS

The months passed and my body continued to heal. I did my best to walk the fine line between pushing myself as hard as I could and not overdoing it. The better I felt, the harder it was not to just go full-on beast mode. I am wise enough to know that the body takes time to finish healing, even after it doesn't hurt anymore. So, it was hard, but I held myself to a conservative plan.

Another thing going on during this time was being right in the middle of an extremely tumultuous relationship with my girlfriend. This was a big distraction and detrimental to my training. However, that desire—that *need* really—to know I can still do my sport overpowered everything and I was able to persevere.

Nationals was in June 2009, just six months after my surgery, and I still wasn't quite healed up enough to compete. I would make it to the Worlds though, via a special invite, and I looked forward to it. The final ten-week countdown would be the real test for my body. I wasn't worried. Not only did my bones heal back together in my pelvis, but I also had a small steel plate attached to both sides of the break. No way both of those things together would fail. And they didn't, that break was healed up good and solid. Thank you, God, we're back!

Worlds would be in Bournemouth, England, November 2009, and Savoy went with me—his first trip ever out of the country.

We enjoyed first class accommodation, and even though the trip was almost eight hours, we were very comfortable the entire time.

And of course, once again, I couldn't make weight. Weigh-ins were from eight to eleven a.m., and then again at one p.m. I couldn't make 181 during the first session, so I missed breakfast and sent Savoy to go eat without me. But by one p.m., I was right on the money, 82.5 kilos. Once I was done, I grabbed Savoy and we went directly out to lunch, I was starving by this point.

My girlfriend showed up the next day—which shocked me because she adamantly said she was not coming. At this point, my girlfriend and I had been together for three years—my longest relationship to date—and I had been getting all kinds of red flags since day one. Things she would say and do, giving me the silent treatment after she would purposely pick a fight, and how it was always right around the time I was starting to train for a huge competition.

When the competition started, I found I was in the second flight of lifters, so I had plenty of time to get ready. Savoy got me all wrapped and ready. We had gone a little conservative, my squat opener was 523.5. No problem, three white lights. Then 584, and that was easy and went right up for three white lights. Now the moment of truth. The bar was loaded with 606.7. I was all set up and I don't know what I was expecting, but I went down past parallel and blasted that weight right up for another three white lights. Easy peasy, now I was really on fire! Bench went well, 264.5, and deadlifts went good as well, 468.9. All in all, a perfect day. A nine for nine day, the kind of day we all dream of every time we compete. And a master-squat record and my own personal best, and now a five-time world champion. This was a great comeback for me. I couldn't have asked for a more perfect day from God. Thank you, thank you, thank you.

Once I got back from England, my life seemed to get a lot more hectic. My relationship with my girlfriend was in full swing and I was completely caught up in the craziness. What I found out later would change my life. I was in a relationship all this time with a total narcissistic, manipulative, lying, cheating, gas-lighting energy vampire. This would explain 2010 clearly. There were a few job stressors and changes, and a few legal issues. You already know I didn't go to jail again; this was more along the lines of moving violations—okay, speeding. I drive fast, what can I say? It seemed like every time I turned around, something else was happening getting under my skin. I still trained but I was so distracted all the time that I just couldn't focus as well as I wanted to. So, I made the decision not to compete in 2010. I wasn't hurt or anything, but my concentration was off, and it felt like my strength was being zapped by my circumstances. Especially the total confusion I was under all the time with my girlfriend. One or two days of getting along and by the end of the week, I'd feel in my spirit this was a big mistake. This cycle happened from the very start, on August 30, 2006. This date is my birthday and should have been a happy day. But that turned upside down as well.

By 2011, I had built up enough resistance to the relationship to compete again. Nationals that year was at Sun Prairie, Wisconsin, and this was where I would make my return. Training had gone well; and I was feeling strong. Derrick and Joe were there to handle me, but Savoy was not able to make this trip with me because he was in school to get another certification for his job. I know he was there in spirit. Once we finally got there, I hopped on the scale to see where I was, and I was once again disappointed to see I was dead on 190 pounds. In fact, it really hurt my feelings this time, I was way far over. Nine pounds to shed by the next day, I was not looking forward to the night to come, this would not be fun, not at all. And oh my, it wasn't.

By the time I was down to 181, I was spent. I was sick as a dog, there was no other way to put it. I felt weak and cranky, cramping, just not happy at all. My friends took me to get something to eat. After that, I felt a little better, but not by much. I really put my body through the ringer this time. I felt sick and very dehydrated, and I had a headache. My muscles were wanting to cramp up on me. This was the worst I'd ever felt going into a competition. I just couldn't get my energy back up. Even the excitement and adrenaline of competition wasn't doing much, I was wiped out. A few friends flew in to support my efforts, my buddy Dr. Soyini Chism a.k.a. Zo, Floyd Powers, and Nee (my girlfriend).

We all met up in the morning, had breakfast, and then went to the competition. I was quiet, and still felt kind of sick and queasy. My back and toes were threatening to cramp at any moment, and there was no one, except me, to blame for my sorry situation.

But it's not a reason and it's not going to be an excuse. I'm going to go out there and lift everything I can, no matter how awful I feel. Because that's what I do.

The guys helped me get suited up, my canvas suit feeling a little looser. Well, I was nine pounds heavier the last time I had it on.

I opened with 529, which I got with no problem. Joe Williams and Derrick Riley were the dream team to handle me on this most important day of my lifting career. My second attempt was 589.5 and that was flawless as well. For my third attempt, we decided to go for 611.7. This would be the New Master's World Record if I got it. Even though I felt weak and sick, my body was strong, and this lift came up faster and easier than the first two! Three white lights and it was official. I had just broken the Master's World Record! I was surprised because the way I felt, I wouldn't have thought I could do it that day.

And then there they were, both Joe and Derrick, looking at me earnestly. "What?" I said, "What are you looking at me for?"

Joe leaned in close and whispered in my ear, "Take a fourth attempt Krista, go for the record. You're there." I hadn't even thought of it. I looked up at Derrick, he nodded his head in agreement. I looked up and I felt Savoy's presence and, for a moment, felt him saying, "Go for it." My heart jumped at the thought, and I had to hurry up and consider it. I was already the last lifter in my flight, and the officials needed to know right away if I was going to take a fourth attempt and try for the record. I guess my guys saw what they needed to see in my face, and Joe was at the official's table in a flash to tell them I was going to take a fourth attempt for the open (meaning any age can attempt) women's 181 class world record.

The bar would be loaded with 628.2 pounds—three and a half times my body weight. I put my headphones on and listened to the calming tones of Sade. And then it was time. As I walked up to the bar, I was asking God for safety and strength. I got under that bar, just like always, and went down, just like always, and I blasted that bar out of the hole as fast as my first three lifts. I had strength to spare. I knew where that came from, and after I racked that bar, I pointed my finger upward. And just like that, it was over. I had just broken the world record! Right now! I just did it! The crowd was cheering, and of course my happy feet came on and I started jumping and jumping all over the platform. The head judge had to grab ahold of me so he could verify my equipment was legit. I stopped for a moment, to let him check me, but when he released me, the jumping continued. The guys were eventually able to corral me and get me back to the warm-up room to get me ready for the bench.

I had been sipping water the whole morning, but once I started warming up for the bench, the muscle cramping intensified. My back and hamstrings were cramping, and every time I used those muscles, the cramping would begin. So, my bench was challenging, but I was able to get 259 pounds. On the deadlift, I got my first two, 429.7 and 446 without too much trouble. Then I had a "Go Big or Go Home" moment and for my last deadlift I tried a very big number, 501 pounds. Let's just say that bar stayed firmly planted on the floor, despite my herculean efforts. Nope, not that day, maybe too much jumping! That's okay. I came here to break the master's record in the squat and that's exactly what I did. I wasn't even thinking about the open record, maybe later in the year at worlds. And then, on June 11, 2011, God decided to bless me with the biggest lift of my life. I finally broke the (open) 181 pounds women's world squat record, 628.2 pounds, twenty-seven years after I picked up my first weights in Tracy, California, homeless, and praying to find my path in life. What can I say? A humble thank you to a mighty God. After it was all over, everyone there for me came to the back warmup area to congratulate me on my success. My girlfriend's response to this great achievement was "That was good." I received no hug, kiss or anything. She didn't seem generally happy for me at all. I knew right then this was envy and jealousy instead of love and support. I wasn't going to let her steal my peace and joy—nope, wasn't happening. From this day on, I would sleep with one eye open. Something was terribly wrong, who acts like that? I have never felt this from any previous girlfriend. Little did I know, it was a gift from God and "I will praise thee, O Lord with all my heart; I will shew forth all thy marvelous works (Psalm 9:1 KJV).

> **"I CAN DO ALL THINGS THROUGH CHRIST" (PHILIPPIANS 4:13 KJV).**

32

REPETITIVE STUPIDNESS

You might remember your grandmother telling you to always go with your first instincts, they are usually right! Vibes don't lie, people do! Follow your gut.

I wish I had listened to her advice. It would have saved me from a fifteen-year toxic relationship with my now-ex narcissist girlfriend.

I experienced what it is like to be with a true narcissist. There were so many red flags, and I recognized all of them only after the fact. I thought, *Surely my girlfriend isn't the worst person walking on this earth.*

This woman is the epitome of a toxic narcissist. The ironic thing about it was she was the longest relationship I have ever had in my lifetime. I say that with a heavy heart, because I think all of us are seeking love, joy, and happiness in our lives, especially if you are in a long-term relationship. That happy ending is usually the goal. I do believe everything happens for a reason; I don't believe in coincidences.

I have experienced manipulation, betrayal, trauma bonding, judgment, love bombing, abandonment, mental abuse, lies, and deceit. If any or all of this resonates in your spirit, and you're getting any red flags from the beginning, middle, or end, I would encourage you to take a closer look at your current relationship and partner. Beware of people who are psychological leeches.

Take it from me. The sick game these people play of using and abusing you is like quicksand. Narcissists inflict repetitive stupidness, i.e., the name of this chapter. I came up with that name based on my experience. My first instinct from day one said, "Something's wrong here!" The energy I felt coming off her was confusing to me. Never had I experienced this before with any other girlfriends. I just couldn't put my finger on it, though, she was married at the time. What I kept hearing was, "Leave! This one is not for you." It was like God Himself telling me, "What part of THOU SHALT NOT don't you understand, Krista?"

I recently confirmed this by going back to 2006 in my journal when we started our relationship to see if my instincts were true. And they were. God closes doors because it's time to move on. He knows you won't start walking until circumstances force you to. That's Gods hand protecting you. He also knows you'd spend every day holding onto hope, trying to see the good in them until they destroyed you. I also believe not everyone is meant to be in your future. Some people are just passing through.

For the longest time, I always thought narcissists were people who just looked at themselves in the mirror a lot and had huge egos. Well, that's the furthest from the truth, especially if they are a toxic narcissist. A friend recommended a book to me called *The Empath's Survival Guide* by Dr. Judith Orloff. In the fifth chapter of the book, it warns you *not* to fall in love with a narcissist, you will be in deep trouble for real! This chapter helped me understand the dangers of being around these people.

There's another thing my grandmother would say, "A hard head makes a soft butt!" Meaning, you can be stubborn all you want until you fall so hard, it's really going to hurt. My saving grace from God was I never fell in love with her. I loved her, but I think it was more compassion, empathy, and sympathy I was feeling because she's very sickly and I felt sorry for her.

So, I dove in and educated myself on narcissism. As I listened to the book on Audible, I couldn't help feeling embarrassed, humiliated, and betrayed. One of the most purposeful but painful kisses is a Judas kiss. I've always thought of myself a smart woman, and a team player, especially when I'm in a relationship. How could I fall for the rope-a-dope? When I finally found out who I was truly dealing with, I began listening to a lot of affirmation videos and researching this toxic behavior. All the pieces started coming together.

You see, I've only been in love one time in my whole life, with an ex-girlfriend (DJW), and she was very reciprocal with that love. We both were running around with that goo-goo-ga-ga look on our faces. The funny thing was that I didn't even know I was in love—I had to call a friend to ask her what the heck I was feeling. She said, "Krista, you're in love!"

I said, "Oh!" and we just laughed about that conversation.

The real crazy part about this story was my now-ex, narcissist girlfriend would say she loved me and was *in* love with me, but knowing what I know now, I'm sure that was an absolute lie.

What is a toxic narcissist? Well, let's look at that for a minute. Psychologists have stated they can be sociopaths, psychopaths, and damaged dreamers. That's why they mirror your life; you possess something they desire but can't obtain. They need people around them to create a life for themselves because their own lives are complacent with no promising future in sight. Narcissists have a ton of insecurities and self-doubt. These emotions stem from jealousy and envy they have toward their partner. Narcissists feed off drama, chaos, and gossip, and often blame shifting, constantly needing their egos stroked.

With these toxic energy vampires, 99.99 percent of the time they are always about themselves. If you really think about it, a person who is at peace with themselves will not find fault with you or anyone else, so please understand these people have no peace within their spirit, and they don't love themselves much either.

Now, let's talk about gaslighting. Narcissists are masters at doing this! Gaslighting is a hot term, becoming increasingly popular in today's world. It's just another word for manipulation.

They will make up some crazy scenario or story to try to distort your reality and then wait for your reaction. And when you react, the narcissist will deny it, minimize it, and get angry. Then the next thing that will come out their mouth is, "YOU'RE CRAZY!"

Let me give you an example of what I mean. Let's say we are having a conversation about the colors red and blue. My comment may be, "Look at that red apple," and then they might say, "No! That's a blue apple." You know good and well an apple is not blue, but if a narcissist says it's blue, then it's blue. Then, two seconds later, you'll say to them, "You said that apple was blue." The first thing a narcissist will say is, "I didn't say that." Their next comment will be, "You don't listen, you don't ever get anything right, and you need therapy." Everything about that conversation was your fault. Even if you're sitting right there in front of them, watching their lips moving, they will swear they never said it.

My narcissist's best attempt at gaslighting me was about two years ago. She said to me, "I think if I wanted to break up with you, you might try to kill me."

I said, "No!" and I laughed. "I'm not going to hell for you or losing my freedom for anyone." She just got quiet because her attempt failed to have me even react to that gaslighting tactic.

You see, these people really think they are grooming you to be this big dumb-dumb. I used to ask her all time, "You really think I'm stupid, don't you?" And she would say no with an innocent voice. Their thought process is that you should just allow them to treat you like crap and agree with everything they say and do, period. Which is just ludicrous!

Don't catch them in a lie, they will gaslight you like crazy. And you'll start thinking to yourself, *Is it me? Did I misunderstand something?* They will have you so confused, you won't know what your own name is.

Toxic narcissist are such great actors and can put on a huge public fake façade that will make you say in your mind, *AND THE OSCAR BELONGS TO . . . !* They are charming to the neighbors, agreeable with strangers, warm and friendly to friends, but to you, behind closed doors, they are controlling, manipulative, downright mean, non-caring, and dishonest.

Narcissist 100 percent act like Dr. Jekyll and Mr. Hyde. They will show you completely two different versions of themselves. And you will never know what side you're going to get next. Sometimes you'll get the nice version, when they love bomb you and put you on a pedestal, giving you breadcrumbs with a twinkle in their eye and say all the right things. The nice side is just a false identity built off manipulation.

And just when you start to get comfortable and truly believe that's who they really are, the other side comes in hard. That other side is the real them. You'll see exactly what's behind that mask. A hateful side. The cold side. A chilling side. You'll spend the whole relationship trying to figure out which side of them is real. It builds so much confusion to go back and forth between one side to the other. Not to mention, you'll be walking on eggshells daily to prevent Mr. Hyde from coming out.

When they don't get their way, they start acting like spoiled, emotional toddlers. And don't you dare call them out on something they did, making them feel exposed. You'll see that rageaholic side coming out of them.

They also use a tactic called stonewalling. That's when they refuse to answer questions by giving evasive replies, stop talking to you, or ghost you entirely. And, when this happens, this is the perfect opportunity for you to get your get-out-of-jail-free card.

Every relationship with a narcissist is doomed one way or the other, no matter how many years it may last, because you're dealing with a fake person. Narcissists are incredibly charismatic, and they will lure you in with all the good until they get you. Then they will turn around, and you'll see a totally different face. Pay attention when people show you who they really are.

And let's not mention the word "accountability." That's like speaking another language to them.

Narcissists also do a thing called discarding you—something they do when they are getting ready to break up with you because they already have a new supply in the queue. So, I'll break this down to you in layman's terms.

Four things narcissists don't want you to know about them:

- They need you more than you need them.
- Nothing about their character is real. They are completely fake, phony, and inauthentic. These people are living a total lie. They are pretending to be someone they are not.
- They are not capable of love, empathy, or respect. In actuality, they are just using you. I also learned never to try to defend yourself against a narcissist. They already know you're right! They just want you to go crazy trying to prove it to them.
- And never go back to these people, no matter what! It's like reading a book repeatedly and already knowing how it ends.

When our breakup happened, I was thinking to myself, *Wow, I've got to start all over again*. Then I changed the way I was thinking about it. I told myself, *This time, I'm not starting from scratch. I'm starting from experience*. Every challenge is an opportunity to grow and build a better you in the process.

If you're in a toxic relationship and have suffered narcissistic abuse, you really should speak with someone about your trauma. In my case, I talked to God a whole lot, friends, acquaintances, and some family members. The truth here is that God and the universe tried so many times to shut the door over the years and so many times I would open it back up and say, "No, God, I got this. I can fix us, I can fix her," and I just wouldn't give up. Once they get their claws in you and lead you on with false hope, they got you.

Someone once told me when something was sent by God, it always comes with confirmation, when it's not from him it comes with hesitation, frustration, and confusion. My story is very interesting because so many people have asked me, "Why did it take you so long to figure this out?" The truth was I didn't know what was going on. You are in a constant state of confusion and in a tailspin of being brainwashed in believing all their lies. It's like being led to a cliff and them telling you to jump because you can *fly*—something a cult leader might emanate. Let me give you an example of what I mean with these "toxic energy people."

Let's go back in time. You might remember this date, November 18, 1978. The People's Temple founder, Jim Jones, led hundreds of his followers to a remote part of the South America nation of Guyana. He believed he was the messiah. Many of Jones's followers willingly ingested a poison-laced punch, while others were forced to do so at gunpoint. The number of adults and children who perished that day was undeniably horrific. Experts had diagnosed Jim Jones as being a total narcissist, with mental disease.

Speaking from my personal experience with being in a relationship with a toxic person, I wish I could have read the warning label like the ones on the side of the cigarette packs stating smoking may be hazardous to your health.

The last thing these narcissists do to trash your name is called a "smear campaign." They tell all these lies to others and their new supply about your relationship to make them sound like the victim and you the villain.

The perfect way to heal from these toxic narcissists is to have NO contact ever again, they start to lose their mind when you don't choose them any longer. Some narcissists' mission is to suck the life right out of you (i.e., energy vampires). So, when you go on and live your life and forgive them and yourself for allowing it to happen in the first place, the peace that follows this act of letting go is so freeing. And they will not take up any more space in your life. You also won't expect them to come back with an apology. You will just simply move on.

One thing is for sure, God gives us all free will. While God is working on your outer and inner to heal you. It's your job to start working on forgiving yourself. There is no need for revenge. "Do not be deceived: God is not mocked, for whatever one sows, that will he also reap" (Galatians 6:7 ESV).

Not all storms come to disrupt your life. Some come to clear your path. We must not hold on to someone who's leaving, otherwise, we won't meet the one who's coming. You don't want to suffer every time you remember what they did to you. Forgiveness is an act of self-love. After some time has passed, you'll stop thinking of them every day.

One week after Nationals. My girlfriend and I called it quits on June 12, 2021, but we were still doing things as couples do. Then the door was shut completely on March 26, 2022. At that time, after four months of no contact, I made a huge mistake. I answered a text from her, and this would start us engaging in conversation again, hanging out again, being friends with benefits, and the vicious cycle started all over, which was my fault because I did not have to answer the text in the first place. So, here's the thing, when you're in a relationship with a narcissist, you might experience a particular area in the relationship you don't have any problems with, then before you know it, you'll find yourself back in bed—literally—with the enemy. We never got back together, but this is where it became really complicated.

Once again, I got myself sucked back into all the chaos and drama you would think I would have learned by now, but *no*! Toward the end, she was cheating on the new supply with me now. What my grandmother said to me about trusting your instinct was absolutely true, my eyes were wide open now. We all know when the trust and communication is gone, the relationship is over.

The official day of ending all this madness was August 17, 2023. To be truthful, our relationship was fifteen years, plus two more years of off-and-on familiarity. For the first time in my life, I am not in a relationship, which is very unfamiliar territory for me, because I absolutely love companionship and having a girlfriend, and that's probably the reason why I have always been in a relationship up to this point in my life. This whole experience and lessons learned has been truly humbling for me.

I saw something long ago that resonated with me. "The sun is alone but still shines brightly." I believe God puts you in places alone sometimes because he needs you to realize you don't need anyone but Him. Everyone will teach you something about yourself. Be thankful for closed doors, and while you're waiting on that next door to open from God, praise Him in the hallway. It's my belief that my next relationship will be a life partner, so I'm not rushing it. I want this love to find me, teach me, and want me. God says, "There is a time for everything, and a season for every activity under the heaven" (Ecclesiastes 3:1 NIV).

I know this how? Let me tell you. I am stronger because I had to be. I'm smarter because of my mistakes. I'm happier and wiser because I've overcome my sadness and confusion. I'm so grateful for my ex because I have learned yet another one of life's lessons.

When God's trying to get your attention and He finally has it, then it's on to the next task at hand that He needs. You to be obedient to His word and take a leap of faith. That's when you fully submit, commit, and surrender your life. That means some friendships you may have to let go, some relationships you can't mess with anymore. All those distractions must go. It's a process you must go through. I have come to realize for myself since being in my isolation season, God's been speaking to me saying, "Krista, I need your undivided attention, no distractions, period. I need you all to myself and I need you to focus." I'm proud to say I have learned so much about myself on this healing journey I'm on.

So, this is what I would like to play forward to anyone reading this chapter about narcissism. What I've learned from my narcissist abuser was: There's nothing wrong with me, my instincts were right. I can heal from a narcissistic, abusive, and manipulative relationship. My hope is that through my experience with this trauma, I can help save someone else too.

In closing, I would like to ask everyone reading this chapter to think about something. There are three types of relationships we can have in this lifetime: Milk, Wine, and Poison. Milk spoils overtime, wine gets better overtime, and poison kills you overtime. Ask yourself: Which kind of relationship are you currently in?

> "AND I WILL RESTORE TO YOU THE YEARS THAT THE LOCUST HATH EATEN" (JOEL 2:25 KJV).

33

BIONIC WOMAN

If you do just a little research, you might be surprised to know that anyone who has ever accomplished anything (big) in life didn't know *how* they were going to do it. They just knew they would.

You see, the *how* (*how it will happen?*) is the domain of God and the Universe. Always knowing the quickest, most harmonist way between you and your goals. Out of your commitment to what you want. The universe will rearrange itself and you'll attract the way. This is called the law of attraction.

It's like having the universe as your catalog and you're placing an order. You might look through it and say, "I would like to have that experience, that career, or a partner like that. etc." Then decide what you want, believe you can have it, believe you deserve it, and believe it's possible for you. We tend to make all these plans for our lives, but God must order the steps. Now! Sit back, relax, and pay attention to what happens next.

It absolutely works! My life is proof, just ask God if you don't believe me.

God sends the *whos*, the *whats*, the *wheres*, and the *hows*, so the vision can be executed properly. Be very vigilant because it's coming!

In the bible, a few stories attest to the laws of the universe with Esther. She went from orphan to queen, Ruth went from gleaning in the fields to owning the fields, Joseph went from prisoner to second in command to Pharaoh through one conversation.

Many years ago, I prayed for a miracle to happen in my life. I asked to retire before sixty years old.

I had no idea how I was going to do this. I saw no strategy, no possibility, I hadn't established longevity with any job, and I certainly had no savings for retirement. However, I realized one very important piece to this puzzle—you can start out with nothing and no way, and a way will be made for you.

On April 15, 2022, God retired me, NOT man, from my last and final job of driving a truck for FedEx ground in 2022 at the age of fifty-five. If that's not God blessing me, I don't know what is. All the years of jumping in and out of that truck, delivering packages, and performing repetitive physical labored jobs my whole life wore my right hip out. At first, I thought I pulled my groin muscle, but my friends would say, "Krista, that's your hip," and I would say, "No, I don't think so." Turns out my friends were right. Once the X-rays and MRI were done, it was official, my right hip was bone-on-bone arthritic and needed to be replaced. A few people were certain this would end my athletic career, but I let all that talk go in one ear and out the other. I was not done; I am no quitter, never have been, never will be. I've always had a gift of focus and, when I get locked in my brain and heart anything I want to achieve, it's getting ready to come true.

Of course, when this hip situation was diagnosed, I was training for APF Senior Nationals 2021. Even though I had been limping around for over a year, squatting didn't hurt as bad as walking—until I needed to squat parallel or below. This is the depth required by the rules when you squat in competition. Having gone through an array of injuries in my career, I have adapted to working around them and still being able to train. After all, I don't have anything to prove to anyone except to my Lord and myself.

When we got to APF Senior Nationals in 2021, Janice Roge-Henderson, my coach who's retired from powerlifting, along with

Savoy, Darrin, Shy Darious, and Gene, all came to handle me. And a host of friends came as well, Dr. Soyini Chism, Gregoryia a.k.a. "Greg" Savoy's wife, and my girlfriend of fifteen years. My goal was to squat five hundred pounds on this bad hip. My squats were a struggle, very painful, and I was getting one red light each time from my right-side judge. I was not able to break parallel on that side, but the other two judges gave me white lights on my depth, and two white lights superseded one red light. That's all you need to continue to your next attempted weight. So, I officially squatted 501.5 pounds. It hurt like heck, let me tell you, it was no picnic. The weight was doable enough, but the pain in my hip radiated all the way down my leg and it was extremely distracting. It's hard to lift when you're distracted with pain, it's challenging to focus on your technique, even for me.

On to the bench press—this was where it got interesting. On my first attempt, Darious lifted off for me as usual and then stepped out of the way so the head judge could see me, but then, out of the corner of my eye, I saw some guy walk up to the bench and stand near the bar and hover there. The reason why this makes no sense is because your head judge *must* have a clear view of the lifter to give you your commands. I don't know what happened, but I couldn't concentrate with him hanging over me like that, and I missed the lift; I found out later it's not a rule, just safety measures they added since the pandemic. I missed my second attempt as well. My foot slid slightly on the mat, and nothing can move while you're lying on that bench. Only one chance left. I had to get this one to stay in the competition. Everything was going fine and then, uncharacteristic of me, I hitched my press on the way up, sometimes we call it a double dip. To explain what I mean by this terminology, you must always be pressing the bar in an upward motion, even if it stalls halfway up, you must push toward the ceiling, the bar can never go downward. So, there went my three attempts. I swore I would never bomb out of another competition. This whole day was a total fluke and for the second time in my thirty-six-year career of powerlifting, I bombed out!

And if that wasn't bad enough, I did it at nationals of all places which was something I never ever did before. I was so embarrassed and disappointed, even if you are the GOAT in your prospective sport, you are not exempt from days like this.

Funny, I thought the squat would be the hardest part, not the bench. I went back into the warmup area and my tears of frustration began to fall. Janice and my crew were there to help me through that moment, and Janice even shed a few tears of her own, knowing exactly what I was going through, with me being able to persevere through three excruciating squats, only to bomb out on the bench.

I felt awful for my crew because I'm not one of those athletes in a mainstream sport with a million-dollar contract deal. Most of the training, traveling, and competing is mainly out of pocket expenses for all of us. Hopefully that will change real soon for myself and my crew. As I was up in my hotel room, sitting on the bed with my head down feeling so disappointed, my girlfriend was there (because we were still in our relationship) and she put on the fakest act of compassion I have ever witnessed. Fortunately it didn't matter because the silver lining here was that we officially ended our fifteen-year relationship for good one week after this nationals on June 12, 2021, as I previously mentioned in chapter thirty-two. After I got showered and pulled together my composure, I met with everyone down in the lobby and we all went out to dinner. I stood up in the restaurant and thanked all my handlers and friends that came to support my efforts and that I was truly sorry for the outcome. They all just said no worries, they were there for me and that would always be the case. At that moment I felt so much better, and I realized my crew was like family to me.

It took a few days, but the silver lining started to show itself. I did accomplish what I set out to do that day. I squatted 501.5, at the young age of fifty-five with a bad hip. But the greatest part of that day was that my loyal friend and number one handler, Savoy Curtis, was with me for the thousandth time. Having him there was the most special part of that day for me, because unfortunately he passed away just two short months afterward (August 16, 2021). Savoy was my "ride or die," my rock, and he was there through the whole climb, and that day was the last time we would be on our journey together. I met him in powerlifting over twenty years ago and he left this earth still loyal to me and by my side. He could handle me at any competition, all by himself if needed, he was that good. We were a team in powerlifting, that's for sure. I will miss him with every fiber in my soul. Savoy Curtis was a great human being, and the world lost a gentle soul when he took his last breath. I am so blessed he came into my life.

I really think Savoy was an angel masquerading around on this earth as a human being. Every Sunday now, out in my garage, when my training starts and the guys show up, I still expect Savoy to come striding up my driveway, ready to train. But not today, not this Sunday—that breaks my heart. I know I will see him again though, when my time comes. Savoy loved the Lord so much, I know he's in heaven, watching over his family and friends like he always did while he was here.

My hip surgery was rescheduled three times due to covid and staff shortages at the hospital. Finally, my right hip was replaced on January 4, 2022. Everything went well and, amazingly, I was up and walking in a few days. I then had another surgery on my left elbow on March 25, 2022. I had recovered enough by August 2022 to start training for worlds, which were to be held in Orlando, Florida, November 4–7, 2022. During my eighth week of a ten-week training cycle, on October 13, 2022, I heard an all too familiar sound—a pop and then tearing.

My heart sank, not again. "Oh, Lord, why? I'm just coming back from one of the biggest surgeries of my life. How can I get hurt again?" I was confused about the timing of this occurrence. The tricep tendon in my left arm had torn completely and it was off to the surgeon again. I think the whole staff at Grady Memorial Hospital knew me by then. Dr. Jackson got me in right away and fixed my tendon and the bone spur that was probably responsible for grating on the tendon enough to tear it completely. That surgery was on October 26, 2022. To date, I've had three major orthopedic surgeries in 2022, and I was determined to come back in 2023, mark my words!

The first time I stood on top of the national/world podium, I was twenty-nine years old. This time, in 2023, I will be fifty-six—no longer the spring chicken.

I would like to tell the story of how I obtained that *cool* name, the Bionic Woman.

There is an awesome orthopedic doctor here in Atlanta, Georgia, named Dr. Steven Wertheim, and he's been my doctor since 2000. He has performed five of fifteen orthopedic surgeries on me. He and his staff gave me the nickname the Bionic Woman after my fifth surgery performed, and it has really stuck over the years because I truly am a medical miracle. Dr. Wertheim was highly recommended to me because of his impeccable orthopedic surgeries performed on a wide selection of world-class Olympic and professional athletes. He's been my favorite doctor in the whole wide world. Close second to him is his buddy, Dr. Douglas Lundy, who performed pelvic surgery back in 2008. Adding to my list of remarkable ortho doctors, there's Dr. Norman Scott in New York who performed my first ever ortho surgery on my left knee ACL tear; Dr. Edward Robert Jackson who did my left arm three times for an elbow, tricep, and graft tear repair; Dr. Christopher Sadlack who gave me a new hip; Dr. Paris Payton was the first Black female ortho doctor I have ever had perform surgery on me—which was an honor—and she did my first ever foot surgery; and the ortho infectious team of Dr. Thomas Moore, Dr. Lenenski, and Dr. Gregory Darrville—this whole dynamic team put me back together again, allowing me to keep competing in my sport for some forty years to date. A standing ovation performance provided by some amazing doctors, I would say. If you were around in the '70s, this would jar your memory for sure.

The Bionic Woman series aired from 1976–1978, featuring Lindsey Wagner as Jamie Sommers who's hired to perform top-secret government missions using her superhuman bionic powers. This series was a spin-off of the 1970s *Six Million Dollar Man*, a science fiction/action television series. These two people were rebuilt with superhuman strength, speed, and vision due to bionic implants and Jamie Sommers was a professional tennis star who suffered near-fatal injuries in a skydiving accident. With cybernetic implants known as bionics, she becomes the first female cyborg.

I think this opening theme suits me well. We can REBUILD her, we have the CAPIBILITY to make the World's first BIONIC WOMAN. Better, stronger, faster.

I feel like we are currently living exactly like these TV series that were aired forty-eight years ago. With all this technology, you can find just about anything via the internet now. I bet I could find any body part I needed on the internet. I also grew up watching cartoon TV shows like *The Jetsons*. This cartoon was a piece of the twentieth century and its futurism. It's easy for some people to dismiss TV shows like *The Jetsons*, *Star Trek*, and *Knight Rider* with Kit being the voice of the car, a 1982 Pontiac Firebird Trans Am. These shows have had a profound impact on the way that Americans think and talk about the future. What's so interesting here is we are living exactly that life now.

Inside my body, I possess cobalt-chromium metal, metal plates, titanium screws, ceramic, and very hard plastics. Here is a list of all the successful orthopedic surgeries I had between 1997 and 2023.

2/14/97	left ACL knee (age thirty)
11/5/00	right ACL knee (age thirty-three)
12/13/02	right golfer's elbow (age thirty-six)
7/27/05	left rotator cuff tear (age thirty-eight)

8/17/05	right rotator cuff tear (age thirty-eight)
12/19/07	left rotator cuff tear again (age forty)
12/17/08	pelvic break (age forty-two)
1/4/22	total right hip replacement (age fifty-five)
3/25/22	left golfer's elbow and bone spurs (age fifty-five)
10/26/22	left tricep tear and elbow bone spurs (age fifty-six)
2/26/23	left tricep graft tear from having it repaired already (age fifty-six) — this retearing brought the conversation up with Dr. Jackson to repair it one more time.
11/13/23	left foot bunion correction surgery (age fifty-seven)
11/17/23	left tricep graft tear reattachment (age fifty-seven)
12/18/23	left tricep infection on cadaver surgery (age fifty-seven)
12/21/23	left tricep infection on cadaver surgery (age fifty-seven)

My friends tease me because I do feel like am a living, breathing, walking, and talking bionic woman in the twenty-first century. The key to my success of gaining back my strength and recovery time is this one fact; you must start your physical therapy immediately. This will help you bounce back on your feet a lot faster than if you prolong it, or don't do it at all. It helps that I have the proper powerlifting equipment to train with. This prevents any unnecessary injuries that may occur.

Remember that two-car garage I so desperately wanted when I purchased my home? Well, now, one side of that garage houses a powerlifting bench, a deadlift platform, two weight trees that hold seven hundred pounds of Ivanko iron plates, and all my barbells needed for squats, bench presses, and deadlifts. And my all-time favorite is a shiny red Monolift I squat out of, which has a sign on it that says, "Ford Tough Blvd," and a giant-colored world map on the wall directly in front of it. This is where the magic happens. It's like having your playground set up in your backyard to practice on. The other side of the garage is empty when we train, but the rest of the time, a fine, automobile with the license plate "STRGWMN" lives there—she's special!

Earlier in this book, I made a vow to come back and compete in 2023. Well, I did just that and some. I started training on April 16, 2023, for APF Senior Nationals to be held in Salt Lake City, Utah, and for the first time ever, at Nationals. The women would have a whole day to ourselves to compete and not have to share the day with the lighter-weight men.

This would be my thirty-fourth year showing up on the platform. My ten weeks of training were amazing, and all my guys were right there for me. I decided to go up a weight class to the 198-Pound Women's Masters Class (fifty-five to fifty-nine age group). In this category, there are two national and two world records I wanted to break in the squat and deadlift. I flew out on June 29, 2023, weigh-ins were on June 30th, and I competed on July 1st. After some complications with the flight, I finally made it and was waiting at the hotel to see if my handlers Derrick and Darious would get on any plane, after having complications of their own. It was apparent they were not going to get out of Atlanta, and the next day flights looked just as bad. This was the Fourth of July weekend, so, it made perfect sense to me why this was happening. I finally told them to go home and thanked them so much for trying.

Here's my problem. I can't compete without my handlers to help me. So, I went downstairs to find Michelle and Scott, the meet directors. I told them my crew was not there and I needed help, and they said they would get on it and find me someone. I just went back upstairs and prayed to God like crazy because this was the first time ever, I hadn't had anyone with me when competing. I was totally alone. I usually had at least one to four of my handlers, my girlfriend, and friends in tow. I just prayed and prayed for a miracle. The next day, after weigh-ins and more praying, I went back downstairs, and Scott came up to me and told me he got a guy. A man walked up to me and said, "Hi, I'm Tristan and I'll take good care of you." It helped he knew who I was in the sport. I came to find out Tristan was on a decent level in powerlifting, so he knew what to do. I thanked him and Scott and went up to my room and just cried and cried and thanked God for my miracle.

God always does this with me, at the stroke of midnight he shows up and shows out. I slept so peacefully and woke up and it was time to do what I did best. There were five flights, A–E, almost seventy women total. I would be in flight E. So, I had more time to warm up and my first, second, and third attempts on squats broke national and world records right off the rip! I ended up with a 501.5-pound squat. Then I took a token bench, which is just fifty-five pounds because of my tricep surgery and the graft retearing.

Then my deadlift was the same as squats, my first, second, and third attempts broke national and world records again, with 407 pounds as the final deadlift. At the end of the day, I had an amazing national. I not only won my thirteenth national champion title, I set records at the young age of fifty-six. I thanked Tristan a hundred times for handling me perfectly the whole day. I thanked Michele and Scott for all their help as well, and I went up to my room, fell on my knees, and thanked God for the gift He just gave me. I refused to doubt God, even when the enemy was trying to distract my thoughts from believing He'd come through for me. You must believe—that's the moral of this story.

> "THEREFORE, I TELL YOU WHATEVER YOU ASK IN PRAYER, BELIEVE THAT YOU HAVE RECEIVED IT, AND IT WILL BE YOURS" [MARK 11:24 ESV].

My vision board, started January 29, 2015. It absolutely works! Two huge things have already manifested for me on my board. To think it is to live

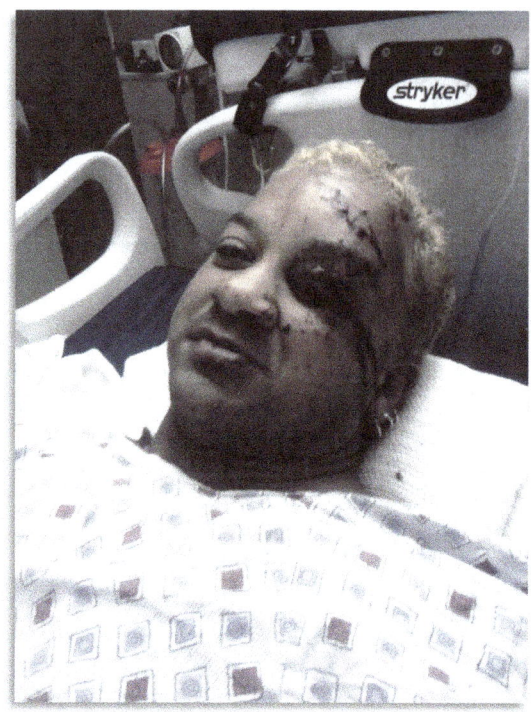

Life threatening auto accident, November 10, 2008.

My car after being T-boned by a school bus, November 10, 2008. GOD is all I have to say!

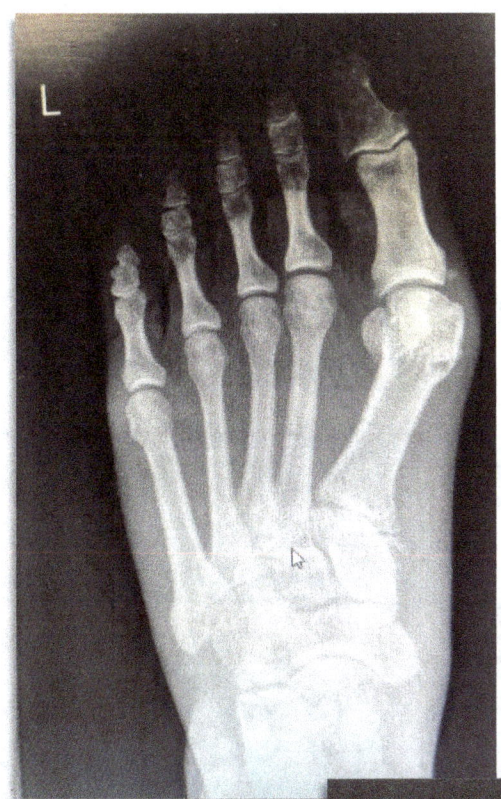

My first foot surgery done by Dr. Paris Payton in December, 2023.

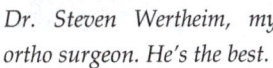

Dr. Steven Wertheim, my ortho surgeon. He's the best.

My first home, bought April 1, 2004, when I was thirty-four years old.

My joys Snap (three and a half dwarf bunny), Babie (floppy eared rabbit), Narita (AKC Morkie), and Meshach (AKC Siberian Husky).

My passion powerlifting deadlifts 500 lbs. in the 181 lbs. open women's class.

APF Senior Nationals, Myrtle Beach, South Carolina, 2012. Squatted 600.7 lbs. in the 181 lbs. open women's class.

My medal display cases and trophies collected over the years.

EPILOGUE

Everyone's heard the expression "paying it forward." Well, I like to say, "playing it forward." Playing sounds fun to do. When I help someone else, it is a great feeling for me. It's something that keeps me smiling while I'm doing it, having fun like we did when we were all children growing up.

Every morning, when I wake up, the first thing I do is talk to God. I thank Him that I'm still here, on this earth. One more day, one more opportunity. Attitude of gratitude is my motto. I thank Him for all He and the universe has given me so far. Every opportunity I have had in my life has been divinely orchestrated. Everything is between me and God.

I pray and talk to God just like He's sitting right next to me, all day, every day. Sometimes I tell Him, "God, you didn't have to save me, but You did. You didn't have to take me from homeless to world champion, but You did. You didn't have to make my dreams come true, but they are, every day." Then I thank Him a million times over. This starts every day off good. I'm going to always choose God over anything and everything.

This entire book is dedicated to my God, the universe, and all the angels walking around on this earth. I made two promises to God, i.e., the name of this book. The first promise was that if God would help me write this book, I would tell the whole world, like John the Baptist, what I've known all along—that without Him there is no *me*. Our Creator plays an all-encompassing part in everyone's life walking on this earth. Walk with Him and you'll have everything your heart desires. The second promise was to give Him all the glory, honor, praise, and homage while He brings to fruition everything I'm praying for. You can have the money, career, cars, house, family, friends, and the success, but none of these matters if you don't have Jesus. He's the backbone of the whole operation. You must believe or what's the point, right?

This world we are living in today is all about social media and how many followers you must have to be successful. Well, I've never been much on posting every day. I guess I've been concentrating on being the best version of myself and the best athlete up to this point. I just never saw any sense in showing the whole world that I ate an egg for breakfast. I refuse to be dragged down that rabbit hole. So, I decided I would surrender my social media to God and let Him navigate the right tribe of people around me to handle that. I'm going to focus on representing Him and not building my following on social media. I will show God, I'm putting Him first and I'll continue to put in the work. In return, I'm confident He'll send me all the provisions I need. God's got this and I'm going to let Him have it. At the end of the day, we all do our very best to live, to be happy, and to treat people as we would want to be treated.

A little girl's promise and a big God's deliverance of one. So, this is me, God, shouting it from the mountaintop. You let me climb with You. All the glory goes to You. You did this, not me. You did this *for* me, your daughter, Krista N. Ford. And I thank You and praise You with all my heart and soul. I couldn't have dreamed up a life any better than this.

A dream come true, and then some. Not just once, but fourteen times as a national champion and seven times as a world champion, a multi-record holder, and the first Black female pioneer of women's bobsled, to all my years of living, being in great health, mind, body, and spirit, to sustaining me financially when I was down to my last dollar, but never losing a thing—not an apartment, home, or having any utilities ever shut off.

EPILOGUE

I would encourage you to have patience and wait for the things you want most, don't chase it. If God wants you to have it, He will give it to you.

God's got this; He's working in your life. Blessings, miracles, favors, signs, and wonders are about to manifest. God is bigger than anything you're facing, He's lining up the right people, places, things, and opportunities for your life. He's arranging things in your favor, and sometimes growth requires new companionships, new location, and a new mindset. What's done is done, what's gone is gone. It's okay to look back on your memories, but never let the past stop you from moving forward.

And then it'll happen—one day you wake up and you're in this place where everything feels right, your heart is calm, your soul is light, your thoughts are positive, your vision is clear, and you're at peace. At peace with where you've been, peace with what you've been through, and peace with where you're headed. God didn't remove the Red Sea, He parted it. Sometimes God doesn't remove your problems, He makes a way through them. Now it's your time to be very intentional with your vision for your life. This time we have here on earth is not refundable. For me, I truly believe in my heart: What you think about, you bring about, and maybe my story will bring about positive energy to you and yours and help you to understand how God plays a huge part in your life. We all have a purpose, and we all have a story to tell. My hope is that my life story can somehow touch yours because I love you though I've never met you. My wish is for you to have an amazing life and *don't you ever give up!* Just look up all around you and know that someone special loves you and it's not just me.

AUTHOR'S NOTES

Nowadays, I spend my time doing what I love. I train and coach several athletes in a variety of other sports, track and field, football, martial arts instructors, MMA fighters, wrestling, and of course powerlifting. These sports require the athletes to be strong. With my strength training and coaching, it will undoubtedly enable them to elevate their performance in their respective sports. And let me tell you there's a deep sense of satisfaction I get from helping others reach their goals. I get to *play* it all forward. I can now pass on all my years of consistency and practice. I have been coached by the best, who were kind enough to teach me the ropes. I'm so grateful for having the opportunity in powerlifting to reach the top and finally break the 181-pound open women's squat world record at the young age of forty-four years old. God not only gave me my gift of strength, through years of developing this knowledge, but also a lifetime's worth of experience. My personal bonus here is that I have developed the wisdom of how to work around injuries and surgeries to maintain my strength. So, now I get to talk, teach, and coach—what better vision to possess than that? I'm free to live my dream and my best life, with this gift of good health and wellness, I can continue living my passion.

My all-time favorite Bible scripture I memorized long ago is Proverbs 3:5, "Trust in the Lord with all your heart" (NIV).

ACKNOWLEDGMENTS

I want to first and foremost Thank God for giving me life.

And to all the people God put on my path, who supported me along the way, and who are still cheering me on. Some have been watching from behind the clouds, Grandma, my Aunt Bobbie, my father (John Ford), my aunt Joyce Poindexter 1936–2022, Bob Sidebottom, Dawn Reshel-Sharon, Big Joe Kennedy, Herb Weinstein, and my beloved friend and handler Savoy Curtis. I'd also like to thank Richard Ader and Erroll "Doug" Woods.

The Women's Sports Foundation, Billie Jean King, and John Inzer (Advanced Inzer design) for his amazing sponsorship of my powerlifting equipment for over thirty years.

To the whole staff at BookLogix who believed in my vision and worked with me on this amazing project. Thank you.

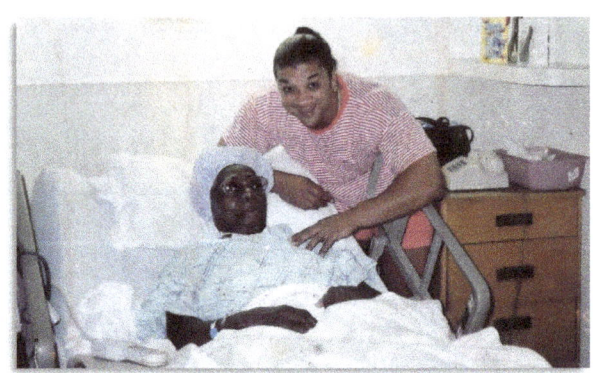

My granny (Florence Huntley).

Myself, Aunt Barbara "Bobbie" Huntley, Tamika (cousin), and Stacey (sister).

My aunt/godmother, Joyce Poindexter.

ACKNOWLEDGMENTS

Friend and handler Joseph Kennedy.

Friend and handler Bob Sidebottom.

Savoy Curtis, my #1 handler and special close friend.

Richard Ader, my God-sent sponsor for my athletic career, and his wife. '97, '98, '00, '01.

Wife Wendy, Herb Weinstein, also my God-sent angel sponsor for my athletic career in '97, and '98, myself, and their daughter Jordon.

John Inzer and I. Icon of powerlifting and owner of Inzer advanced designs. He's been my sponsor for all my powerlifting equipment for over thirty years to now.

ABOUT THE AUTHOR

Krista Noelle Ford, a professional athlete, has been called a living legend pioneer of the sports world. She's defied gender norms in the male-dominated sport of powerlifting for more than forty years. During this time, she's earned the title of national champion fourteen times and world champion seven times, setting multiple records along the way. Krista has also broken race barriers by being the first Black female bobsledder for the US Women's team. She also was a part of the first women's team to earn a silver medal at the International Women's Bobsled Race 1998 Winterberg Germany.

While training others and competing as a professional powerlifter, Krista plays it forward in other ways. Her philosophy of talk, teach, and coach can be seen in how she shares her experience, knowledge, and passion for living the magic of life. It is this philosophy that has allowed her to be free, strong, and power-filled even through adversity.

www.ingramcontent.com/pod-product-compliance
Lightning Source LLC
Chambersburg PA
CBHW052132070526
44585CB00017B/1799